SEXUAL MURDERERS

SEXUAL MURDERERS

A Comparative Analysis and New Perspectives

Edited by

Jean Proulx
University of Montreal

Éric Beauregard
University of South Florida

Maurice Cusson
University of Montreal

and

Alexandre Nicole
Institut Philippe-Pinel, Montreal

With a Preface by William L. Marshall
Translated by Steven Sacks

BICENTENNIAL
1807
WILEY
2007
BICENTENNIAL

John Wiley & Sons, Ltd

Other Wiley Editorial Offices

John Wiley & Sons Inc., 111 River Street, Hoboken, NJ 07030, USA

Jossey-Bass, 989 Market Street, San Francisco, CA 94103-1741, USA

Wiley-VCH Verlag GmbH, Boschstr. 12, D-69469 Weinheim, Germany

John Wiley & Sons Australia Ltd, 42 McDougall Street, Milton, Queensland 4064, Australia

John Wiley & Sons (Asia) Pte Ltd, 2 Clementi Loop #02-01, Jin Xing Distripark, Singapore 129809

John Wiley & Sons Canada Ltd, 6045 Freemont Blvd, Mississauga, ONT, L5R 4J3

Wiley also publishes its books in a variety of electronic formats. Some content that appears in print may not be available in electronic books.

Anniversary Logo Design: Richard J. Pacifico

Library of Congress Cataloging-in-Publication Data

Sexual murderers : a comparative analysis and new perspectives/edited by Jean Proulx, Eric Beauregard, and Maurice Cusson ; with a preface by William L. Marshall ; translated by Steven Sacks.
    p. cm.
Includes bibliographical references and index.
ISBN 978-0-470-05953-1 – ISBN 978-0-470-05954-8
1. Sex offenders. 2. Sex offenders–Québec (Province) 3. Murderers. 4. Murderers–Québec (Province) 5. Sex crimes–Psychological aspects. 6. Criminal psychology. 7. Criminology. I. Proulx, Jean. II. Beauregard, Eric. III. Cusson, Maurice.
    HV6556.S435 2007
    364..152'3–dc22   2007006918

British Library Cataloguing in Publication Data

A catalogue record for this book is available from the British Library

ISBN 978-0-470-05953-1 (hbk) 978-0-470-05954-8 (pbk)

Typeset in 10/12pt Palatino by Thomson Digital
Printed and bound in Great Britain by TJ International, Padstow, Cornwall
This book is printed on acid-free paper responsibly manufactured from sustainable forestry in which at least two trees are planted for each one used for paper production.

CONTENTS

List of Figures   vii

List of Tables   ix

About the Editors   xiii

List of Contributors   xv

Preface   xvii

Acknowledgements   xix

Introduction
Sexual Murderers: Myth and Reality   1
Maurice Cusson

PART I   THE MONTREAL STUDY   7

1 Sexual Murder: Definitions, Epidemiology and Theories   9
Jean Proulx, Maurice Cusson and Éric Beauregard

2 Sexual Murderers and Sexual Aggressors: Developmental
  Paths and Criminal History   29
Alexandre Nicole and Jean Proulx

3 Sexual Murderers and Sexual Aggressors: Psychopathological
  Considerations   51
Jean Proulx and Nadège Sauvêtre

4 Sexual Murderers and Sexual Aggressors:
  Intention and Situation   71
Sabine Chéné and Maurice Cusson

5 The Factors Distinguishing Sexual Murderers from Sexual
  Aggressors: A Multivariate Analysis   87
Alexandre Nicole and Jean Proulx

6 Serial Killers and Sexual Murderers 99
Élisabeth Campos and Maurice Cusson

7 Sadistic Sexual Offenders 107
Jean Proulx, Etienne Blais and Éric Beauregard

8 Angry or Sadistic: Two Types of Sexual Murderers 123
Éric Beauregard, Jean Proulx and Michel St-Yves

9 The Motivation and Criminal Career of Sexual Murderers 143
Maurice Cusson and Jean Proulx

PART II   THE BIRMINGHAM STUDY 157

10 A Comparison of Rapists and Sexual Murderers on
Demographic and Selected Psychometric Measures 159
Caroline J. Oliver, Anthony R. Beech, Dawn Fisher and Richard Beckett

11 Identification of Motivations for Sexual Murder 175
Dawn Fisher and Anthony R. Beech

PART III   PRACTICAL ISSUES 191

12 The Role of Profiling in the Investigation of Sexual Homicide 193
Éric Beauregard

13 Psychotherapeutic and Psychodynamic Issues with
Sexual Murderers 213
Monique Tardif, Benoît Dassylva and Alexandre Nicole

Conclusion 229
Jean Proulx

References 233

Index 249

LIST OF FIGURES

Figure 2.1   Empirical model   45
Figure 4.1   Model of the escalation process   76
Figure 4.2   Decision tree for the outcome of the attack   79
Figure 4.3   Decision tree for the severity of the attack   81
Figure 12.1   Graphical representation of a Bayesian Belief Network   199

LIST OF TABLES

Table 1.1 Sociodemographic and developmental
characteristics of three types of violent criminals   20

Table 1.2 Psychological characteristics of three types of
violent criminals   22

Table 1.3 Characteristics of the pre-crime and crime
phases in three groups of violent criminals   23

Table 1.4 Characteristics of serial and nonserial
sexual murderers   25

Table 2.1 Prevalence of victimization-related events
(prior to age 18) in sexual offenders   34

Table 2.2 Prevalence of inappropriate adolescent
behaviours in sexual offenders   36

Table 2.3 Characteristics of the three developmental profiles   37

Table 2.4 Static and dynamic parameters of criminal
career in sexual offenders   39

Table 3.1 Empirical studies of personality disorders among
sexual murderers   58

Table 3.2 Percentage of sexual aggressors and sexual
murderers with DSM-IV axis I mental disorders   60

Table 3.3 Percentage of sexual aggressors and sexual
murderers with DSM-IV axis II personality disorders   61

Table 3.4 Percentage of sexual aggressors and sexual
murderers with base-rate scores above 84 (*disorder*)
and between 75 and 84 (*trait*) on the MCMI
personality disorder scales   61

Table 3.5 Base-rate MCMI scores for two personality
disorder profiles among sexual aggressors and
sexual murderers   62

Table 4.1 Logistic and multiple regression of the
escalation process (*R* and ß)   77

Table 5.1 Bivariate comparison (percentage or mean)
of the variables included in the multivariate analysis   89

Table 5.2 Correlation matrix of the variables included in
the multivariate analyses
(Pearson's r, phi, point biserial)   90
Table 5.3 Hierarchical logistic regression analysis of
the type of crime committed (sexual
assault/sexual murder)   91
Table 6.1 Childhood characteristics   102
Table 6.2 Adolescent characteristics   102
Table 6.3 Adult characteristics   103
Table 7.1 Mean scores and percentages of sadistic and
nonsadistic sexual aggressors of women on
the MCMI personality scales   116
Table 7.2 Characteristics of the pre-crime phase of sadistic
and nonsadistic sexual aggressors of women
during the 48 hours prior to the offence   117
Table 7.3 Offence characteristics of sadistic and
nonsadistic sexual aggressors of women   118
Table 7.4 Crime scene characteristics of sadistic and
nonsadistic sexual murderers   119
Table 8.1 Characteristics of typological studies
of sexual murderers   124
Table 8.2 Summary of the types of sexual murderers
in the typological studies corresponding to
the angry, sadistic and witness-elimination types   125
Table 8.3 Summary of the sadistic sexual murderer   127
Table 8.4 Summary of the angry sexual murderer   128
Table 8.5 Distribution of subjects in the two profiles
of offending process: crime phase   130
Table 8.6 Distribution of subjects in the two profiles
of offending process: supplemental
crime-phase variables   131
Table 8.7 Distribution of subjects in the two profiles
of offending process: affect prior to crime,
precipitating factors (48 hours prior to crime)
and predisposing factors (1 year prior to crime)   132
Table 8.8 Distribution of subjects in the two profiles
of offending process: crime-related attitudes   133
Table 10.1 Differences in background characteristics   166
Table 10.2 Percentage of rapists and sexual murderers
with BR scores over 74 and over 84 on the
personality and clinical syndrome scales
of the MCMI-III   169
Table 10.3 Differences in mean scores on the antisocial
personality questionnaire (APQ)   169

Table 10.4 Differences in victim and offence
characteristics   170
Table 11.1 Offence characteristics of men grouped
by the presence/absence of Dangerous
world/Male sex drive is uncontrollable
implicit theories   187

ABOUT THE EDITORS

Jean Proulx is Professor and Director of the School of Criminology at the University of Montreal, and Researcher at the International Centre of Comparative Criminology of that university. His main research interests are personality profiles, sexual preferences, treatment issues, and recidivism risk factors among sexual murders, rapists, child molesters and incest offenders. Over the last twenty years, he has published four books and more than 100 book chapters or refereed articles, in French and English. Since 1989, he has been active, both as Researcher and Clinical Psychologist, in treatment programmes for sex offenders at the Philippe-Pinel Institute, a maximum-security psychiatric institution

Éric Beauregard is an Assistant Professor in the Department of Criminology at the University of South Florida. His PhD dissertation, completed at the School of Criminology, University of Montreal, was on the hunting patterns of serial sex offenders. Before joining USF in 2005, Dr. Beauregard worked as a clinical criminologist for Correctional Service Canada, where he was responsible for the phallometric and criminological assessment of sex offenders. He evaluated more than 1200 different sex offenders either during their admission process or before their release. He has published a number of studies on the offending process of sexual offenders, criminal profiling, and sexual preferences of sex offenders.

Maurice Cusson is Professor at the School of Criminology at the University of Montreal and Researcher at the International Centre of Comparative Criminology at that university. Over the last thirty years, he has written ten books and more than 50 book chapters or refereed articles, in both French and English. He has received four prizes for his books, including two from the Académie des Sciences Morales et Politiques de l'Institut de France. His main research interests are homicide, crime prevention, the rational-choice perspective in criminology, and national security.

Alexandre Nicole is a clinical criminologist for the sex offender treatment programme at the Philippe-Pinel Institute of Montreal, a maximum-security psychiatric hospital. The institute is affiliated to the University of Montreal and M. Nicole also collaborates to various research projects related to sexual offending

LIST OF CONTRIBUTORS

Éric Beauregard, Assistant Professor, Department of Criminology, University of South Florida, 4202 E Fowler Avenue, SOC107, Tampa, Florida, 33620-8100, USA.

Richard Beckett, Head of Forensic Psychology and Research Service, The Oxford Clinic, Littlemore Hospital, Sanford Road, Oxford, 0X4 4XN, UK.

Anthony R. Beech, Professor and Chair in Criminological Psychology, Centre for Forensic and Family Psychology, University of Birmingham, Edgbaston, Birmingham, B15 2TT, UK.

Etienne Blais, Assistant Professor, School of Criminology, Université de Montréal, CP 6128, Succursale Centre-Ville, Montreal, Quebec, H3C 3J7, Canada.

Élisabeth Campos, Researcher, Institut Phillippe-Pinel de Montréal, 10905, boul. Henri-Bourassa Est, Montreal, Quebec, H1C 1H1, Canada.

Sabine Chéné, Head of Project, École Nationale d'Administration Pénitentiaire, 440 Avenue Michel Serres, BP 28 47916 Agen Cedex 9, France.

Maurice Cusson, Professor, School of Criminology, Université de Montréal, CP 6128, Succursale Centre-Ville, Montreal, Quebec, H3C 3J7, Canada.

Benoît Dassylva, Psychiatrist, Institut Phillippe-Pinel de Montréal, 10905, boul. Henri-Bourassa Est, Montreal, Quebec, H1C 1H1 Canada.

Dawn Fisher, Head of Psychology, Llanarth Court Hospital, Llanarth, Raglan, Usk, Gwent, NP15 2YD, UK.

Alexandre Nicole, Clinical Criminologist, Institut Philippe-Pinel de Montréal, 10905 boul. Henri-Bourassa Est, Montreal, Quebec, H1C 1H1, Canada.

William L. Marshall, Director, Rockwood Psychological Services, Suite 403, 303 Bagot Street, Kingston, Ontario, K7K 5W7, Canada.

CarolineJ.Oliver, Research Fellow, Centre for Forensic and Family Psychology, University of Birmingham, Edgbaston, Birmingham, UK.

Jean Proulx, Professor and Director, School of Criminology, Université de Montreal, CP 6128, Succursale Centre-Ville, Montreal, Quebec, H3C 3J7, Canada.

Nadège Sauvêtre, Criminologist, Centre International de Criminologie Comparée, Université de Montreal, CP 6128, Succursale Centre-Ville, Montreal, Quebec, H3C 3J7, Canada.

Michel St-Yves, Forensic Psychologist, Behavioral Science Unit, Sûreté du Québec, 1701 rue Parthenais, Montreal, Quebec, H2K 3S7, Canada.

Monique Tardif, Professor, Department of Sexology, Université du Québec à Montréal (UQAM), CP 8888, Succursale Centre-Ville, Montreal, Quebec, H3C 3P8, Canada.

PREFACE

Sexual murderers quite rightly attract significant public attention. Indeed, they are among the most consistently noted sexual offenders to appear in the public media. As a result, considerable attention has been given to those offenders in the professional literature. Unfortunately much of this literature, until quite recently, reflected no more than the untested opinions of clinicians who had worked with these men (and they are almost all men, a point not all authors attend to). As a more empirically based literature has appeared, it has become clear that many of the purportedly distinguishing features of these offenders do not distinguish them from other sexual offenders. This, in fact, is the essential and most important feature of the evidence reported in Proulx et al.'s excellent book.

Sexual murderers, as Proulx et al. make clear, are a mixed group, a fact often overlooked in empirical studies. The FBI researchers, who have been among the foremost authors on this topic, characteristically include serial sexual murderers, sexually sadistic murderers and sexual murderers with just one victim where there is no evidence of sadism. Proulx et al. sensibly distinguish these groups and focus all but one of their studies on the single-victim sexual murderers by comparing them with nonmurderous sexual aggressors (i.e., rapists of adult women). Their other study compared sadists with nonsadistic sexual aggressors.

The *Introduction* to this book provides an excellent overview of the results of the Montreal studies of sexual murderers, revealing, as noted above, that these men have far more in common with sexual aggressors who do not murder than a reading of the prior literature would imply. The Montreal studies also reveal that the murder of a victim occurring in the course of a sexual assault has various causes (e.g. to silence the witness, an expression of rage, a response to victim resistance and as a result of sadistic impulses). However, the Montreal group generated a 'decision tree' revealing that four features are strongly predictive of the occurrence of murder during a sexual crime: pre-crime anger; a stranger victim; offender has a weapon; and victim resistance. This latter feature is quite disappointing, since feminists at one time advocated training women to fight back in the event that they might be sexually attacked, and presumably fighting back reduces the tendency of victims to blame themselves for the abuse.

The valuable chapters by the Montreal group of researchers are followed by two outstanding contributions by the Birmingham group, whose studies produced findings essentially matching those of the Montreal researchers. The addition, in the Birmingham reports, of a comparison between sexual murderers and rapists on demographic features and psychometric results adds to the overall picture of sexual murderers.

Finally there are two chapters that focus on what are said to be practical features. I must say I was surprised to learn that work over the past few years on profiling has revealed utility to this approach. However, the authors are careful to point out that too many practitioners overemphasize the 'art' or 'semi-mystical' aspect of applied profiling. Apparently, adhering carefully to the empirically established rules of profiling can result in very valuable information that can assist investigators. The last chapter treads where few authors have gone before to suggest ways to therapeutically intervene with sexual murderers. While there are good suggestions made for treatment, these need to be subjected to empirical analysis, although one problem that besets such endeavours is the fact that few sexual murderers get released from prison and those that do are quite old at the time of release. Since we now know that age at release markedly alters the likelihood of reoffending among sexual offenders, this latter feature will always remain a confounder in examining the effects of treatment on sexual murderers.

I found this book to be very valuable and I congratulate the authors on their top-class work. The topic of sexual murderers has been of considerable interest to me in my work over the past 38 years of treating sexual offenders. At last I feel I have some empirical guides to help me in my work with these men.

William L. Marshall, OC, PhD, FRSC

ACKNOWLEDGEMENTS

The editors wish to thank the SSRC for its financial support, without which the Montreal Study could not have been conducted. We would also like to thank Correctional Service Canada for its support throughout the study. In particular, we would like to draw special attention to the professionalism and availability of Jacques Bigras, a senior psychologist with CSC.

In addition, we would like to thank Martine Giovanola and Nicole Pinsonneault, secretaries in the Centre International de Criminologie Comparée (CICC), as well as Francine Packwood, of the Centre de Recherche de l'Institut Philippe Pinel de Montréal (IPMM), for having typed the various versions of this book. We would be remiss if we did not mention the significant contribution of Steven Sacks, who translated the book into English. We would also like to thank the directors of the CICC (Jean-Paul Brodeur) and the research centre of the IPPM (Gilles Côté) for their financial support for the publication of this book. Finally, we are grateful to Gillian Leslie, Sarah Tilley, Nicole Burnett and Tessa Hanford at John Wiley & Sons for their skilful shepherding of the manuscript to publication.

INTRODUCTION
SEXUAL MURDERERS: MYTH AND REALITY

Maurice Cusson

Why is it that sexual murder elicits such a striking mixture of revulsion and fascination from us? Perhaps it is because the sexual murderer, although a figure of evil, bridges the gap between the two antithetical realities of unbridled violence and sexual pleasure. Krafft-Ebing believed that this association can be traced back to the Marquis de Sade, that regular guest of French asylums and prisons from 1763 until his death in 1814. Sadism – for that is the name we know it by today – appeared to Kraft-Ebing to be the key, the direct link between violence and sexual pleasure.

Since then, the shadow of de Sade has hovered in the background of every study of sexual murder. Sexual murder is the culmination of an attack prepared with the express purpose of seeking pleasure, even orgasm, in the subjugation, rape and suffering of a carefully selected woman. Indeed, it is precisely because they obtain pleasure in the suffering and humiliation of women that sexual murderers torture and kill their victims. Most authors believe that this aberrant motivation originates in long-nurtured fantasies in which cruelty and sexual pleasure are intermingled. Once a sadist has experienced the pleasure of sexual murder, he develops an obsession for it and sets out on murderous hunts over and over again. Hardly surprising, therefore, that of all sexual murderers, it is the serial killer who predominates in literature – both professional and fictional. It goes without saying

Sexual Murderers: A Comparative Analysis and New Perspectives Edited by Jean Proulx, Éric Beauregard, Maurice Cusson and Alexandre Nicole

that such monsters are clearly distinct from the run-of-the-mill lot of habitual thieves, violent criminals and, even, rapists. They are in a category of their own: obsessed by their fantasies, serial sexual murderers have only scorn for the petty crimes of robbery and assault.

When we began the research that forms the basis of most of the chapters of this book, we did not have the temerity to question the apparently implacable logic of the classic model of sexual murder. We did, however, know that the empirical foundation of this conceptual edifice was fragile, and that every relevant study had generalized from either a few cases or from small and unrepresentative samples, and furthermore that statistically valid conclusions were few and far between, and controversial in any event. To elucidate the phenomenon of sexual murder, it seemed to us, the logical next step was to rigorously verify the scientific validity of this apparently coherent and valid model. We therefore constructed a representative sample of sexual murderers, and systematically investigated the criminological, sexological, psychological and social characteristics of its members. Specifically, we approached every inmate incarcerated in Quebec in 1998 and 1999 for the sexual murder of a woman. Of the 57 inmates approached, 40 agreed to respond to our questions and submit to our tests. This sample is clearly different, in terms of both size and systematic recruitment, from other samples reported in the literature. It is in no way simply a collection of 'good cases' or 'monsters'.

Science often proceeds on the basis of comparison, and criminology is no different: criminals are compared to noncriminals, yesterday's patterns to today's. Consistent with this approach, we investigated the distinctive characteristics of the sexual murderers in our sample, through comparison of this group to sexual aggressors in a similarly constructed sample. To this end, every inmate incarcerated in federal penitentiaries in Quebec between 1995 and 2000 for the sexual assault of a woman was asked to participate in the study and respond to the same questions posed to sexual murderers. In all, 101 agreed. We also compared the sexual murderers in our sample to a sample of American serial murderers, and compared sadistic and nonsadistic offenders in our sample.

As the comparisons progressed, we had no choice but to face the obvious: our results raised serious questions about the dominant theory of sexual murder. The first surprises were that only a minority of sexual murderers were sadistic, and that sadism was much less important in the dynamics of murder than we had first thought. Another unexpected finding was the widespread similarity of sexual murderers and sexual aggressors: with very few exceptions, the two groups had similar criminal histories and personality disorders. This last similarity led us to a further discovery: the criminal histories of incarcerated sexual murderers and incarcerated career criminals were strangely similar. In both cases, the most common crimes were crimes against property and nonsexual assault.

The final surprise was a big one: among all the sexual murderers incarcerated in Quebec, there was only one serial killer of women (who refused to participate in our study). The conclusion was inescapable: unless one is to believe that Quebec police officers are incapable of catching serial murderers, this type of criminal is extremely rare in Quebec. Serial murderers are, it is true, more numerous in the United States, but the population there is some 45 times greater than that of Quebec. And even in the United States, they are hardly legion: Ressler interviewed only 36 in the entire American prison system. The illusion of numbers is only the product of media and literary frenzies.

In addition, a comparison of the single-victim sexual murderers in our sample and Ressler's serial killers revealed that the American serial killers were clearly more disturbed. It would thus be an error to equate sexual murderers and serial killers.

In summary then, sexual murderers are not as sadistic as we had thought, and are in fact little different than the sexual aggressors and broad-spectrum habitual criminals so familiar to criminologists. Can they then truly be called sexual murderers in the strictest sense of the term, i.e. members of a distinct category of criminals with a specific personality, history and criminal career? This answer is far from clear. What *is* clear, is that they had committed a sexual murder. And so we must ask: why? The reader will find the answer revealed bit by bit in the following pages. Without giving everything away, however, we would like to outline a few ideas that run through all our analyses, and which are more fully developed in the following chapters.

Among the sexual murderers in our sample, some exhibited a particularly strong intention for murder; in these, the primary intention – driven by rage, vengeance or sadism – was to kill. On the other hand, some murders started out as sexual assaults, with the death of the victim resulting from the murderer's excessive violence in the face of resistance to sexual relations, or the need to silence the only person capable of identifying him.

Sexual murder may be understood as the outcome of three factors: the murderer's personal history; the murderer's state of mind at the moment of the crime; and the specific circumstances of the attack. Most of the murderers in our sample (more than 60%) had substantial criminal records, typified by thefts of all kinds (the most common type of crime), nonsexual violent crimes and drug-related crimes. But virtually similar criminal records were also found among the sexual aggressors. Most sexual murders were thus preceded by a succession of varied, and in most cases nonsexual, crimes. This suggests that the general criminal proclivity invoked by criminologists to explain recidivism is also a factor in sexual murder. It can be further hypothesized that the commission of a crime as serious as murder requires a profound contempt for human life, and indeed for all rules, that is reinforced by a long history of unpunished transgressions.

If sexual murderers and sexual aggressors are so similar, why does the first group kill? Our results point to a nexus of developmental, intentional and situational factors. The sexual murderer is a man possessed by anger, if not rage, who drinks to excess, and who has a weapon close to hand. Which is to say that sexual aggressors who progress to murder are unhindered by inhibitions and scruples, in part because of alcohol consumption and their criminal background, and are so overcome with rage that they formulate a plan to kill or attack with ultimately fatal force.

And the sadists? Here we found a portrait similar to that reported by our predecessors – but only partially. As far as sexual preferences are concerned, we found essentially the classic clinical portrait. Once well ensconced in their reveries, the sadists in our sample – regardless of whether they had committed a murder or a sexual assault – wallow in fantasies of domination and violence. Phallometric evaluation revealed their preference for humiliating and violent scenarios. In particular, they like violent pornography. They are more likely than nonsadists to prepare their crime, and to choose their victims carefully. During the commission of the murder or sexual assault, they give full rein to their perverse nature, humiliating their victims and indulging in wanton violence much more often than nonsadists, and going as far as torture and mutilation.

Where our observations part company with the dominant model is on the question of the similarity of sadists and ordinary recidivists. The dominant model sees these two groups as quite distinct, the sadists being seen as exceptions by virtue of the fact that they lack criminal records. But this was not true in our sample: sadists had committed as many thefts and nonsexual violent crimes as nonsadists. This suggests that sadistic killing takes more than the mere contemplation of fantasies of humiliation and torture: it also takes fertile criminal soil.

Similarly, our results with regard to the role of anger and sexual motivation in sadistic sexual murder forced us to question the classic model. The sadists in our sample did not act in cold blood, and were motivated by more than the mere quest for orgasm. Even more so than the nonsadists, they hated women and were driven by rage, which rendered their attacks even more violent than they would have been had they been motivated by sexual desire alone. The personal histories of the sadists, riddled with hate and resentment, are consistent with this interpretation. Very early in their lives, future sadistic criminals are the object of humiliation, which leads them to social isolation and to take refuge in an imaginary world in which they keep their wounds green. Coupled with an aversion to women, this resentment nourishes an obsessive desire for vengeance.

For several reasons, we believe that rage is a factor in most sexual murders, although it may operate in two different ways. In nonsadistic murderers, rage is impulsive, an explosive reaction to frustration (for example, a woman's rebuffing of the murderer's advances). On the other hand, in sadistic murderers, it appears that hate long nurtured in solitude leads to a premeditated attack. Filled as they are with resentment, and accustomed to associating violence and pleasure, sadists are predictably drawn to murder. And in fact this is what we found: sexual murders were twice as common among sadists as among nonsadists. In the latter group, sexual assault is the predominant crime, and is three times more prevalent than murder.

This book is composed of 13 chapters. Chapters 1 to 9 present the results of the *Montreal Study of Sexual Murderers*. Chapter 1 outlines our view of sexual murder, summarizes current knowledge on its frequency and critically reviews the principal explanatory theories. Chapter 2 adopts a developmental perspective. It presents our results concerning the childhood and adolescence of sexual murderers, compares them to those of sexual aggressors and examines the criminal careers of both groups. Chapter 3 examines the personality characteristics of sexual murderers and sexual aggressors, as measured by psychological tests, in order to identify any psychopathologies specific to sexual murderers. In Chapter 4, the focus is on the sexual murder as an event. What were the murderer's intentions at the time of the crime? What happened afterwards? Why did an attack which could have ended in sexual assault only in fact end in the death of a woman? Chapter 5 presents the results of a multivariate analysis in which all the variables presented in Chapters 2–4 that appear to contribute to the discrimination of sexual murderers from sexual aggressors were studied simultaneously. This statistical procedure revealed the existence of several factors which are related to the lethality of the sexual assault. This analysis is followed in Chapter 6 by a comparison of our sample of sexual murderers and the FBI sample of serial sexual murderers analysed by Ressler. Chapter 7 discusses sexual sadism. After a detailed examination of the literature, we compare the sadistic sexual aggressors in our sample to the nonsadistic sexual criminals (in this case, the samples of sexual murderers and sexual aggressors were merged). This comparison gave rise to a novel portrait of sadistic criminals. This analysis is further developed in Chapter 8, which is concerned with the distinction between the angry and sadistic types of sexual murderers: the first acts primarily out of anger and in a disorganized manner, while the second acts in a premeditated manner, and the suffering of his victim is the core component of his crime. In Chapter 9, the results of qualitative analyses are presented. Case studies are relied on heavily in our attempt to answer two questions: What motivates sexual murderers to commit their crimes? What was the criminal career of our subjects before they committed their last and worst crime? Chapters 10 and 11 present the results of the *Birmingham Study of Sexual Murderers*. Chapter 10 presents a comparison of sexual aggressors of women (rapists) and sexual murderers of women, whereas Chapter 11 contains an analysis of sexual murderers' motivations. Chapters 12 and 13 discuss *Practical Issues* related to sexual murderers. Chapter 12 discusses criminal profiling, a popular but controversial technique, while Chapter 13 formulates recommendations for treatment of sexual murderers.

PART I
THE MONTREAL STUDY

Chapter 1
SEXUAL MURDER: DEFINITIONS, EPIDEMIOLOGY AND THEORIES

Jean Proulx, Maurice Cusson and Éric Beauregard

In the popular mind, the archetypal sexual murderer is someone like Ted Bundy, the intelligent, charming and manipulative American psychopath responsible for the death of scores of women. Because of the extensive media coverage of sexual murders, there is a widespread belief that this type of crime is common and that every woman is in fact in danger of becoming one of these monsters' next victims. But is this perception of sexual murderers and their crimes a true reflection of reality?

This chapter will summarize current understanding of sexual murders and sexual murderers. A definition of sexual murder will first be proposed. This will be followed by a presentation of the epidemiological data related to sexual murder, a review of the biological, psychological and sociological theories of sexual murder, and a description of the comparative studies that have identified characteristics specific to sexual murderers. Lastly, the conceptual framework of this book, as well as some methodological issues, will be discussed.

DEFINITIONS

The first obstacle to characterizing sexual murder is the absence of any legal definition. As Roberts and Grossman (1993) point out, the *Criminal*

Sexual Murderers: A Comparative Analysis and New Perspectives   Edited by Jean Proulx Éric Beauregard, Maurice Cusson and Alexandre Nicole

Code of Canada contains no provision specific to sexual murder. While the *Code* does of course contain sections related to murders committed during sexual crimes, the only charge prescribed by these is first-degree murder, regardless of premeditation. In fact, the sexual nature of a sexual murder is considered relevant only for the purposes of determining sentence. Furthermore, application of the sections concerning murder committed during a sexual crime presupposes that the homicide has actually being identified as a sexual murder – a difficult task in the absence of victim testimony.

When investigators attempt to solve a murder and decide whether it is sexual in nature, they rely on two types of information: testimony, of either the murderer or someone else, and material evidence, of which the crime scene is the key source. Ressler, Burgess and Douglas (1988) consider a murder sexual if at least one of the following is true: (1) the victim is found totally or partially naked; (2) the genitals are exposed; (3) the body is found in a sexually explicit position; (4) an object has been inserted into a body cavity (anus, vagina, mouth); (5) there is evidence of sexual contact; (6) there is evidence of substitutive sexual activity (for example, masturbation and ejaculation at the crime scene) or of sadistic sexual fantasies (for example, genital mutilation). The main obstacle to the exploitation of this type of evidence is the failure of some police officers to recognize it as sexual.

The definition of sexual murder also poses problems of a purely lexical nature. In practice, the terms 'sexual murder', 'serial murder', 'mass murder', and 'sadistic (lust) murder' are often used interchangeably (Langevin, 1991; McKenzie, 1995; Myers, 2002). However, a murder should only be classified as a mass murder if it results in at least three deaths at the same location and time. In contrast, a serial murder comprises a series of events separated from one another by emotional cool-off periods. Mass and serial murders may or may not be sexual, and serial and nonserial sexual murders may or may not be sadistic. These lexical confusions can result in research weaknesses: while some published studies have used samples comprising solely sadistic sexual murderers, others have relied upon heterogeneous samples comprising both sexual and nonsexual serial murderers. Our understanding of the specific features of sexual murder has been hindered by the extreme difficulty of comparing the results of such diverse studies to one another.

A final problem related to the definition of sexual murder has been the failure of some researchers to take into account differences in the sex and age of the victims. In several cases, murders of women, of men and of children have been considered to belong to a single category, despite the fact there is no evidence that these types of sexual murders are part of a homogeneous phenomenon. Because of the absence of any such evidence, on the contrary, it is essential that definitions of sexual murder take into account the age and sex of the victims.

EPIDEMIOLOGY

In Canada, between 1974 and 1986, there were 305 sexual murders, i.e. approximately 23 murders annually (Roberts & Grossman, 1993). These represented approximately 4% of all murders in this period. In 1999, there were 22 sexual murders, representing 4.1% of all murders (Porter & Woodworth, 2001). The Canadian rate of sexual murder thus appears to have remained stable over the last three decades. The victims have been overwhelmingly female (85%) and younger than 30 years (69%). Virtually all (99%) the sexual murderers have been male, and half have been between 16 and 25 years old (Roberts & Grossman, 1993).

In the United States, the situation appears to be different. Between 1991 and 1995, sexual murders accounted for only 0.9% of all murders (Meloy, 2000). An average of 199.6 sexual murders were committed annually over this period, equivalent to a rate of 0.09 sexual murders per 100,000 people per year. The rate of sexual murder in Canada in 1999 was also 0.09 per 100,000 people. There was thus no difference in the rate of sexual murder in the two countries. However, because the overall murder rate is much higher in the United States than it is in Canada, the percentage of murders represented by sexual murder is much lower than it is in Canada (Cusson, 1999).

Serial sexual murderers account for only a small proportion of all sexual murderers. In the United States, between 1975 and 1999, 153 serial murderers were responsible for more than 1400 deaths, a rate of approximately 70 victims per year. Overall, 60% of serial murderers are sexual murderers as well (Geberth, 1995). Thus, between 1975 and 1999, serial sexual murderers were responsible for 42 victims annually, i.e. for almost 20% of all sexual-murder victims. Because serial sexual murderers kill an average of 10 victims each, it follows that they account for approximately 2% of all sexual murderers in the United States. The situation is similar in Canada, where serial sexual murderers account for only 3% of incarcerated sexual murderers (Beauregard & Proulx, 2002). Given these statistics, it is surprising that publications on serial sexual murderers are so prevalent in the literature on sexual murder. This state of affairs led Fox and Levin (1999) to conclude that 'there may be more scholars studying serial murder than there are offenders committing it' (p. 166). Clearly, studies of sexual murder that focus on serial killers shed limited light on the phenomenon of sexual murder as a whole.

In the previous section, it was pointed out that ambiguous evidence or testimony may result in the sexual nature of some murders going undetected (Ressler et al., 1988). This may result in the underestimation of the number of sexual murders. Hickey (1997) mentions two other situations that lead to the underestimation of sexual murders: the destruction of the body of a victim; and the failure to report the disappearance of a victim to the police. In the former, the crime will be considered a missing persons case. In the latter case, common when the victim is socially marginal or lacks well-established social networks, e.g. a prostitute, the crime will not even be considered a missing persons case. Nonetheless, as Roberts and Grossman (1993) point out, almost all the victims of sexual murder are indeed correctly classified, and the solution rate for these crimes is approximately 75%.

THEORIES

Several theories of sexual murder have been advanced. Unfortunately, empirical evidence for any of them is limited. Several of the theories rely solely on clinical observations, and some are based on small study groups. Furthermore, many of the theories are derived from populations comprising only a single type of sexual murderer, namely serial sexual murderers or sadistic sexual murderers, both of which represent only a small percentage of incarcerated sexual murderers (Fox & Levin, 1999). A final caveat is that in no case do the theories take into account more than a limited number of factors. Despite these limitations, these theories make valuable contributions, and the following sections discuss their principal features and empirical bases. The theories can be grouped into three broad categories: biological theories, psychological theories and sociological theories.

Biological theories

Money's (1990) biological theory of sadistic sexual murder (erotophonophilia) is based on a single clinical case and the scientific literature on the biological basis of violence. In this theory, the sexual stimulation of the sadistic sexual murderer arises from the physical and psychological suffering of the victims in his sexual fantasies or actual crimes. According to Money, the main cause of sexual sadism is a tumour in, or trauma to, the limbic system (comprising the hippocampus, hypothalamus and amygdaloid nucleus), the region of the brain that controls sexual and attack behaviours. Lesions of this system are thought to cause sexual sadism by facilitating the transmission of messages that simultaneously trigger sexual and attack behaviours. The lesions may be quite subtle, and impossible to detect through medical examination. Also, as with epilepsy, the cerebral dysfunction is episodic.

Although Money (1990) considers neurological factors to be the primary cause of sadistic sexual murder, he points out that endocrinological and genetic factors are also at play. Thus, sadistic murderers may have testosterone deficits that result in diminished virility, which in turn causes compensatory hypermasculine behaviours such as sexual murder. This type of criminal may also possess a genetic predisposition towards emotional instability (for example, rage or sexual arousal) and impulsive behaviour.

Money believes that sexual sadism may also have psychological roots. For example, a history of childhood sexual abuse or dysfunctional family relationships may increase the risk of sexual sadism. Furthermore, some intercurrent mental disorders – such as dissociative syndrome, bipolar disorder, or even epilepsy – may facilitate sadistic sexual murder.

While Money's model is coherent, it is not derived from actual research on the role of biological (neurological, endocrinological or genetic) factors in sexual murder. In fairness, however, it should be noted that there is some evidence of a noteworthy prevalence (18–40%) of neurological disorders among sexual criminals (Gratzer & Bradford, 1995; Hucker, 1997; Hucker et al., 1988; Langevin, 1991; Langevin et al., 1988; McKenzie, 1995; Stone, 1994). Nevertheless, this evidence is insufficient to establish a causal relationship between any biological variables and the commission of sexual murder. Consequently, the biological factors included in Money's model remain only *possible* causes of sexual murder: empirical studies are required to clarify their role.

Psychological theories

Classical (respondent) conditioning

Meloy (2000) posits that sexual arousal in sexual murderers is a conditioned response to the conditioned stimuli of coercion and violence. As an illustration of this process of classical conditioning, consider an adolescent who watches horror films in which naked women are killed by monsters. In Phase 1, the sight of naked women is an unconditioned stimulus that triggers sexual arousal as an unconditioned response. However, violent behaviour towards women (i.e. a neutral stimulus) triggers no such response. In Phase 2, the neutral stimulus (violent behaviour towards women) becomes a conditioned stimulus through its repeated association with the unconditioned stimulus (naked women). In Phase 3, the conditioned stimulus (violent behaviour towards women) is sufficient to provoke a conditioned response of sexual arousal.

MacCulloch, Snowden, Wood and Mills (1983) note that the observed progressive escalation of the violence of fantasies and crimes can be explained by the process of habituation. According to these authors, the sexual arousal generated by a violent sexual fantasy or violent sexual crime decreases with repetition, driving sexual murderers to increasingly violent stimuli (fantasies, crimes) in order to obtain the same, high, level of sexual arousal.

Operant conditioning

MacCulloch et al. (1983) have also suggested that sadistic sexual fantasies constitute operant behaviours that diminish feelings of incompetence.

Consider the sexual murderer whose interpersonal difficulties with women make him feel incompetent. In such an individual, sadistic sexual fantasies may result in feelings of power and control. The probability of such fantasies recurring when the murderer experiences feelings of incompetence is increased by the efficacy of these fantasies in reducing such feelings (negative reinforcement).

Classical and operant conditioning theories appear to be promising avenues of explanation for the initiation and progression of violent sexual fantasies and behaviours. However, the hypotheses have yet to be tested in empirical studies.

Psychodynamic approaches

According to Revitch and Schlesinger (1981, 1989), there are two types of sexual murders: catathymic and compulsive. Catathymic murders are a form of symbolic matricide, in which the murderer's intense and invasive rage towards his mother is displaced to another woman. Such rage may have many origins, including: (1) an overprotective mother; (2) a seductive mother; (3) a mother with inappropriate sexual behaviour (for example, prostitution); and (4) a mother who infantilizes or feminizes her son. The catathymic process comprises three phases: (1) incubation, during which tension and rage are accumulated; (2) the murder itself; (3) relief following the expression of the rage (Revitch, 1980). In general, catathymic murder is an isolated event that involves only one victim, specifically a woman known to the murderer (Revitch, 1965).

Compulsive sexual murders are the work of loners who nurture feelings of rage towards women (Revitch & Schlesinger, 1989), and spend considerable time lost in sadistic sexual fantasies (Schlesinger, 2000). These fantasies induce a state of sexual tension which, when finally unbearable, precipitates a murder. The emotional and sexual gratification attendant on the murder reduces this tension. Compulsive sexual murderers usually attack victims unknown to them. A great many of them become serial sexual murderers (Schlesinger & Revitch, 1997).

Revitch and Schlesinger's model of sexual murder is based on their clinical analysis of 43 individuals, only nine of whom were sexual murderers. While their theory of catathymic sexual murder is based on an empirically unverifiable psychodynamic paradigm (Fox & Levin, 1999), it should be noted that the displacement process they invoke has been demonstrated in laboratory experiments (Tedeschi & Norman, 1985). Their explanation of compulsive murder, on the other hand, is inherently descriptive (sadistic sexual fantasies, sexual tension, sexual murder, sexual gratification) and therefore includes few interpretative elements.

The theme of matricentric rage is also at the heart of Stone's (1994) explanatory model of sexual murder. After clinical analysis of 42 biographies of serial sexual murderers, Stone concluded that sexual murder is always an act of displaced vengeance against a mother who humiliated the murderer or exhibited inappropriate sexual behaviour.

According to Meloy (2000), matricentric rage stems from an abnormal child–mother differentiation process. This conclusion is based on Stoller's (1978) theory, which argues that boys who are unsuccessful in differentiating themselves from their mothers develop not only an ambiguous masculine identity but also sexual perversions that allow them to indirectly express their rage against their dominating and controlling mothers.

Finally, Liebert's (1985) psychodynamic model is based on the theories of Klein (1948) and Kernerg (1975). According to this model, maternal hostility during a child's early psychological development favours splitting, an archaic defence mechanism, which enables the child to cope with its paranoid anguish. This results in a vision of interpersonal relations in which the Other is either totally good or totally evil. Sexual murderers see their victims as the embodiment of evil, and displace their rage, from their hostile mothers to surrogate female victims.

The motivational model

A group of researchers associated with the Federal Bureau of Investigation (FBI) have developed a motivational model of sexual murder (Burgess et al., 1986; Burgess et al., 1994; Douglas et al., 1992; Ressler et al., 1988; Ressler, Burgess, Douglas et al., 1986; Ressler, Burgess, Hartman et al., 1986). This model is based on data collected during interviews with 36 sexual murderers who had killed a total of 118 victims. The majority of the subjects in this study (25/36) were serial sexual murderers. The majority of victims were female (82%) and older than 13 years (88%).

According to the FBI researchers, both the fantasy and the act of sexual murder are inappropriate coping strategies used by murderers in the face of stressful situations. This propensity for sexual murder is the result of a long process that comprises the following steps:

1. In early childhood, the absence of care and affection establishes a problematic attachment style characterized by detachment and hostility.
2. During childhood and adolescence, sexual, physical or psychological victimization experiences result in social isolation and favour the emergence of violent sexual fantasies which compensate for the absence of real-life control. Masturbatory activities reinforce the coping role of fantasies in the psychological world of the developing sexual murderer.
3. The negative personality traits (rebelliousness, aggressivity, feelings of entitlement, desire for vengeance) that develop in the preceding steps interfere with the development of gratifying social relationships, prosocial values and empathy. Consequently, both social isolation and preferential reliance on sexual fantasies as a substitute source of affective

stimulation grow. In these fantasies, the future murderer, unconstrained by reality, assumes a grandiose and omnipotent role.

4. Aggressive fantasies are concretized as nonlethal destructive actions such as arson, animal cruelty and physical, sexual and psychological violence towards those both close to and unknown to the future murderer. The future murderer experiences these behaviours both as an extension of the power he assumes in his fantasies and vengeance for injustices he has experienced.

5. The first sexual murder is precipitated by an intense stressor, such as conflict with a woman (59%), conflict with parents (53%) or financial difficulties (48%).

6. Following the first murder, the murderer's fantasies become richer and even more invasive. When the next stressful episode occurs, the murderer plans his next crime, in which he not only attempts to reduce the risks of being caught, but also maximizes the congruence of the crime to his fantasies.

This motivational model of sexual murder has many strengths. Firstly, it has an empirical basis, namely in-depth interviews with, and official files (police reports, court files) related to, 36 sexual murderers. Furthermore, the model is particularly comprehensive, as it takes into account developmental factors, personal characteristics and situational factors. Nevertheless, the model does have some limitations. First, the study group is not a random sample (Godwin, 2000), and serial sexual murderers are over-represented in it. Secondly, it is not possible to identify factors specific to sexual murderers, as the FBI study did not use a comparison group. Finally, the study does not differentiate between sexual murderers of women, of men and of children – all of whom were present in the study group – despite the fact that these three types of murderers may be so different as to justify separate studies (Beauregard & Proulx, in press; Beauregard et al., in press).

Social isolation and deviant sexual fantasies are the two central elements of the FBI's motivational model. The conclusions of other studies agree with those of the FBI and underscore the importance of these two factors. McKenzie (1995), for example, found that 55% of the 20 serial sexual murderers he studied were socially isolated, and Grubin (1994) considered sexual murder to be directly and indirectly related to social isolation. In the latter's opinion, social isolation is a symptom of a psychopathology that itself leads to sexual murder; furthermore, in the absence of interpersonal contacts, sexual murderers rely on their inner worlds and fantasies for emotional gratification. Finally, Marshall (1989a) has mentioned that loneliness is a source of psychological suffering and can engender violence.

Brittain (1970) considered deviant sexual fantasies to be at the heart of the process that culminates in sexual murder. In his view, these fantasies are the mechanism by which individuals compensate for low self-esteem. In fact, sexual murderers, in their fantasies and crimes, perceive themselves to be superior to others, and even omnipotent (see also Hazelwood & Warren, 1995; MacCulloch et al., 1983; Meloy, 2000). In addition, Prentky, Burgess et al. (1989) suggest that such fantasies are the cause of serial sexual murders. This is supported by their finding that 86% of serial sexual murderers in their study ($N = 25$), but only 23% ($N = 21$) of nonserial sexual murderers, reported homicidal fantasies. Other studies have also reported a high prevalence of aggressive sexual fantasies among serial sexual murderers (Myers, Burgess & Nelson, 1998; Ressler et al., 1988; Warren, Hazelwood & Dietz, 1996). With repetition, the fantasies preceding the first sexual murder lose much of their gratifying power (due to habituation), which precipitates a quest for emotional intensity that culminates in a sexual murder that concretizes the fantasies (Gacono & Meloy, 1994). In sexual murderers, coercive sexual fantasies are also thought to facilitate the progression from the first murder to subsequent ones, as they are reinforced by masturbatory activities (Meloy, 2000). Furthermore, as new elements are introduced into the fantasies, the murderer is stimulated to undertake new murders that concretize them.

Paraphilias and sexual murder

Several studies have reported the presence of a high prevalence of paraphilias among sexual murderers (Arrigo & Purcell, 2001; Dietz, Hazelwood & Warren, 1990; Gratzer & Bradford, 1995; Langevin et al., 1988; McKenzie, 1995; Prentky, Burgess et al., 1989). The most frequently encountered paraphilias are sexual sadism, fetishism, exhibitionism and voyeurism. According to Prentky, Burgess et al. (1989), individuals who exhibit paraphilias prefer the world of fantasy to that of reality, and are constantly searching for new fantasies that increase their sexual pleasure. Because of habituation, the maintenance of a high level of pleasure requires an escalation of the coercive nature of the murderer's sexual fantasies and behaviours. Voyeurism, exhibitionism, rape and sexual murder are thus simply stages of a paraphilic continuum.

Psychopathologies and sexual murder

Several divergent positions have been taken with regard to the role of psychopathological factors in sexual murder. Some authors believe that sexual murderers are schizophrenic (Revitch, 1965), while others suggest dissociative disorders (Watkins, 1984) or obsessive-compulsive disorders (Brown, 1991) are at play. In addition, sexual murder appears to be associated with a variety of personality disorder, including psychopathy (Dietz, 1986), antisocial personality disorder (Yarvis, 1995), borderline personality disorder (Gacono & Meloy, 1994) and schizoid personality disorder (Myers & Monaco, 2000). Debate over the relationship between sexual murder and psychopathological factors will be discussed in Chapter 3.

Sociological theories

Leyton (1986) developed a socio-historical theory of serial sexual murder in which this crime transcends temporary personal frustrations and the quest for immediate gratification. According to this theory, sexual murder is 'a kind of sustained sub-political campaign directed towards the timelessness of oppression and the order of power' (p. 331). The specific features of sexual murder are thus reflections of specific socio-historical contexts: 'It is precisely at the point in time when a single class is most threatened that we expect to find some members of that class beginning to fantasize about killing members of another class' (p. 376).

Serial sexual murders were rare before the nineteenth century. In traditional communal societies, most people enjoyed a modest standard of living, and mutual help was the rule, competition the exception. In this world, sexual murderers were members of a select social group – nobles – and their prey were members of the peasantry. The constructed meaning of sexual murders committed by nobles is rooted in the crisis of feudalism that started at the end of the Middle Ages. These crimes were the expression of a desire to restore the absolute power of the nobility, which was threatened by the claims of peasants and merchants.

In the nineteenth and early twentieth century, serial sexual murderers were members of the petite bourgeoisie, and their victims were servants or prostitutes. The social meaning of their crimes can be found in the murderers' need to negate the insecurity associated with their newly acquired social position. Servants and prostitutes with their coarse and vulgar ways were the cesspool into which they feared to return.

The new social dynamics that emerged after the end of the Second World War resulted in yet another change in the face of the serial sexual murderer. The sexual murderer is now an ambitious, but untalented, young man from the middle class, and his victims belong to the social class to which he aspires. Thus, sexual murder has become a way of exacting revenge on an unattainable social class, an outlet for failed aspirations. In this analysis, the relatively high rate of serial sexual murder in the United States can be understood as a reflection of a dominant culture that exalts upward social mobility and tolerates violence as a problem-solving strategy.

From a strictly intellectual perspective, Leyton's model is seductive. However, it rests on a tenuous empirical base, namely the biographies of only a few serial sexual murderers. Furthermore, Leyton's theory is rhetorically unsatisfying. For if sexual murder does indeed fulfil a political function – the struggle against oppression – why are there so few murderers of this type? Furthermore, the selection of biographies of pre-twentieth-century sexual murderers is subject to sampling bias, as it is probable that the crimes of the nobility or bourgeoisie elicited greater interest than those of the peasantry or proletariat. Finally, it is possible that the choice of victims is a function of criminal opportunity, and is totally unrelated to social conflict (Cohen & Felson, 1979; Miethe & McCorkle, 1998). It should be recalled, in this connection, that in the nineteenth century servants and prostitutes were common, in contrast to 'guardians' likely to interfere with the criminal intentions of a serial murderer.

It is possible to see the biological, psychological and sociological theories of sexual murder as various levels of description of the same phenomenon: that is, as complementary rather than mutually exclusive explanations. However, given the current level of understanding of sexual murder, it is essential to conduct empirical studies designed to verify the hypotheses derived from these theories. A further necessity is the performance of comparative studies in order to identify the characteristics that differentiate serial sexual murderers from nonserial sexual murderers and from sexual aggressors. The following section takes up this theme.

COMPARISON OF NONSERIAL SEXUAL MURDERERS, SEXUAL AGGRESSORS AND SERIAL SEXUAL MURDERERS

To our knowledge, very few studies of nonserial sexual murderers have included a comparison group composed of other types of sexual offenders. In fact, only three studies have compared nonserial sexual murderers to sexual aggressors of women (Grubin, 1994; Langevin et al., 1988; Milsom, Webster & Beech, 2001), and only one study has compared nonserial and serial sexual murderers (Prentky, Knight et al., 1989). This section will first present the results of these studies, and subsequently interpret them in the light of the theories of sexual murder outlined in the preceding section.

Nonserial sexual murderers and sexual aggressors of women

Langevin et al. (1988) conducted the first, and still the most comprehensive, comparative study of nonserial sexual murderers. Although a broad range of developmental, psychological and criminological variables were analysed, the generalizability of their results is seriously limited by the small number of subjects studied (13 nonsexual murderers, 13 nonserial sexual murderers and 13 sexual aggressors of women). A further limitation is the study's biased sample, as only sexual aggressors having committed nonviolent sexual assaults were included. Grubin (1994) compared nonserial sexual murderers $(N = 21)$ to sexual aggressors of women $(N = 121)$. While this study is noteworthy for the significant number of subjects, it investigated a narrower range of variables, particularly psychological and developmental ones, than did Langevin et al.'s (1988). Finally, Milsom et al. (2001) studied a limited number of variables in two small samples, namely 19 nonserial sexual murderers and 16 sexual aggressors of women.

Table 1.1 Sociodemographic and developmental characteristics of three types of violent criminals

Characteristics	Langevin et al. (1988)			Grubin (1994)		Milsom et al. (2001)	
	NSM (N = 13)	SM (N = 13)	SAW (N = 13)	SM (N = 21)	SAW (N = 121)	SM (N = 19)	SAW (N = 16)
Sociodemographic							
Age (years)				30	26*		
Number of jobs held	3	7	1				
Developmental							
Social isolation prior to age 18				43%	19%*	+	–
Behaviour problems at school	18%	45%	83%				
Running away from home	11%	80%	0%*				
Enuresis beyond age 5	33%	62%	33%				
Temper tantrums	40%	83%	100%*				
Cruelty towards animals	10%	39%	40%				
Father present prior to age 10				76%	52%		
Father violent		+	–				
Mother present prior to age 10				71%	65%		
Mother controlling						+	–
Deviant sexual fantasies prior to age 18						+	–
Violent hobbies	40%	17%	83%	50%	50%		
Previously charged with a sexual crime	0.33	0.67	3.0*	29%	7%		
Previously charged with a violent crime				50%	50%		

* $p < 0.05$

An examination of the developmental variables presented in Table 1.1 reveals that nonserial sexual murderers are more likely than sexual aggressors of women to have experienced social isolation (Grubin, 1994; Milsom et al., 2001) and to have run away from home (Langevin et al., 1988). The prevalence of controlling mothers (Milsom et al., 2001), as well of violent fathers (Langevin et al., 1988), was higher among sexual murderers than among sexual aggressors. Finally, the prevalence of deviant sexual fantasies was higher among sexual murderers (Milsom et al., 2001).

These results highlight certain developmental characteristics that distinguish sexual murderers from sexual aggressors of women. Several of them – social isolation (Brittain, 1970; Ressler et al., 1988), hostility towards a dominant mother (Revitch & Schlesinger, 1989) and deviant sexual fantasies that compensate for a lack of control in the real world (MacCulloch et al., 1983; Ressler et al., 1988) – have found a place in theories of sexual murder. It is worth emphasizing that these comparative studies confirm the theoretical relevance of developmental factors in attempts to understand nonserial sexual murderers. These studies also indicate that sexual murderers and aggressors share a number of problematic behaviours, such as cruelty towards animals and temper tantrums.

Turning now to psychological factors, we see, in Table 1.2, that overcontrolled anger is more prevalent among sexual murderers (Grubin, 1994). Furthermore, a diagnosis of antisocial personality was more common among sexual murderers than among sexual aggressors of women (Langevin et al., 1988), although the former scored lower on the psychopathy scale (Minnesota Multiphasic Personality Inventory, MMPI) than did sexual aggressors. How should we interpret this contradiction? A plausible explanation is that clinicians have a tendency, in judicial contexts, to formulate judgements about the crime – in this case, sexual murder, the ultimate antisocial act – rather than about the criminal. The MMPI, in contrast, evaluates the sexual murderer rather than the murder.

In Langevin et al.'s (1988) study, sexual murderers exhibited higher IQs and higher testosterone levels than did sexual aggressors. This latter result is consistent with Money's (1990) biological model. However, sexual murderers were little different than sexual aggressors with regard to the frequency of brain damage, which was relatively common in both groups of sexual offenders and totally absent in nonsexual murderers.

Paraphilias were more common among sexual murderers than among sexual aggressors of women (Grubin, 1994; Langevin et al., 1988). The most frequently reported paraphilias were voyeurism, transvestism and sadism. Sexual murderers also exhibited phallometric responses consistent with a sexual preference for sadistic behaviours. The results of these comparative studies with regard to paraphilias agree with Prentky, Knight et al.'s (1989) model.

Table 1.3 summarizes the comparative studies' results with regard to the pre-crime phase. Adult sexual murderers were more socially and sexually

Table 1.2 Psychological characteristics of three types of violent criminals

Characteristics	Langevin et al. (1988)			Grubin (1994)		Milsom et al. (2001)	
	NSM (N = 13)	SM (N = 13)	SAW (N = 13)	SM (N = 21)	SAW (N = 121)	SM (N = 19)	SAW (N = 16)
Personality							
Psychopathy (MMPI score)	88	60	67				
Antisocial personality (DSM)	15%	58%	11%				
Personality disorders	54%	83%	58%				
Overcontrolled anger				38%	18%*		
Hypochondria				52%	20%		
IQ (mean)	104	109	93				
Biological factors							
Brain damage	0%	40%	60%				
High testosterone level	14%	71%	33%				
Paraphilias							
Paraphilia				43%	26%		
Voyeurism	17%	54%	38%*				
Transvestism	8%	54%	0%*				
Sadism (behaviour)	8%	75%	0%*				
Sadism (phallometry)		44%	13%				

* $p < 0.05$
NSM: nonsexual murderer; SM: sexual murderer; SAW: sexual aggressor of women

Table 1.3 Characteristics of the pre-crime and crime phases in three groups of violent criminals

Characteristics	Langevin et al. (1988)			Grubin (1994)		Milsom et al. (2001)	
	NSM (N = 13)	SM (N = 13)	SAW (N = 13)	SM (N = 21)	SAW (N = 121)	SM (N = 19)	SAW (N = 16)
Pre-crime (older than 18)							
Deviant sexual fantasies				5%	7%	+	—
Social isolation				29%	5%*		
Lives alone				43%	22%*		
No sexual partner				38%	15%*		
Little sexual experience				62%	19%*		
At least one characteristic of social isolation				86%	45%		
Pre-crime (preceding 48 hours)							
Anger	25%	69%	25%	50%			
Alcohol/drugs	54%	25%	50%	43%			
Crime							
Age of the victim (years)	36	20	28*	38.3	28.2*		
Victim unknown to criminal	8%	69%	82%*				
Victim female	38%	92%	100%*				
Use of a weapon	100%	100%	42%	24%	39%		
Murder by strangulation	8%	71%					
Murder by firearm	46%	8%					

* $p < 0.05$

NSM: nonsexual murderer; SM: sexual murderer; SAW: sexual aggressor of women

+: subjects in this group exhibited the characteristic in question more often than did the group indicated by–

isolated than were sexual aggressors of women (Grubin, 1994). However, deviant sexual fantasies appear to be virtually absent in both groups. These astonishing results probably reflect the forensic context of the data collection. It must be recalled that sexual offenders are only likely to reveal their sexual fantasies if they believe such revelations will not have negative consequences; this condition does not appear to have been true in Grubin's study. Nevertheless, these results unequivocally confirm the importance of social and sexual isolation, reported in Brittain's (1970) seminal clinical profile of sexual murderers.

In sexual murderers, the dominant feature of the hours preceding the crime is anger (Grubin, 1994; Langevin et al., 1988; Milsom et al., 2001), whereas in sexual aggressors of women it is intoxication with psychoactive substances. According to Langevin et al. (1988), these pre-crime differences can be explained by the fact that sexual murderers may experience less sexual pleasure when they are intoxicated. It may also be that control over the offending process, which is incompatible with excessive consumption of alcohol and drugs, is more important to sexual murderers.

There is little difference in the features of the crime phases of sexual murderers and sexual aggressors. Both types of offenders, in most cases, choose victims who are female and unknown to them (Langevin et al., 1988). The differences with regard to victim age and the use of weapons reported by Grubin and by Langevin et al. may reflect differences in sampling procedures. A final noteworthy finding is that sexual murderers most often killed their victims by strangulation, while nonsexual murderers used firearms.

Overall, the results of these three comparative studies are consistent with the theories of sexual murder outlined previously. In summary, nonserial sexual murderers can be distinguished from sexual aggressors of women by their greater social isolation and anger, and by a higher prevalence of deviant sexual fantasies and paraphilias. These results should be interpreted prudently, however, given the studies' limitations, already outlined.

Nonserial sexual murderers and serial sexual murderers

Prentky, Knight et al.'s (1989) study is the only one, to our knowledge, to compare serial sexual murderers (i.e. murderers responsible for at least three deaths) to nonserial sexual murderers (i.e. murderers responsible for one or two deaths). The serial-murder group was composed of 25 of the 36 murderers in the FBI study (Burgess et al., 1986), while the nonserial-murder group comprised seven subjects from the FBI study and 10 subjects from the Massachusetts Treatment Center (MTC). The constitution of the nonserial-murder group is less than ideal, as it relied on recruitment from two different sources: whereas the FBI researchers interviewed each

Table 1.4 Characteristics of serial and nonserial sexual murderers

Characteristic	Serial murderers ($N = 25$)	Nonserial murderers ($N = 17$)
IQ > 110	58%	29%
Exhibitionism	25%	7%
Voyeurism	75%	43%*
Fetishism	71%	33%*
Transvestism	25%	0%*
Deviant sexual fantasies	86%	23%*
Compulsive masturbation	70%	50%
Planned crime	42%	41%
Organized crime scene	68%	24%*

*$p < 0.05$
Source: Prentky et al., 1989

subject in person and analyzed his police file, the MTC study relied solely on the subjects' clinical files. In addition, different sampling strategies were used to construct the groups. Despite these methodological flaws, however, the study sheds new light on both serial and nonserial sexual murders.

The characteristics of serial and nonserial sexual murderers are presented in Table 1.4. The most striking feature is the significant proportion of serial sexual murderers with superior intelligence, i.e. IQs above 110. Serial sexual murderers also reported deviant sexual fantasies more often than did nonserial sexual murderers, and were associated with organized crime scenes more often than were nonserial sexual murderers. According to Prentky, Knight et al. (1989), a high IQ is unrelated to the content or vividness of deviant sexual fantasies, but does favour the transposition of these fantasies to reality, i.e. the degree of organization of the crime. These authors also hypothesize that deviant sexual fantasies are the cause of repetitive sexual murder. However, they emphasize that the presence of deviant sexual fantasies does not in itself explain sexual murder, serial or not.

The prevalence of paraphilias was also higher among serial sexual murderers than among nonserial sexual murderers. More specifically, the two groups differ with regard to the prevalence of voyeurism, fetishism and transvestism. According to Prentky, Knight et al. (1989), these paraphilias reinforce the sexual fantasy world of sexual murderers, to the detriment of appropriate interpersonal relationships. The results concerning sexual murderers' fantasies and paraphilias are consistent with the FBI's motivational model. In fact, the presence of fantasies and paraphilias is proportional to the intensity of the criminal activity of both serial and nonserial sexual murderers.

THE MONTREAL STUDY OF SEXUAL MURDERERS OF WOMEN

Objectives

Virtually all theories of sexual murder rest on limited empirical bases. In some cases, there is a limited amount of data from a limited number of subjects (Leyton, 1986; Money, 1990). In others, the sample is biased by the overrepresentation of serial murderers (Burgess et al., 1986). In yet others, sexual murderers of women, of children and of men are grouped together, despite the fact that it is possible that the three types of sexual murderers differ with respect to their development, motivation and offending process. Finally, it should be noted that the narratives of sexual murderers are often the only source of data available.

Comparative studies identify the factors that distinguish sexual murderers from sexual aggressors, as well as the characteristics of serial sexual murderers. Unfortunately, few comparative studies have been conducted, and those few have significant limitations. These limitations include small study groups, which restricts the generalization of the results, and the analysis of only a small number of variables, which reduces the scope for comparisons.

The main objective of the Montreal Study was therefore to determine whether there are characteristics that distinguish sexual murderers of women from sexual aggressors of women. In order to avoid the pitfalls of previous studies, care was taken to ensure that the two samples were both of respectable size and, as they included only murderers of women, relatively homogeneous. Care was also taken to avoid the over-representation of serial sexual murderers. In fact, our sample, which is almost a population in itself, includes 70.7% of the sexual murderers incarcerated in the province of Quebec (approximate population of Quebec in 2000: 7 million) at the time of data collection. However, our sample included no serial murderers, and there was only one among the potential subjects who refused to participate in the study. As we can see – and contrary to popular belief – Ted Bundy is hardly the archetype of the sexual murderer.

The variables analysed were selected to ensure an exhaustive inventory of developmental, psychological and situational factors related to sexual murder. Finally, to improve the quality of the results, data was collected from both official records (police reports, victim statements, correctional files) and subject narratives.

Methods

Subjects

In this study, 40 nonserial sexual murderers of women (i.e. of females at least 14 years old) were evaluated. Five murderers had killed two victims.

Subjects with close emotional relationships with the victims (spouses, ex-spouses) were excluded, as such relationships influence the modus operandi (St-Yves, Granger & Brien, 1998). The mean age of the murderers at the time of incarceration was 32.3 years (s.d. 10.4 years). At the time of their crimes, 75% were single, 7.5% were separated, divorced or widowed, and 17.5% were in traditional or common-law marriages. The majority of these murderers were white (95.0%); blacks and other groups each accounted for 2.5% of the sample. These murderers represent 70.7% of the population of sexual murderers of women ($N = 57$) incarcerated in Quebec at the time of data collection (1998–99).

The comparison group was composed of 101 sexual aggressors of women (i.e. of females at least 14 years old). None had close emotional relationships with their victims. The mean age of the sexual aggressors at the time of incarceration was 32.8 years (s.d. 8.9 years). At the time of their crimes, 48.5% were single, 13.0% were separated, divorced or widowed, and 38.5% were in traditional or common-law marriages. Whites accounted for 78.2% of the sample, blacks for 15.8%, Aboriginal peoples for 5% and other groups for 1.0%. This group of 101 sexual aggressors represents 93.5% of the 108 subjects whose participation in this study was requested from 1995 to 2000.

At the time of data collection, all 101 sexual aggressors and 13 of the sexual murderers of women were incarcerated at the Centre Régional de Réception (Sainte-Anne-des-Plaines, Quebec, Canada), a maximum-security penitentiary of Correctional Service Canada. During their stay of approximately six weeks at this institution, the subjects were evaluated by members of a multidisciplinary team composed of psychologists, criminologists, sexologists, vocational training professionals and correctional agents. This evaluation was carried out both for the purposes of this study and to determine the appropriate treatment and degree of security for each criminal. The 27 other sexual murderers of women in this study were evaluated during their incarceration in another Quebec penitentiary of Correctional Service Canada.

In cases in which a subject had assaulted more than one victim, we used only the information concerning the last victim. This decision reflects our premise that it is the most recent modus operandi that most accurately reflects the sexual preferences of the experienced offender (Kaufman et al., 1996).

Procedure

All study participants signed a consent form that stipulated that the information collected was for research purposes. Each was subjected to a battery of psychometric instruments (Chapter 3). Information on developmental factors (Chapter 2) and modus operandi (Chapter 4) was collected during semi-structured interviews based on the Computerized Sex Offenders Questionnaire (CSOQ) (St-Yves, Proulx & McKibben, 1994). This was complemented by information from official records (police files, victim statements). In cases of divergent information from the two sources, the information from official sources was considered more reliable, and retained.

The methodological outline presented here is applicable to the results discussed in Chapters 2 to 9. Each of these chapters also presents methodological information specific to its subject matter. The comparison of sexual aggressors to sexual murderers occupies Chapters 2 to 5: developmental factors are discussed in Chapter 2, psychopathological factors in Chapter 3, situational factors in Chapter 4 and an integrative model in Chapter 5. In Chapter 6, our sample of nonserial sexual murderers is compared to the sample of serial murderers in the FBI study (Ressler et al., 1988). Chapter 7 discusses differences in developmental, psychopathological and circumstantial factors in sadistic and nonsadistic sexual aggressors of women. Finally, typological analyses of modus operandi and criminal motivation are the subjects of Chapters 8 and 9.

Chapter 2

SEXUAL MURDERERS AND SEXUAL AGGRESSORS: DEVELOPMENTAL PATHS AND CRIMINAL HISTORY

Alexandre Nicole and Jean Proulx

This chapter approaches sexual offending from the perspective of developmental criminology (Blumstein et al., 1986, Blumstein, Cohen & Farrington, 1988; LeBlanc, 1986; Loeber & LeBlanc, 1990). In it, we investigate whether sexual aggressors can be distinguished from sexual murderers on the basis of their personal development and criminal career. We hypothesize that sexual murderers of women have more disturbed personal histories and more severe criminal careers than do sexual aggressors of women.

DEVELOPMENTAL FACTORS

Sexual aggressors of women

Marshall and Barbaree (1990) consider a problematic family environment during childhood and adolescence to be a key determinant of the development of violent attitudes and behaviours. In their view, children exposed to, or victims of, inadequate parental models (violence, sexual abuse, substance abuse, parental criminality) develop numerous socialization deficits, and are more likely to reproduce these inappropriate models later in life. Furthermore, the peri-pubertal period is seen as critical in the development

Sexual Murderers: A Comparative Analysis and New Perspectives Edited by Jean Proulx Éric Beauregard, Maurice Cusson and Alexandre Nicole

of deviant sexual preferences. In this view, therefore, most sexual aggressors are predisposed to developing coercive sexual behaviours in adolescence because of the inadequate family environments in which they were raised. In a similar vein, Marshall, Hudson and Hodkinson (1993) consider that inadequate parent–child relationships hinder the development of a secure attachment style. Children with 'insecure' attachment run a high risk of developing antisocial and dysfunctional interpersonal behaviours. Furthermore, their relational problems lead them to live in emotional isolation, which in turn favours the adoption of violent behaviours. Marshall (1989a) illustrates the relationship between emotional isolation and the transition to actual violent acts thus:

> [T]hey (sexual aggressors) have history of emotional isolation from others. The experience of emotional loneliness which, no doubt, causes the unskilled male to experience considerable frustration. If this frustration is experienced as emotional isolation from effective relations with women, then it may express itself in violence, or sexual aggression (rape, indecent assault or exhibitionism) directed at women, since adult females may be seen by these men as the cause of their loneliness (p. 498).

Finally, Malamuth, Heavy and Linz (1993) proposed a dual-path predictive model of the sexual coercion of women. The first path takes the form of sexual promiscuity (initial sexual contact at an early age, very many partners), a pattern of behaviour whose earliest precursor is an inadequate family environment (parental violence, sexual abuse). This hostile environment leads the child to socialize with delinquent peers, adopt antisocial behaviours, and, ultimately, become a delinquent himself. The second path takes the form of hostile masculinity, which is composed of four components that feed violence: the need to dominate; attitudes facilitating aggression against women; hostility towards women; and sexual arousal by rape. In the authors' view, these attitudes stem from perceptions of rejection and feelings of anger from childhood all the way to adulthood. Developmental factors thus occupy an important place in this model.

Sexual murderers

As the FBI's motivational model (Ressler et al., 1988) has already been presented in detail (Chapter 1), here we will only discuss its developmental factors associated with sexual murder. According to this motivational model, an inadequate family environment during childhood, and victimization during childhood and adolescence, are at the root of coercive sexual behaviour. More specifically, Burgess et al. (1986) have identified physical and sexual abuse, inadequate attachment (i.e. the absence of appropriate parent–child emotional ties, which engenders feelings of insecurity), inadequate interpersonal relationships, unreliable parental care and deviant parents as contributory developmental factors. These factors have a powerful impact on the development of a maladapted personality characterized by social isolation, aggressiveness, habitual lying and a preference for autoerotic activities. Furthermore, in both children and adolescents, such social maladaptation leads to cognitive coping strategies characterized by a preference for fantasy worlds in which domination, violence, power, torture and rape predominate. Developmental factors are thought to have an impact on both juvenile delinquency and adult criminality, and ultimately lead to sexual murder.

Hickey (2002) has proposed a trauma-control model that specifies the predisposing and disinhibiting factors that may lead an individual to commit serial sexual murder. Predisposing factors may be familial (e.g. a dysfunctional family environment), psychological (e.g. mental illness, personality disorder) or biological (e.g. extra Y chromosome). Like the FBI model (Burgess et al., 1986; Ressler et al., 1988), the trauma-control model posits that traumatic events at a young age, such as psychological, physical or sexual victimization, may disrupt normal personal development. Hickey (2002) also notes that the traumatic events' effects may be exacerbated by an inadequate family environment. These traumatic events engender low self-esteem, as well as feelings of rejection, despair, powerlessness and self-loathing, and are followed by the development during adolescence of fantasies and daydreams that are surrogates for deficient social relationships. In the end, the adolescent develops a distorted perception of himself and his social circle, and the fantasies become the preferred coping strategy for re-establishing psychological equilibrium. The adolescent thus takes refuge in a fictional world in which he dominates others. Over the years, various other negative experiences (e.g. failed relationships) reinforce this distorted perception. Furthermore, disinhibiting factors such as pornography and alcohol promote a search for deviant activities (Hickey, 2002), which – in conjunction with the other components of the model – culminates in the commission of murder.

Arrigo and Purcell's (2001) model of the emergence of paraphilias and sadistic sexual behaviours is largely based on theoretical considerations. However, their model also incorporates the assumption – drawn from the work of the FBI (Burgess et al., 1986; Ressler et al., 1988) and Hickey (1997) – that predisposing factors and traumatic events during personal development favour cognitive coping that takes the form of wallowing in deviant sexual fantasies that lead to sexual murder. The innovative element of their model is their assertion that criminal sexual acts arise from the interaction of deviant sexual fantasies and paraphilias (e.g. exhibitionism, sexual sadism). These paraphilias emerge from a cyclical process that comprises the following interactive elements: fantasies, paraphilic stimuli, orgasmic conditioning and disinhibiting factors (pornography, alcohol, drugs). As the fantasies become increasingly violent, the intensity, duration and frequency of the paraphilic activities increase. The need for more intense stimulation subsequently leads to sexual murder.

Thus, the hypothesis that developmental factors favour the transition to actual acts of sexual coercion is supported by the FBI's motivational model (Burgess et al., 1986; Ressler et al., 1988), the trauma-control model (Hickey, 2002), Arrigo and Purcell's model (2001) and models of sexual aggressors (Malamuth et al., 1993; Marshall & Barbaree, 1990) However, despite the importance these models accord to developmental factors, only a few variables (family environment, sexual development) have been investigated empirically. Furthermore, some models (Arrigo & Purcell, 2001; Hickey, 1997; 2002) have never been empirically verified.

CRIMINAL CAREER

While few studies have examined the criminal career of sexual offenders, the available results suggest that these criminals exhibit a polymorphic criminality. For example, Heritage (1992) found that a high proportion of sexual offenders (79%) had criminal records for nonsexual crimes, and Hazelwood and Warren (1989) found the criminal records of 41 serial rapists to contain a variety of crimes.

Soothill et al. (2000) specifically set out to determine whether sexual offenders are 'specialists' or 'generalists'. While their sample contained no sexual murderers, their results are nevertheless of interest. They concluded that sexual offenders are both specialists and generalists: although they have criminal records comprising a wide range of crimes, they 'specialize' in sexual assault. In other words, sexual assault occupies a special place among the many crimes they commit.

Boutin (1999) also analysed the criminal career of sexual offenders. She concluded that sexual offenders, both paedophiles and sexual aggressors of women, have an unspecialized criminal profile, since their criminal careers are far from exclusively sexual. In fact, criminal sexual activity accounted for two-thirds of all convictions in only 1.4% of sexual offenders, and in only 37% of cases were convictions following an initial sexual crime also for sexual crimes (Boutin, 1999).

In addition, few studies have investigated whether the authors of sexual crimes with objectively high severities have a more active, more varied or more serious criminal career. The criminal career of sexual murderers has not been extensively investigated, and what little is known comes from case studies; the criminal career of sexual aggressors has been investigated in recidivism studies. Some predictors of sexual assault (number of previous convictions, age at first crime) are common to other types of recidivism, while others (number of previous sexual crimes, deviant sexual preferences) are specific to sexual assault (Hanson & Bussière, 1998; Marshall & Barbaree, 1988; Proulx et al., 1997; Quinsey, Rice & Harris, 1995).

AIM OF THIS STUDY

The preceding literature review of developmental factors indicates that many sexual aggressors and sexual murderers grew up in chaotic family environments, and exhibited problematic behaviours even as children. Several authors have concluded that disturbed personal development is associated with childhood and adolescent criminal acts, and that these acts lead to adult criminality (Blumstein et al., 1986, Blumstein, Cohen & Farrington, 1988; LeBlanc, 1986; Loeber & LeBlanc, 1990; Malamuth et al., 1993; Marshall & Barbaree, 1990; Ressler et al., 1986; 1988).

These studies confirm the necessity of studying the personal development and criminal career of sexual offenders. Our study was undertaken to determine whether the severity of a sexual offender's last crime is related to his developmental profile and the characteristics of his criminal career. In other words: Does a sexual offender's personal development have an impact on the lethality of his sexual crimes? Our model, derived from previous research, postulates that disturbed personal development (inadequate social environment, experiences of victimization) in childhood and adolescence favours cognitive coping that in turn favours the development of deviant sexual fantasies. These conditions lead developing males to engage in criminal acts while still quite young. The greater the duration, frequency, variety and volume of juvenile criminal activity, the more likely the individual is to commit criminal acts early in adulthood, which in turn favours a more intense form of adult criminal activity (LeBlanc, 1986). The sexual crimes are hands-off (minor sexual crimes such as voyeurism and exhibitionism) in early adulthood, but subsequently progress to hands-on. Our theoretical model postulates that the severity of sexual crimes (sexual murder vs. sexual assault) is dependent on the inadequacy of the criminal's personal development and the intensity of his criminal career.

METHODOLOGY

The primary source of information on developmental factors was interviews with the subjects. Information on the adult criminal career of the subjects was obtained from the Royal Canadian Mounted Police's FPS (Fingerprint System) files.

RESULTS

Developmental factors

Exposure to inadequate models

The prevalence of exposure to inadequate models prior to the age of 18 was higher, although not statistically significantly so, among sexual murderers of women than among sexual aggressors of women. In fact, more than half the subjects in each group reported having been exposed to abusive alcohol consumption and psychological violence, and almost half of the subjects in both groups reported having witnessed physical violence.

Sexual aggressors and sexual murderers did not exhibit significantly different scores on a global, duration-weighted scale of exposure to inadequate models. Scores on this scale were calculated by multiplying the score on a dichotomous scale corresponding to the presence or absence of inadequate models by the duration of exposure to these models (age at last exposure minus age at first exposure). The internal consistency of the scale (Cronbach's alpha = 0.71) exceeds the standard threshold of 0.70. Sexual murderers scored higher on this scale than did sexual aggressors (19.79 vs. 16.44), although this difference was not statistically significant.

Victimization

The prevalence of victimization-related variables in both groups of sexual offenders prior to the age of 18 is presented in Table 2.1. Sexual murderers were the victims of physical violence more often than were sexual aggressors of women (64.1% vs. 41.6%), and more frequently reported having been victims of incest (20.5% vs. 5.9%). The prevalence of three of the four other victimization-related variables was higher in sexual murderers than in sexual aggressors, although this difference was not statistically significant. Parental abandonment was the only variable which was more prevalent among sexual aggressors than among sexual murderers.

The two groups of sexual criminals in this study did not exhibit significantly different scores on a global scale of victimization. This scale is analogous to the global scale of exposure described above, but takes into

Table 2.1 Prevalence of victimization-related events (prior to age 18) in sexual offenders

Victimization	Sexual aggressors (N = 101)	Sexual murderers (N = 40)	Coefficient of association (phi or eta)
Psychological violence	46.5%	56.4%	0.089
Physical violence	41.6%	64.1%	0.202*
Incest	5.9%	20.5%	0.218**
Sexual violence	25.7%	33.3%	0.076
Parental abandonment	44.6%	38.5%	0.055
Victimization scale[a] (0–176)	37.86	49.80	0.121

Notes: [a] presence (1) or absence (0) x (age at last victimization − age at first victimization) x (frequency)
*p< 0.05; **p < 0.01

account the frequency as well as the duration of victimization. The internal consistency (Cronbach's alpha = 0.58) of the scale was less than the recommended threshold of 0.70 but nevertheless acceptable, given the scale's high theoretical relevance. In fact, withdrawing items in order to improve the alpha coefficient would have been contrary to the objective of establishing a global profile of the victimization suffered by each subject.

Consumption of alcohol and drugs

The prevalences of regular use and abuse of alcohol, and of alcohol dependence, were not significantly different in the two groups of sexual offenders, although the prevalences of all three patterns of consumption were higher among sexual murderers. However, sexual murderers did begin drinking regularly at a younger age than did sexual aggressors (14.7 vs. 17.7; eta = 0.25, $p < 0.05$). A high proportion of subjects (43.6% of sexual aggressors, 38.0% of sexual murderers) in both groups reported being or having been dependent on alcohol.

Regular use and abuse of drugs, and drug dependence, were more prevalent among sexual murderers than among sexual aggressors, although this difference was not statistically significant.

Sexual murderers began consuming and abusing drugs regularly at a younger age than did sexual aggressors (consumption: 15.8 vs. 19.4; eta = 0.27, $p < 0.05$; abuse: 17.3 vs. 21.6, eta = 0.28, $p < 0.01$). The prevalence of drug dependence was notable in both groups (37.6% among sexual aggressors, 48.7% among sexual murderers).

Inappropriate behaviours

Inappropriate behaviours in childhood were more prevalent among sexual murderers than among sexual aggressors. This was true of social isolation (54.1% vs. 30.6%; phi = 0.22, $p < 0.01$), daydreaming (43.2% vs. 20.2%; phi = 0.23, $p < 0.01$), habitual lying (40.5% vs. 20.0%; phi = 0.21, $p < 0.01$), running away from home (27.0% vs. 10.1%; phi = 0.21, $p < 0.05$) and reckless behaviours (24.3% vs. 2.0%; phi = 0.36, $p < 0.001$). In addition low self-esteem was more prevalent among sexual murderers (56.8% vs. 26.3%; phi = 0.29, $p < 0.01$). The mean total of inappropriate childhood behaviours was higher among sexual murderers than among sexual aggressors (4.4 vs. 2.3; eta = 0.37, $p < 0.001$).

The prevalence of inappropriate adolescent behaviours in both groups of sexual offenders is presented in Table 2.2. Such behaviours were more prevalent among sexual murderers than among sexual aggressors, be they daydreaming (48.6% vs. 24.5%), social isolation (56.8% vs. 33.7%), habitual lying (59.5% vs. 21.3%) or reckless behaviours (32.4% vs. 16.2%). In addition, sexual murderers exhibited a higher prevalence of low self-esteem (78.4% vs. 34.3%) and phobias (32.4% vs. 15.3%). The mean total score of inappropriate adolescent behaviours was higher among sexual murderers

Table 2.2 Prevalence of inappropriate adolescent behaviours in sexual offenders

Inappropriate behaviour	Sexual aggressors ($N = 101$)	Sexual murderers ($N = 40$)	Coefficient of association (phi or eta)
Daydreaming	24.5%	48.6%	0.233**
Social isolation	33.7%	56.8%	0.210*
Habitual lying	21.3%	59.5%	0.368***
Enuresis	6.1%	10.8%	0.081
Rebellious attitudes (e.g. resistance to authority)	50.5%	59.5%	0.080
Nightmares	12.1%	10.8%	0.018
Cruelty to animals	3.0%	10.8%	0.157
Low self-esteem	34.3%	78.4%	0.393***
Angry temperament	28.9%	40.5%	0.112
Sleep disorders	13.3%	24.3%	0.134
Phobias	15.3%	32.4%	0.191*
Running away from home	24.5%	37.8%	0.132
Reckless behaviour (e.g. reckless driving)	16.2%	32.4%	0.179*
Headaches (migraines)	9.2%	10.8%	0.025
Self-mutilation	3.0%	8.1%	0.111
Physical complaints	7.0%	10.8%	0.062
Total, adolescence	3.12	5.29	0.351***
Total, developmental period (childhood, adolescence)[a]	5.44	9.71	0.379***

Note: [a] Cronbach's alpha $= 0.73$
$*p < 0.05$; $**p < 0.01$; $*** p < 0.001$

than among sexual aggressors (5.3 vs. 3.1). Furthermore, the mean number of inappropriate behaviours during childhood and adolescence was higher among sexual murderers (9.7 vs. 5.4).

Education

Sexual murderers appear to have had a significantly lower educational level than did sexual aggressors of women (grades 7/8 vs. grades 10/11; phi $= 0.22$, $p < 0.01$). Sexual murderers reported having had more discipline problems at school than did sexual aggressors (62.9% vs. 43.8%; phi $= 0.14$, $p < 0.05$). There was no significant difference in the prevalence of learning disabilities in the two groups of sexual offenders, with almost half of both groups reporting having had them.

Atypical sexual behaviours

The frequency of atypical sexual behaviours during childhood (e.g. consumption of pornography, use of phone-sex services, compulsive masturbation) was very low in both groups. The relative frequencies of these activities were slightly higher in adolescence than during childhood, but there were no significant differences between the two groups. Both groups reported a comparable total score of atypical sexual behaviours (murderers: 1.11, aggressors: 0.95) for the period of development (prior to age 18).

Sexual fantasies

Sexual murderers more frequently reported having had deviant sexual fantasies during childhood and adolescence than did sexual aggressors (39.5% vs. 22.7%; phi $= 0.17$, $p < 0.05$). Nondeviant sexual fantasies during this same period were extremely common in both groups of sexual offenders (murderers: 94.4%; aggressors: 88.4%).

Developmental profiles

For this analysis, sexual aggressors and sexual murderers of women were merged into one group, and a K-means cluster analysis of individual total scores on the scales described above was performed. This type of analysis clusters the entire sample into relatively homogeneous subgroups on the basis of personal development variables. As indicated in Table 2.3, the

Table 2.3 Characteristics of the three developmental profiles

		Type I (N = 57)	Type II (N = 38)	Type III (N = 28)
***	Inadequate-model exposure scale (0–73)	8.75	18.28	40.29
***	Victimization scale (0–176)	6.72	58.63	109.92
**	Learning disability	44.7%	52.1%	69.9%
***	Discipline problems at school	34.1%	49.2%	72.3%
n.s.	Alcohol-consumption scale (0–3)	1.15	1.21	1.43
n.s.	Drug-consumption scale (0–3)	1.19	1.22	1.24
***	Inappropriate behaviours during childhood and adolescence, total (0–32)	4.57	8.21	15.82
***	Atypical sexual behaviours during childhood and adolescence, total (0–16)	0.94	1.22	1.68
*	Deviant sexual fantasies	19%	31%	45%

$*p < 0.05$; $**p < 0.01$; $***p < 0.001$
n.s.: not significant

analysis resulted in the identification of three distinct profiles that differ significantly for all scales, with the exception of the alcohol and drug consumption scales. Furthermore, there is a gradient of pathology in the profiles, with Type I subjects presenting the least disturbed personal development and Type III subjects presenting the most disturbed. The two groups of sexual offenders present different profile distributions. In sexual aggressors of women, the distribution is: Type I: 56.9%, Type II: 25.6%, Type III: 17.4%. In sexual murderers, the distribution is: Type I: 21.6%, Type II: 43.2%, Type III 35.1%. There is a strong association (phi = 0.26, $p < 0.01$) between the type of sexual offender and the type of developmental profile.

Criminal career

In both groups of sexual offenders, the majority of subjects had previous criminal records (murderers: 71.8%, aggressors: 80.9%). Criminality parameters are presented in Table 2.4 for each type of sexual offender. Criminal careers were determined on the basis of official criminal records of previous and current crimes. In addition, in order to quantify the severity of the criminal career, the number of charges for each type of crime was multiplied by the Wolfgang severity score (NSCS) for that crime (Wolfgang et al., 1985). To render the subjects comparable, this result was then weighted as a function of the subjects' age, by dividing the previous result by the number of years for which the subject was at risk of committing crimes (i.e. current age – 18). This provided a global severity score for each type of crime for each subject.

Sexual aggressors of women had a higher mean global severity score for adult crimes against property than did sexual murderers (112.74 vs. 49.51). In addition, the global severity score for crimes against persons was almost twice as high for sexual murderers as for sexual aggressors (64.73 vs. 33.51). Finally, the mean number of charges for 'other' crimes (related to driving, failure to appear in court, escaping from prison, etc.) was higher among sexual aggressors (7.42 vs. 2.23). Sexual murderers committed their first crime at a younger age than did sexual aggressors (17.0 vs. 20.6); age at first crime was determined on the basis of self-reporting. No significant differences were observed for any other measure of criminal career parameters.

DISCUSSION

Exposure to inadequate models prior to age 18

There was no significant difference in the exposure of sexual murderers and sexual aggressors to inadequate models. More than half of the subjects in both groups were exposed to abusive alcohol consumption and psychological

Table 2.4 Static and dynamic parameters of criminal career in sexual offenders

	Sexual aggressors (N = 101)	Sexual murderers (N = 40)	Eta
Crimes against property, mean	4.71	3.05	0.10
Severity of crimes against property, total	112.74	49.51	0.14*
Crimes against persons, mean	4.68	5.20	0.03
Severity of crimes against persons, total	33.51	64.73	0.15*
Sexual crimes, mean	2.12	2.43	0.06
Severity of sexual crimes, total[1]	17.42	7.66	0.09
Other crimes, mean	7.42	2.23	0.18*
Total crimes, mean	18.94	12.90	0.13
Wikstrom index (sexual crimes/total crimes)	0.17	0.22	0.12
Types of crimes (variety)	5.58	5.13	0.06
Convictions, total	5.49	4.25	0.14
Age at first crime (adult, official)	24.29	23.55	0.04
Age at first crime (self-reported)	20.6	17.0	0.14*
Age at first crime against property	23.44	23.54	0.006
Age at first crime against persons	25.99	25.86	0.06
Age at first crime, sexual	30.67	29.12	0.07
Age at first crime, other	23.72	24.68	0.05
Lambda[2], total crimes	4.59	2.82	0.13
Lambda, crimes against property	0.96	0.78	0.05
Lambda, crimes against persons	1.66	1.06	0.07
Lambda, sexual crimes	0.43	0.43	0.00
Lambda, other crimes	1.54	0.52	0.15

Notes: [1]Other than the sexual murder for which the murderer is incarcerated. [2]Annual rate of crime.
*$p < 0.05$

violence, while approximately half of the subjects in both groups witnessed physical violence. Our results are in agreement with those of Langevin et al. (1988), who reported that 60% of the fathers of sexual murderers and 43% of the fathers of sexual aggressors were alcoholic, and that conjugal violence had been present in more than half of the families of both types of sexual offenders. Pithers et al. (1988, 1989) reported even higher percentages – 86% of the 64 sexual aggressors in their study came from chaotic families. Scully (1990) also noted that half of the sexual aggressors in her sample had witnessed conjugal violence and had had childhoods characterized by fragile family ties. Interpreting these results in the light of Bandura's (1977) model of social learning, the violence of our subjects (both sexual aggressors and sexual murderers) is a repetition of what they observed in their family environment.

Victimization prior to age 18

There was little difference in the victimization of sexual aggressors and sexual murderers. Sexual murderers were more likely to have been victims of physical violence and incest than were sexual aggressors. Slightly more than one-quarter of sexual aggressors and slightly more than one-third of sexual murderers reported at least one incident of extrafamilial sexual victimization. Aubut et al. (1993) reported comparable results: in that study 20% of sexual aggressors and 35% of sexual murderers had been victims of sexual abuse prior to 18. However, 76% of Hazelwood and Warren's (1989) sample of 41 serial sexual aggressors reported having experienced sexual abuse prior to adulthood. In the studies of 36 sexual murderers (several of whom were serial murderers) conducted by Ressler, Burgess, Douglas et al. (1986) and Ressler et al. (1988), sexual abuse prior to age 12 was reported by 43% of the subjects, and sexual abuse between ages 13 and 18 by 32%.

Several hypotheses may be advanced to explain the disparity between these results. Firstly, the majority of the studies do not clearly distinguish between intra- and extrafamilial victimization. Secondly, some studies have used samples that contain both serial sexual aggressors and serial sexual murderers (Hazelwood & Warren, 1989; Ressler et al., 1988). These studies report higher percentages than those observed in our two samples. This confirms our hypothesis that a more serious sexual victimization during childhood or adolescence is related to more serious criminal outcomes (several victims) in adulthood. Finally, the divergent results could be due to the scope of the definition of sexual assault, which may extend from sexual touching to rape with mutilation. Thus, our results, as well as those of the various studies cited, support the hypothesis that previous sexual victimization is linked to the severity of later coercive sexual behaviours, although they do not establish a direct causal relationship.

In our study, sexual murderers reported experiencing physical violence more often than did sexual aggressors (64.1% vs. 47.2%). These results are broadly comparable to those of Langevin et al. (1988), who found that 54% of sexual murderers and 62% of sexual aggressors in their sample had been victims of either physical or psychological violence from their mothers, while 74% of sexual murderers and 57% of sexual aggressors had been victims of physical or psychological violence from their fathers. Thus, the severity of sexual crimes appears to be related to the violence experienced during childhood.

All these results concerning the victimization of sexual offenders agree with the model of Malamuth et al. (1993), which postulates that an inadequate family environment is a precursor of sexual coercion. Marshall (1984) claims that a chaotic family environment leads to feelings of solitude and emotional isolation, as well as difficulties establishing significant emotional ties – all of which favour recourse to sexual violence. Although they do not inevitably lead to sexual crime, victimization and exposure to inadequate models are thought to be 'distal' causes of sexual offences against women. Thus, as

Bumby and Hanson (1997) have pointed out, there is an indirect link between exposure to familial violence and sexual assault. It is, however, impossible to conclude that these factors are either specific to sexual assault or common to other types of criminality, given the absence of control groups (nonsexual offenders) in our study and in the literature.

Consumption of alcohol and drugs

Our results indicate that a high proportion of both groups of sexual offenders had drug and alcohol problems, and that sexual murderers had begun to regularly consume alcohol and regularly abuse drugs at significantly younger ages than did sexual aggressors. Langevin et al. (1988) reported that 62% of sexual murderers and 55% of sexual aggressors in their sample had alcohol problems, half the sexual murderers and 55% of sexual aggressors had drug problems, and 25% of sexual murderers, but no sexual aggressors, had problems with both types of substances (alcohol and drugs). Grubin (1994) reported that 43% of the 21 sexual murderers in his study had alcohol-related problems. Results from other studies confirm the high prevalence of substance abuse among sexual aggressors (Baxter et al., 1984; Gratzer & Bradford, 1995; Hazelwood & Warren, 1989; Kruttschnitt, 1989; McKenzie, 1995; Scully, 1990). A plausible explanation of these results is that children who grew up in inadequate environments become maladapted young adults for whom alcohol and drug consumption become outlets.

Inappropriate behaviours

Sexual murderers reported having had significantly more inappropriate childhood and adolescent behaviours than did sexual aggressors. In both childhood and adolescence, sexual murderers were more likely than sexual aggressors to have been socially isolated and habitual liars, suffer from low self-esteem and engage in dangerous behaviours (including setting fires). In addition, sexual murderers were more likely than sexual aggressors to have run away from home in childhood, have had daydreams ('Any cognitive activity representing a shift of attention away from a task', Prentky, Burgess et al., 1989, p. 889) and have suffered from phobias in adolescence.

Many studies have reported a high prevalence of social isolation in sexual offenders. In Kruttschnitt's (1989) study of sexual aggressors, 70% of the subjects were socially isolated in adulthood. The prevalence of social isolation among the 41 serial sexual aggressors studied by Hazelwood and Warren (1989) was considerably higher than among the sexual aggressors in our study, but comparable to the (nonserial) sexual murderers. Although the results reported by the FBI group (Ressler et al., 1988) for sexual murderers are higher than in our study, it should be recalled that their sample of 36 sexual murderers (responsible for 118 victims) comprised 25 serial sexual murderers. These results support Grubin's (1994) hypothesis that differences in the escalation in violence exhibited by the two types of sexual offenders he studied (121 sexual aggressors, 21 sexual murderers) are partially attributable to differences in social isolation. In fact, in the absence of gratifying interpersonal relationships, sexual crimes appeared to be a compensatory source of emotional stimulation.

Our results clearly highlight the tendency of sexual murderers to report a greater number of inappropriate behaviours than do sexual aggressors. We in fact observed a gradient of inappropriate behaviours that is directly associated with the severity of criminal sexual activity. Furthermore, it was demonstrated that more serious offenders (serial sexual aggressors and murderers) report even more seriously disturbed developmental profiles.

Education

Our results indicate that sexual murderers had a significantly lower educational level than did sexual aggressors. Furthermore, the prevalence of self-reported discipline problems at school was significantly higher among sexual murderers. Both groups were indistinguishable, however, with regard to learning disabilities, as almost half of both groups reported such problems. Our results agree with those of other studies (Alder, 1984; Baxter et al., 1984; Hazelwood & Warren, 1989; Kruttschnitt, 1989; Ressler et al., 1988). In light of these results, it is possible to hypothesize that the more dysfunctional environment of sexual murderers is the source of their poorer educational results. Furthermore, sexual murderers' lower self-esteem would tend to lead them to be socially isolated. All in all, the developmental environment of sexual murderers would have undermined their chances of educational success.

Atypical sexual behaviours

Many researchers and clinicians have investigated the role of the consumption of pornography, prostitution, resort to prostitutes and other atypical sexual behaviours in adult sexual offenders. As our study only examined atypical sexual behaviours prior to age 18, it was not possible to assess the impact of these factors in adult offenders. For the period studied, however, no significant difference was observed between sexual aggressors and sexual murderers, and the relative frequency of all variables was very low. Analysis of the association between the type of sexual crime and the prevalence of atypical sexual behaviours in adulthood would perhaps have been fruitful, but it may nevertheless be pointed out that sexual aggressors and sexual murderers do not appear to present any specific problematic sexual activities prior to age 18.

Deviant sexual fantasies

The sexual murderers in our sample more frequently reported deviant sexual fantasies than did sexual aggressors (39.5% vs. 20.7%). Grubin (1994) obtained comparable results, deviant sexual fantasies having been reported by 38% of sexual murderers and 27% of sexual aggressors in his sample. As well, the presence of deviant sexual fantasies was a predictor of recidivism in his study, as the prevalence of such fantasies was higher among serial sexual aggressors. In fact, Warren et al. (1996) reported that 80% of the subjects in their sample of serial murderers had deviant sexual fantasies.

Deviant sexual fantasies appear to play a crucial role in the transition to actual coercive sexual acts. However, it should be recalled that not all sexual aggressors have violent sexual fantasies, and not all men who have violent sexual fantasies actually commit sexual assault. Furthermore, deviant fantasies do not always involve murder, but may focus on victim control. The nature and frequency of deviant sexual fantasies are thus good predictors of the severity of the offence.

Developmental profiles

The approximately 200 developmental variables analysed were used to establish 10 scales. Using these scales, typological analyses were then conducted, in order to identify developmental profiles. The profiles exhibit a pathological gradient for each developmental factor, with Profile I individuals exhibiting the fewest problems and Profile III individuals the most. Profile I (associated with the least disturbed development) contained the highest proportion of sexual aggressors, while Profiles II and III (associated with the most disturbed development) contained two-thirds of the sexual murderers. These results thus confirm the hypothesis that the severity of the crimes committed by sexual offenders of adult women is a function of the extent to which their personal development was disturbed. Typological analysis confirmed the hypothesis, advanced by Hickey (1997, 2002), that the cross-product of the various disruptive factors of personal development is a better predictor of the severity of adult sexual offending than is any independent factor.

Criminal career

The analysis of the criminal careers of the sexual offenders in our two study groups clearly reveals that the vast majority of them had had previous convictions (80.9% of sexual aggressors and 71.8% of sexual murderers). These results are similar to those of Langevin et al. (1988), who found that 85% of sexual aggressors and 92% of sexual murderers in their study had criminal records. Furthermore, in our study, there was no significant difference in the prevalence of convictions for sexual crimes in the two groups. However, sexual aggressors had a higher mean severity score for crimes against property, and sexual murderers had a higher mean severity score for crimes against persons. Thus, sexual murderers tended to present a more violent criminal record than did sexual aggressors, a finding confirmed by other researchers (Alder, 1984; Baxter et al., 1984; Davies, 1997; Grubin, 1994; Heritage, 1992; Jackson & Bekerian, 1997; Langevin et al., 1988).

What emerges from these results, and is consistent with results reported by other researchers, is that sexual crimes against women appear to be more closely associated with polymorphic antisocial behaviour than with any specific sexual problem (Alder, 1984; Soothill et al., 2000). Several arguments support the hypothesis that sexual assaults and sexual murders are part of a polymorphic repertoire of antisocial behaviours rather than of specialized, strictly sexual, pathways. Our results, consistent with those of other studies, demonstrate that nonsexual crimes predominate in the criminal career of sexual aggressors and sexual murderers. Nevertheless, the criminal career of sexual aggressors is more oriented towards property while that of sexual murderers is more oriented toward persons.

However, some caveats are in order. Firstly, our study, as well as almost all the studies cited, had no control groups composed of non-sexual criminals. Furthermore, it should be recalled that our two samples were drawn from the federal penitentiary system (which means that all subjects were serving at least a two-year sentence). Since the number and variety of previous convictions are recognized to aggravate sentencing of sexual aggressors, the polymorphic criminal career observed in the sexual aggressors in our study (who were serving federal sentences) may simply reflect this sentencing bias. It should be noted that this bias does not affect sentencing of sexual murderers, who receive statutory life sentences. Lastly, our study only examined 'official' sexual aggressors and sexual murderers. Ouimet (1998) has suggested that approximately 10% of sexual crimes are reported to police, and that only half of reported cases result in convictions.

THE EMPIRICAL MODEL

Our objective was to determine whether the type of sexual crime (sexual assault vs. sexual murder) was associated with specific developmental factors or with criminal career parameters, and whether these elements were related to the severity of the sexual offences. Our results indicate that sexual murderers are more likely than sexual aggressors to have developmental impairments, exhibit deviant sexual fantasies and possess a more violent criminal record (Figure 2.1).

The general theories of sexual assault developed by Marshall and Barbaree (1990) and by Hall and Hirschman (1991), as well as the empirical study by Malamuth et al. (1993), highlight the role of developmental factors in the aetiology of sexual criminality. A motivational model of sexual murder was presented by the FBI (Ressler et al. 1988), and extended by Hickey (1997) and by Arrigo and Purcell (2001), all of whom highlighted the crucial role of developmental factors. In the same vein, comparative studies by Langevin et al. (1988) and Grubin (1994) demonstrated that sexual murderers are more likely to have developed in dysfunctional environments. Although our results support these hypotheses, it should be pointed out that the sexual aggressors and sexual murderers in our study exhibited several similarities. However, while several of the slight differences that were observed appear nonsignificant when considered in isolation, their cumulative effect is highly significant. Thus, the developmental and criminal background of sexual aggressors and sexual murderers do present certain differences, although they are not diametrically opposed.

Inadequate developmental factors				Deviant sexual fantasies	
	Type I	Type II	Type III		
Sexual aggressors	56.9%	25.6%	17.4%	Sexual aggressors	22.75%
Sexual murderers	21.6%	43.2%	35.1%	Sexual murderers	39.5%

Juvenile delinquency		
	Sexual aggressors	Sexual murderers
Age at first crime	20.6	17.0

Adult criminality		
	Sexual aggressors	Sexual murderers
Criminal record, nonviolent crime	++	+
Criminal record, violent crime	+	++

Minor sexual crimes
(voyeurism, exhibitionism, etc.)

Sexual assault

Sexual murder

Figure 2.1   Empirical model

CASE STUDIES

As a qualitative complement to the quantitative analyses presented above, we present brief case studies, including a discussion of developmental features of a Profile I sexual aggressor, a Profile II sexual murderer and a Profile III sexual murderer.

Robert: Profile I sexual aggressor

Personal history

Robert is the youngest of seven children. From a very young age, Robert was timid and had low self-esteem. He stated that his father was a very introverted man who was often absent from home. He believed that his mother had not been affectionate enough. His parents never separated but often argued over money. Robert stated that people around him often looked down on his family because they came from a poor rural environment. At school, children made fun of him, especially because he was small, poor, and smelled of the farm. As a result, he tended to keep to himself.

Robert dropped out of school at 17 to work. At 21, he returned to school to complete his high school diploma. He then resumed working, but experienced corporate and personal bankruptcy. Soon after these setbacks, he began university and completed a bachelor's degree. After university, he had only a few contracts and had to make ends meet by doing occasional renovation work. Robert said that he had been drinking regularly for 15 years, and that he became more aggressive when he had been drinking.

Over the course of his life, Robert had had some 60 sexual partners. Of these, he had had stable and appropriate relationships with five. He has been with the same partner for the last eight years. Although he would have preferred to have had sex with her once per week, the actual frequency was once per month. He was very dissatisfied with the gap between reality and his expectations. He masturbated daily, and reported no sexual dysfunction. For sexual stimulation, he used magazines and occasionally frequented bars featuring exotic dancers. He admitted having had an extramarital affair. Robert admitted to having a confrontational attitude towards women, which he believes is due to the negative view he had of his mother, his sisters, the nuns who taught him, and his first girlfriend, all of whom he had conflicts with.

Robert was not forthcoming about his sexual fantasies. He admitted being a voyeur since adolescence, initially toward his sisters, and later towards women otherwise unknown to him. He also admitted having a fetish for brassieres. He denied having committed sexual offences other than those for which he had been arrested. He did, however, admit having often thought of sexually assaulting women.

His previous criminal record consists of a single conviction for a series of acts of gross indecency against women (touching the breasts of women otherwise unknown to him). For these offences, he was put on probation for two years. He admitted having been violent to his partner (holding her wrists during an argument). He also had been violent towards furniture and household objects.

The pre-crime and crime phases

In the months preceding the last crime for which he was convicted, Robert often argued with his partner, particularly about communication and their sex life. He could not accept the fact that his partner, who held a stable job, made a bigger contribution to the family finances. This situation caused him much distress, and he drank more than usual. He was increasingly dissatisfied with his relationship with his partner, and continued to feel devalued. Under the effect of alcohol, he became more aggressive and his sexual desire was high.

Robert stated that he was exhausted on the day of his crime. He had worked the whole day and had had a drink with his friends in a bar. On returning home, he saw an adolescent girl walking down the street. He followed her in his car for a while before parking. The police report states that the victim was seized from behind by the hair and had no chance of seeing her assailant. She was thrown violently to the ground and her head was hit against a bus shelter several times. She experienced multiple injuries as a result of this attack. Robert touched her breasts and succeeded in inserting a finger into her vagina; he also licked one of her ears. Passers-by, witnessing the scene, alerted the police.

Serge: Profile II sexual murderer

Personal history

Serge is the youngest of five children; he claimed to have always gotten along with his siblings ever since childhood. He described his childhood as 'normal'. He was surrounded by an 'affectionate and over-protective' mother and a strict father. He added that he never witnessed any conjugal violence at home and had never been the victim of physical, psychological or sexual abuse. His father died when he was 12 years old. He confided that he had taken his father's death very hard.

Serge had only vague memories of his schooling, but claimed not to have had any major problems. He dropped out of school once, around the age of 15, when he was in Grade 8. He returned to school, in order to obtain his high school diploma, when he was unemployed and receiving welfare.

Work is Serge's only source of valorization and satisfaction. Since he was 15, he has had many jobs of many types, typically involving manual labour and requiring few social skills. In recent years, he had worked primarily in the delivery business.

Serge said that he had never been attracted to drugs, and had his first drink when he was 16. Although he initially drank only occasionally, his drinking became more regular when he was 25. He described himself as a social drinker, someone who consumes a few beers on the weekend but never lapses into excess. He said that he drank to relax.

Serge's sexual development revealed no hint of any problem. He had never been a victim of abuse. He had his first heterosexual contact when he was 12, and complete sexual relations five years later. He sporadically watched pornographic films portraying consensual relations between a man and a woman, and rarely bought pornographic magazines. Speaking of the frequency of his sexual relations, he stated that he had them when the opportunity presented itself.

At the time of his arrest, Serge, then 41 years old, still lived with his mother, a woman he described as anxious and controlling. In fact, she appeared to be quite vindictive and still reprimanded him when he left the house without her permission, except when he went to work. She did not like him coming home late and did not allow him to invite friends of either sex home. Serge submitted to her requests, justifying his attitude by a desire to spare his sick mother, avoid causing her heartache and avoid arguments. His mother's control was not limited to his comings and goings but also extended to his relationships. In fact, she had always judged the women that he was interested in before she even met them.

Serge stated that he had four or five significant romantic relationships. He said this without any great conviction but was able to name a woman with whom he had had a relationship for four years. However, given the distance that separated them, this relationship had primarily taken the form of letters rather than a sexual relationship – which was in fact the reason he gave for their break-up. He added that he subsequently went through several break-ups, which only intensified his low self-esteem. He reminded us that his mother had been the major obstacle to other relationships with women.

Serge had a very limited social network. He had no one to confide in, nor even the slightest significant friendship. He admitted having had very few friends in his life. He described himself as a loner who rarely dared to start a discussion. Over the years, Serge had developed a permanent feeling of solitude, and doubted not only his ability to have a relationship with a woman, but also his sexual performance.

The pre-crime and crime phases

In the months preceding the crime, Serge worked compulsively. He accepted even the smallest contracts and all overtime work. In the previous year, he had become dissatisfied with the frequency of his sexual relationships, although he had been powerless to change this state of affairs. One week before the crime, Serge had felt rejected by the victim, a waitress in the bar he frequented. Although he saw her as an inaccessible woman, he took the risk of inviting her to a group activity. She refused, explaining that she had a boyfriend, and wasn't available the day in question.

The evening of the murder, as was his habit on Saturday nights, he took great care to tell his mother that he was finishing work at midnight; this was false, but gave him the freedom to go to the bar he frequented. He spent the night at the bar playing video poker. The victim was working there that night, but he stated that he only spoke to her to order drinks: three large beers and two small beers, while playing video poker. Serge knew that the victim decided the bar's closing time, on the basis of the number of customers. Towards one o'clock, the next-to-last client left, and 15 minutes later Serge decided to go as well.

As he was leaving the bar, something snapped in him and he grabbed the victim by the throat without premeditation, strangling her as hard as he could. She managed to ask him to stop, but he continued to squeeze her throat: 'I had no choice, she had to die, because if she didn't she would talk, she would turn me in. At one point, she became stiff, she stopped breathing, I was sure she was dead, I let go of her.'

Afterwards, Serge undressed her and noticed that she was menstruating. It was at that point that he came to himself and realized what he had done. To camouflage the motive of his crime, he left with the cash receipts and took care to lock the door before leaving, discarding the key on the road.

Sylvain: Profile III sexual murderer

Personal history

Sylvain remembers having been the victim of psychological violence from his father. His immediate family environment was very strict and devoid of expressions of affection. Until he was eight, he lived with his maternal grandparents five days a week. His maternal grandfather was the only person who he felt loved him, and his death, when Sylvain was an adolescent, was a great trial to him. Sylvain said that his grandfather's death made him feel the most depressed he has ever been. When he was 12, his parents separated, after years of arguments, only to reconcile two years later. While his parents were separated, Sylvain lived with his mother; he fought intensely with her, going as far as to threaten her life. His relationship with his older brother had always been strained, and as a result, Sylvain didn't see him.

Sylvain wet his bed up until the age of 13, and began to exhibit behavioural problems with the onset of puberty; for example, he was cruel to animals and committed arson. He recalled that he put his dog in a cage with a radio playing full blast to record the animal's suffering and laugh at it with his friends. On other occasions, he set fire to cats and mice, hung them by their tails, or dropped them from great heights. Shortly before he was 12, he and his friends set fire to two acres of woodland. One year later, he amused himself by setting fires in school lockers or throwing matches at his friends.

He stated that at school both boys and girls often made fun of him and insulted him, but that the humiliation was much worse when it came from a girl. He was disciplined for fighting and was often absent from school.

As an adult, Sylvain often drove through city streets at high speed despite his passengers' fears, and he drove a motorcycle without a licence. When he was convicted for impaired driving, he failed to respect court-imposed restrictions. In addition, he was attracted to gambling, and went to the casino at least once a month.

At the age of 16, he began working as an apprentice electrician and has since then held a variety of jobs. He worked steadily from that time on, except during slow periods between contracts. He stated that he stopped working, by choice, more than one year before the crime 'because I spent all my time taking drugs'. Sylvain began drinking at the age of 13, and began smoking marijuana and hashish at the age of 14. Over the three years preceding the crime, he consumed alcohol and drugs daily. His favourite substances were marijuana, cocaine (smoked or snorted), hashish, magic mushrooms, LSD and PCP.

Sylvain did not mention any problematic or abusive event that could have disrupted his psychosexual development. Toward the age of 18, he thought of having 'grown-up' sexual relations with his cousins, but it was only a year later that he had his first sexual relations. He mentioned having had 15 partners, although he was not convinced that all of them were completely consensual. Only once did he frequent a prostitute.

Sylvain took marked pleasure in describing his sexual fantasies. He reported having developed, from the age of 16, fantasies in which he dominated, raped, tortured and even killed women. He also said that he was sexually aroused by mutilation and by fantasies involving sexual relations with an unconscious or even dead person whom he could dominate and do with as he wanted. Taking a woman by force, killing her and sexually assaulting her constituted the apotheosis of sexual pleasure for him. Sylvain reported having sexually assaulted women who had not pressed charges. He admitted that he had once restrained a woman with handcuffs, scratched her and hit her breasts with his hands.

Pornographic films did not arouse him a great deal, although the sight of blood and savage attacks did. He preferred films portraying bloody murders or stories of serial murderers.

He masturbated compulsively from the age of 13 onwards, sometimes many times a day for several consecutive days. He was also a voyeur. He explained that when he felt frustrated, his reflex was to turn inwards, isolate himself and take refuge in deviant sexual fantasies, finally finding release in masturbation. Phallometric evaluations conducted after his incarceration indicated a mixed 'deviant' profile, with reactions to both deviant and nondeviant scenarios.

The pre-crime and crime phases

During the summer, a friend (the eventual victim of the attempted sexual assault described below) came to live with him. Theirs was a problematic relationship. It appears that his friend was alarmed by Sylvain's attitudes and behaviours. He stated that he never hit her, despite having wanted to. Sylvain admitted that she was afraid of him and that he had gotten to the point of 'having murderous thoughts' when they broke up for a period of three months. One month before the murder, they began to see each other again to smoke marijuana, but she remained afraid of him. Sylvain admitted that he had 'thoughts of assaulting her pretty violently' from the end of the summer onwards.

The day of the murder, he offered to drive her to a friend's home. He had decided that this was to be the big day, the day he would realize his violent fantasies. Sylvain stated that he had consumed alcohol and cocaine before the attack. After stopping the car, he took her by the throat and attempted to kiss her. She screamed and fought, and despite his efforts to subdue her, fought him off and escaped. He admitted that she had been lucky: he would have 'raped her, penetrated her', hit her in order to get her to obey, and would not have hesitated to use his knife to make her obey. He admitted that this sexual assault was a failure.

Once the sexual assault had failed, he recalled, he went to his parents' hunting lodge, where he continued to drink, take cocaine and listen to music. Thinking about what he had just done, he said, he became 'paranoid'. The failed sexual assault, the unveiling of his true nature and the possible denunciation by his friend only fanned the hate he had for her.

The next morning, his friend's mother called him and asked him to come over to her house, which he did. 'She insulted me, told me that I was a good for nothing, a rapist, that I had no future.' He asked her to explain what she meant, but the discussion degenerated into a fight. Sylvain recounted that he hesitated, but finally took out his knife and stabbed his friend's mother 29 times. Despite the absence of sexual behaviours during the murder, Sylvain reported that the murder was sexually arousing (for further details, see Chapter 3).

CONCLUSION

All our analyses indicate that sexual aggressors and sexual murderers resemble each other more than they differ. However, while the slight differences may appear nonsignificant when considered in isolation, their cumulative effect is significant. Thus, sexual aggressors and sexual murderers do not present diametrically opposed developmental trajectories but can be distinguished from one another on the basis of the degree of their developmental disturbance.

Chapter 3

SEXUAL MURDERERS AND SEXUAL AGGRESSORS: PSYCHOPATHOLOGICAL CONSIDERATIONS

Jean Proulx and Nadège Sauvêtre

The role of psychopathological factors in sexual murder has been the object of some debate. This is hardly surprising, since 'the utterly primitive sadism and violence make one think of psychotic illness; the criminal activity in itself is suggestive of antisocial personality and/or a variety of sexual disorders; the repetitive nature of the crimes suggest obsessions and compulsions; and the abused childhoods of the killers suggest dissociation' (Brown, 1991, p. 16).

There are several explanations for the profusion of suggested underlying psychopathological disorders. First, it must be emphasized that many of the hypotheses have no valid empirical basis. Some are based on indirect data, such as biographies or newspaper articles. Others are based on dubious reasoning such as: (1) sexual murderers have no empathy for their victims; (2) psychopaths have no empathy for their victims; (3) therefore, sexual murderers are psychopaths. Research based on data obtained directly from sexual murderers has been primarily conducted by clinicians such as Brittain (1970). Such research provides interesting insights into the psychopathological characteristics of sexual murderers, but frequently lacks scientific rigour, as the sampling procedure and diagnostic procedures are often unexplained. For these reasons, it is possible that the multiplicity of diagnoses associated with sexual murderers is due to the deficient scientific

Sexual Murderers: A Comparative Analysis and New Perspectives   Edited by Jean Proulx Éric Beauregard, Maurice Cusson and Alexandre Nicole
© 2007 John Wiley & Sons, Ltd.

rigour of many of the studies. However, it should be noted that a few studies have provided clear descriptions of their samples and used rigorous assessment protocols such as psychometric instruments (e.g. MCMI, MMPI) and standardized clinical criteria (e.g. DSM-IV).

Notwithstanding the above-mentioned criticisms, it is nevertheless possible that the multiplicity of psychopathological factors reflects a reality, namely that the population of sexual murderers is heterogeneous. In fact, several typologies of sexual murderers have been developed (see Chapters 8, 9 and 12), and it is possible that each of the proposed categories (for example, sadistic, anger-driven) is associated with a specific psychopathological dimension. Thus, the heterogeneity of diagnoses associated with sexual murderers may actually be a valid observation rather than a methodological artefact.

Another factor that must be taken into account when examining the range of diagnoses associated with sexual murderers is the evolution of the diagnostic criteria for specific psychopathologies. In fact, prior to the publication of the DSM-III (American Psychiatric Association, 1980), research on sexual murderers relied on imprecise diagnostic criteria for personality disorders and psychoses that often varied from author to author. A further difficulty is that the theoretical frameworks of some more recent studies have been inconsistent with the descriptive diagnostic criteria of the various versions of the DSM (III, III-R, IV).

In light of the methodological problems of, and taxonomic and theoretical issues related to, some of the studies of the psychopathological features of sexual murderers, the literature review presented below must be interpreted with care. In order to facilitate the critical review of the studies discussed, a clear distinction will be made, for each mental disorder, between valid data, clinical opinion and logical inference. The first section will present the results of research on serious mental disorders (psychosis, dissociative syndrome, obsessive-compulsive disorder and sexual sadism), while the second will discuss research on personality disorders (antisocial, narcissistic, borderline and schizoid) and psychopathy.

SERIOUS MENTAL DISORDERS

Psychosis

Revitch (1965) claimed that 20% of sexual murderers are schizophrenic, while Rada (1978) believed the majority of sexual murderers to be psychotic. However, these clinical opinions are based on very broad conceptions of psychosis. In fact, as Liebert (1985) has pointed out, strict application of modern nosographic criteria would result in most sexual murderers being diagnosed with some sort of personality disorder. For this reason – and despite the criminals' apparent madness from a lay point of view – the majority of researchers and clinicians do not currently believe sexual murderers to be psychotic (Brittain, 1970; Dietz, 1986; Geberth, 1995; Levin & Fox, 1985; Leyton, 1986; Meloy, 2000; Myers et al., 1993).

Notwithstanding this majority view, some recent authors have considered the psychological processes of sexual murderers to include psychotic features. For example, Brown (1991) considers that 'the ability to relieve intense anxiety through the physical enactment of violent inner destructiveness may prevent a psychotic regression' (p. 17). Similarly, Myers and Blashfield (1997) reported paranoid ideations in a significant proportion (62%) of their sample of adolescent sexual murderers; however, none of the adolescents satisfied the diagnostic criteria of the DSM-III-R (American Psychiatric Association, 1987) for psychosis. It should be noted that in the DSM-IV (American Psychiatric Association, 1994), paranoid ideation is one of the diagnostic criteria for borderline personality disorder.

Dissociative syndrome

According to Watkins (1984), some sexual murderers exhibit dissociative syndrome, i.e. multiple personality disorder. In order to illustrate his point, he presents the case of Bianchi, a serial sexual murderer. In Watkins' view, Bianchi's two personalities, Ken and Steve, are totally different from one another and ignorant of each other's existence. In fact, 'the alternations of personality (behaviour, perception, motivation, speech, mannerisms, handwriting, attitudes, amnesias and Rorschach responses) and the consistencies within each of the respective personalities, all point out to a real dissociation' (p. 94). This position is, however, not widely held – most researchers and clinicians regard sexual murderers who appear to present dissociative syndrome to be, in reality, manipulators (Hickey, 1997; Myers, 2002).

Obsessive-compulsive disorder

Because of the disturbing and invasive nature of sadistic sexual fantasies, some clinicians have hypothesized that serial sexual murderers suffer from obsessive-compulsive disorder (Brown, 1991; Revitch, 1980). However, there is no empirical support for this position. What is more, as Myers (2002) points out, sadistic sexual fantasies are a source of sexual pleasure, despite their invasive nature, and do not generate psychological distress. Consequently, these fantasies cannot be said to constitute obsessions in the clinical sense of the term.

Sexual sadism

Convergent results from several studies suggest that sexual murderers have a propensity for sexual sadism (Dietz, 1986; Dietz et al., 1990; Geberth, 1995;

Money, 1990; Myers et al., 1993; Stone, 1998). These results must, however, be interpreted with caution, as several studies are tainted by significant methodological limitations, such as data sources of dubious validity (books, newspaper articles), data from only a single – and inadequately described – case, and unspecified diagnostic criteria. Furthermore, as Meloy (2000) points out, a diagnosis of sexual sadism can only be applied to organized sexual murderers. Despite that, however, sexual sadism appears to be the only serious mental disorder observed in a significant proportion of sexual murderers. In fact, several authors consider sexual murder to be driven by the combination of this sexual disorder and psychopathy (Dietz et al., 1990; Geberth, 1995; Ressler, Burgess, Douglas et al., 1986; Vetter, 1990).

PERSONALITY DISORDERS

Antisocial and narcissistic personality disorders, and psychopathy

In many ways, Hare's (1991, 1996) definition of psychopathy overlaps with the DSM-IV's (American Psychiatric Association, 1994) definitions of anti-social personality disorder (both including, for example, antisocial lifestyle and the absence of empathy, remorse and guilt) and narcissistic personality disorder (both including, for example, inflated self-esteem, absence of empathy, remorse and guilt, manipulative behaviour). In addition, anti-social personality disorder and narcissistic personality disorder exhibit strong comorbidity (American Psychiatric Association, 1994). Although these diagnostic categories will therefore be discussed together, it should be borne in mind that their diagnostic criteria have evolved rapidly over the last 30 years, and that multiple conceptualizations of the same nosological entity may have coexisted at various points in the past.

With regard to personality disorders in sexual murderers, the most frequently encountered opinion is that the latter are psychopathic, antisocial and narcissistic (Dietz, 1986; Dietz et al., 1990; Fox & Levin, 1999; Liebert, 1985; Myers, 2002; Vetter, 1990). During their crimes, sexual murderers feel no empathy for their victims, and subsequently feel neither remorse nor guilt. Finally, they have inflated self-esteem, as they are convinced that they are so intelligent that they will not be caught by the police. This psychological model adequately characterizes their criminal activities, but is it enough to qualify them as psychopaths? According to Brittain (1970), 'it is useless, though it is sometimes done, simply to label such a person a psychopath [. . .] it is also not accurate' (p. 198).

Brittain (1970) concluded, on the basis of his clinical experience, that sadistic sexual murderers are anxiety-ridden, shy and reserved in their interpersonal relations. They also tend to shun human company in favour of an imaginary world in which they are omnipotent. Applying the diagnostic criteria of the DSM-IV (American Psychiatric Association, 1994), one would probably classify these murderers as avoidant and schizoid. Sexual murderers, who behave psychopathically only towards their victims, therefore appear to be distinct from psychopaths, who are dominant, manipulative and hostile in every sphere of their lives. On this point, Brittain (1970) states that 'he may feel himself to be an inferior being except as regards his offences. The planning and contemplation of these acts can make him feel superior to the other men, someone special or even god-like. Others then become to him inferior creatures, without rights to be used in any way he wishes for his gratification' (p. 199). What can empirical research add to these clinical opinions and theoretical considerations regarding psychopathy in sexual murderers?

Although a few studies have suggested that sexual murderers are psychopaths or antisocial (Geberth & Turco, 1997; Langevin et al., 1988; Stone, 1998; Yarvis, 1995), these findings must be interpreted with caution. Both Yarvis' (1995) and Langevin et al.'s (1988) studies – which reported antisocial personality disorder in 90% (9/10) and 58% (7/13) of sexual murderers respectively – used the DSM-III's (American Psychiatric Association, 1980) diagnostic criteria, which have been widely criticized for overdiagnosing antisocial personality disorder in prison inmates. Geberth and Turco (1997) reported that the majority of serial sexual murderers in their study satisfied the DSM-IV's antisocial personality disorder criteria, which are much more restrictive than those of the DSM-III, and are consistent with the items on Hare's (1991) psychopathy scale (PCL-R). Unfortunately, the study's methodology leaves much to be desired, as the authors arrived at their diagnoses through analysis of biographies, police reports and clinical files, without any direct contact with their subjects. Stone (1998) also based his diagnosis on the biographies of serial murderers, the majority of whom (74/77) scored higher than 25 on Hare's psychopathy scale. Finally, 58% (7/13) of sexual murderers in Langevin et al.'s (1988) study scored higher than 70 on the MMPI scale of psychopathy (Pd). Despite its name, the Pd scale is poorly correlated with Hare's psychopathy scale (Hare, 1985), and in fact primarily evaluates impulsiveness and social maladaptation.

In brief, the few empirical studies that suggest that sexual murderers are psychopaths all suffer from methodological limitations, namely small sample size, over-representation of serial sexual murderers, reliance on obsolete diagnostic criteria, questionable data sources, and psychometric instruments that are inadequate for the comprehensive evaluation of psychopathy.

Evidence that sexual murderers may not be psychopaths comes from Myers and Blashfield's (1997) study of 14 adolescent sexual murderers. In that study, the murderers' mean score on Hare's psychopathy scale was 22.4 (range: 7.1–30.6), less than the threshold of 30 for a diagnosis of psychopathy. Further evidence that adult sexual murderers are not psychopaths comes from Langevin et al.'s (1988) study, in which the scores of six adult sexual murderers on the MCMI scales of antisocial and narcissistic personality disorder were not clinically significant.

In an attempt to shed light on the question of psychopathy in sexual murderers, Meloy and colleagues conducted a series of studies in which the responses of sexual murderers to Rorschach tests were compared to those of psychopaths (Gacono & Meloy, 1994; Gacono, Meloy & Bridges, 2000; Meloy, Gacono & Kenney, 1994). The Rorschach tests were scored using the Exner system, and psychopathy was defined as a score of more than 30 on the PCL-R scale. Both the sexual murderers and the psychopaths exhibited intense anger, and tended to suffer from inflated self-esteem (Meloy et al., 1994), but the two groups differed in several respects. While all the psychopaths exhibited emotional detachment, 28% of the sexual murderers exhibited a thirst for all-consuming, if not frankly monomaniacal, relationships (Gacono et al., 2000; Meloy et al., 1994). Sexual murderers also exhibited a broader emotional repertoire, albeit one dominated by negative emotions such as anxiety and hopelessness, than did psychopaths (Gacono & Meloy, 1994). In this connection, Meloy et al. (1994) noted that 'although the psychological operations of psychopaths facilitate rapid discharge of unmodulated affect and primitive impulse, and bolster grandiosity, sexual homicide perpetrators seem to contain, and then be overwhelmed, at time, by such affect and impulse' (p. 63). Finally, the two groups differ with regard to psychological content, sexual murderers being noteworthy for their frequent and plaintive brooding. All in all, the results of these comparative studies suggest that sexual murderers have some points in common with psychopaths but also possess distinct characteristics. Alternatively, these comparative studies could be seen as indicating that sexual murderers constitute a heterogeneous group composed of psychopaths and nonpsychopaths.

Meloy (2000) has proposed a typological approach to personality disorders among sexual murderers. On the basis of the comparative studies presented above, he concludes that two-thirds of sexual murderers are psychopaths (antisocial, narcissistic) and that the others exhibit an amalgam of personality disorders in which psychopathy plays a secondary role. This view is in good agreement with that of Schlesinger (2000), who considers compulsive sexual murderers to be psychopaths, and catathymic sexual murderers to suffer from borderline and schizoid personality disorders.

Borderline personality disorder

According to Myers (2002), the impulsiveness, anger, emotional lability and chaotic interpersonal relationships of sexual murderers are evidence of borderline personality disorder. Gacono and Meloy (1994) concluded that some sexual murderers exhibit a borderline personality organization; it should be noted that their diagnoses were based on the work of Kernberg (1975) rather than on the criteria of the most recent versions of the DSM. According to them, sexual murderers have an inner world dominated by anxiety, rage and hopelessness, and alternate between periods of intimacy and emotional detachment. Finally, in order to cope with these affects, they resort to defence mechanisms such as projection, denial and projective identification. Other authors (Liebert, 1985; Schlesinger, 2000) also believe that at least some sexual murderers exhibit a borderline personality organization.

Schizoid and schizotypal personality disorders

The adolescent sexual murderers ($N = 14$) in Myers and Blashfield's (1997) study exhibited schizoid (38%) and schizotypal (38%) personality disorders, as evaluated by the SNAP (Schedule for Nonadaptive and Adaptive Personality, whose diagnostic criteria are compatible with those of the DSM-III-R). Antisocial and borderline personality disorders were rare in these murderers, whose scores on the SNAP personality scales indicated introversion and inhibition. This personality profile is consistent with schizoid and schizotypal disorders. Myers and Monaco (2000) consider that this clinical portrait:

> is not clinically inconsistent with their crimes. These diagnoses [schizoid, schizotypal] are in the odd, eccentric category of personality disturbance, and signal aloofness, disturbed interpersonal functioning, idiosyncratic thinking, and perhaps a greater reliance on fantasy for fulfilment due to impairment in their capacity for relationships with others. Their emotional detachment may well have been an important ingredient in the cascade of factors leading to their crimes (p. 700).

The serial sexual murderers studied by Stone (1994) exhibited both schizoid personality disorders (40%) and psychopathic traits, and were emotionally detached and socially withdrawn, with neither empathy for their victims nor remorse for their crimes. These results are consistent with those of Myers and Monaco (2000), and suggest that the emotional detachment of sexual murderers could profitably be conceptualized as a form of schizoid, rather than psychopathic, disorder. However, as interesting as they are, Stone's results should be interpreted with caution, as the diagnoses were arrived at on the basis of the sexual murderers' biographies, rather than direct interview.

AIM OF THE STUDY

The prevailing opinion among clinicians and researchers concerning serious mental disorders among sexual murderers is that these individuals are not psychotic and do not suffer from dissociative syndrome or obsessive-compulsive disorder. However, many believe that a significant proportion of sexual murderers exhibit signs of sexual sadism.

On the other hand, the situation with regard to personality disorders is unclear (see Table 3.1). Despite the fact that psychopathy (antisocial and narcissistic behaviour) is the most common diagnosis associated with sexual murderers, clinical opinion, as well as research data, indicates that some sexual murderers have schizoid or borderline personality disorders.

The diversity of personality disorders attributed to murderers may be due to the methodological limitations of the studies which have addressed this issue. Several studies have relied on small samples, and in those cases where larger samples were used, the data sources have been of dubious validity (for example, biographies). In addition, serial sexual murderers are

Table 3.1 Empirical studies of personality disorders among sexual murderers

Study	Number of subjects	Data sources	Personality disorder
Brittain (1970)	Unknown	Clinical experience	Schizoid Avoidant
Dietz, Hazelwood and Warren (1990)	22 sexual murderers (17 serial)	Clinical and correctional files	Psychopathy Narcissistic
Gacono, Meloy and Bridges (2000)	68 sexual murderers (serial)	Biography, clinical and correctional files (DSM-IV criteria)	Antisocial
Geberth and Turco (1997)	38 sexual murderers 32 psychopaths	Rorschach, PCL-R	Borderline Antisocial Narcissistic
Langevin et al. (1988)	13 sexual murderers 13 murderers 13 sexual aggressors	MMPI, MCMI, clinical examination (DSM-III criteria)	Psychopathy Antisocial Schizoid Avoidant Dependent
Meloy, Gacono and Kenney (1994)	18 sexual murderers 23 psychopaths	Rorschach, PCL-R	Borderline Antisocial Narcissistic
Myers and Blashfield (1997)	14 sexual murderers (adolescents)	Clinical examination (DSM-III-R criteria), PCL-R, SNAP	Schizoid Schizotypal
Schlesinger (2000)	77 sexual murderers (serial)	Biography	Schizoid Psychopathy
Stone (1998)	Unknown	Clinical experience	Psychopathy Borderline Schizoid
Yarvis (1990, 1995)	10 sexual murderers	Interview (DSM-III criteria)	Antisocial

over-represented in many studies, and obsolete diagnostic criteria and variations in theoretical frameworks hinder comparison of the results of the various studies. Finally, it is possible that the heterogeneity of personality disorders identified among sexual murderers reflects a real diversity of sexual murderers. For all these reasons, further studies are needed on the personality disorders of sexual murderers.

The objective of the present study was to evaluate and compare the prevalence of serious mental disorders and personality disorders among sexual murderers and sexual aggressors of women. To avoid the weaknesses of some previous studies, the data in this study was collected in a relatively large sample of nonserial sexual murderers $(N = 40)$. Furthermore, data collection was direct: each sexual murderer in the sample was interviewed, and completed a standardized psychometric instrument, the MCMI.

Methodology

Subjects

Clinical diagnoses were obtained for all 101 sexual aggressors and for 30 sexual murderers. The missing data in the latter group is due to incomplete clinical files or obsolete diagnoses (i.e. diagnoses based on versions of the DSM prior to DSM-IV).

The MCMI (Millon Clinical Multiaxial Inventory) (Millon, 1983) was completed by 75 sexual aggressors and 25 sexual murderers; 26 sexual aggressors and 5 sexual murderers either refused to complete the questionnaire or were unable to do so because of reading deficits.

Instruments

- DSM-IV – The diagnoses for axes I and II of DSM-IV were taken from the clinical files of Correctional Service Canada's (CSS) Regional Reception Centre (RRC) in the case of sexual aggressors, and from the clinical files of the RRC and other correctional institutions of CSS's Quebec region in the case of sexual murderers.
- MCMI – A French version of the MCMI, validated in a sample of Quebec francophones (Landry, Nadeau & Racine, 1996), was used to evaluate the personality disorders of the subjects. This objective instrument consists of 175 true-or-false questions. In the first stage of the evaluation procedure, raw scores are obtained for 11 personality disorders: schizoid, avoidant, dependent, histrionic, narcissistic, antisocial, obsessive-compulsive, passive-aggressive, schizotypal, borderline and paranoid. In the second stage, the raw scores are transformed into base-rate scores, by reference to the prevalence of each personality disorder in clinical populations.

Finally, the base-rate scores are compared to cut-off scores: a base-rate score of 75–84 indicates the presence of characteristics specific to a personality disorder (*trait*), while a base-rate score of 85 or more strongly indicates the presence of such characteristics (*disorder*).

Results

The prevalence of clinically diagnosed axis I DSM-IV mental disorders among sexual aggressors and sexual murderers is presented in Table 3.2. Sexual sadism was the only axis-I mental disorder present in a significant percentage (16.7%) of sexual murderers. Other paraphilias were rare among the sexual murderers in this sample. Similarly, psychotic conditions were extremely rare among these subjects, and dissociative, anxiety and mood disorders were completely absent. Finally, axis I mental disorders were extremely rare among sexual aggressors of women, and their prevalence was not statistically different from that observed among sexual murderers.

The prevalence of clinically diagnosed axis II DSM-IV mental disorders among sexual aggressors and sexual murderers is presented in Table 3.3. The most common personality disorders among sexual murderers were antisocial (35.7%), borderline (28.6%) and narcissistic (25%) disorders. The prevalence of narcissism was statistically higher among sexual murderers than among sexual aggressors (25% vs. 9.9%, phi $= 0.18$, $p = 0.04$). No other significant difference was observed between the prevalence of personality disorders among sexual murderers and sexual aggressors.

Table 3.2 Percentage of sexual aggressors and sexual murderers with axis I DSM-IV mental disorders

Mental disorder	Sexual aggressors (N = 101)	Sexual murderers (N = 30)
Psychotic disorders		
Schizophrenia	1.0%	0.0%
Delusional disorder	1.0%	3.3%
Other psychotic disorder	0.0%	3.3%
Mood disorder	0.0%	0.0%
Dissociative disorder	0.0%	0.0%
Anxiety disorder		
Obsessive-compulsive	0.0%	0.0%
Paraphilias		
Sexual sadism	7.9%	16.7%
Exhibitionism	4.0%	0.0%
Fetishism	3.0%	6.7%
Masochism	1.0%	6.7%
Transvestism	0.0%	6.7%
Voyeurism	4.0%	6.7%

Table 3.3 Percentage of sexual aggressors and sexual murderers with axis II DSM-IV personality disorders

Personality disorder	Sexual aggressors (N = 101)	Sexual murderers (N = 30)
Schizoid	1.0%	0.0%
Avoidant	3.0%	0.0%
Dependent	7.9%	14.3%
Histrionic	0.0%	7.1%
Narcissistic*	9.9%	25.0%
Antisocial	25.7%	35.7%
Obsessive-compulsive	0.0%	3.6%
Passive-aggressive[a]	2.0%	3.6%
Schizotypal	0.0%	0.0%
Borderline	16.8%	28.6%
Paranoid	0.0%	0.0%
Sadism[a]	1.0%	0.0%

Note: [a] Part of the 'Not otherwise specified personality disorders' category
*$p < 0.05$

The prevalence of personality traits and disorders (base-rate scores of 75–84 and ≥ 85, respectively, on the MCMI personality disorder scale) among sexual aggressors and sexual murderers is presented in Table 3.4. The most commonly observed personality disorders (base rate ≥ 85) among sexual murderers were dependent (32%), avoidant (28%), passive-aggressive (24%) and schizoid disorders (20%). There was no significant difference between the prevalences of disorders among sexual murderers and sexual

Table 3.4 Percentage of sexual aggressors and sexual murderers with base-rate scores above 84 (*disorder*) and between 75 and 84 (*trait*) on the MCMI personality disorder scales

Personality disorder	Sexual aggressors (N = 75)		Sexual murderers (N = 25)	
	Disorder	Trait	Disorder	Trait
Schizoid	22.7%	8.0%	20.0%	8.0%
Avoidant	21.3%	16.0%	28.0%	4.0%
Dependent	44.0%	14.7%	32.0%	20.0%
Histrionic	2.7%	4.0%	0.0%	16.0%
Narcissistic	10.7%	20.0%	12.0%	28.0%
Antisocial	6.7%	14.6%	8.0%	24.0%
Obsessive-compulsive	4.0%	4.0%	0.0%	4.0%
Passive-aggressive	18.7%	9.3%	24.0%	0.0%
Schizotypal	1.3%	5.4%	4.0%	0.0%
Borderline	2.7%	16.0%	4.0%	8.0%
Paranoid	8.0%	10.3%	0.0%	16.0%

Table 3.5 Base-rate MCMI scores for two personality disorder profiles among sexual aggressors and sexual murderers

Personality disorder	Profile 1 (N = 56)	Profile 2 (N = 44)
Schizoid*	39.7	81.3
Avoidant*	42.1	87.5
Dependent*	55.9	88.1
Histrionic*	57.9	43.5
Narcissistic*	72.4	44.3
Antisocial*	67.8	45.9
Obsessive-compulsive*	66.0	48.5
Passive-aggressive*	31.2	75.9
Schizotypal*	51.6	66.5
Borderline*	50.4	68.8
Paranoid	64.9	61.3

*$p < 0.001$

aggressors. The most frequently observed pathological personality traits (base-rate scores of 75–84) among sexual murderers were narcissistic (28%), antisocial (24%), dependent (20%), paranoid (16%) and histrionic (16%) disorders. Once again, there was no significant difference between the prevalences of pathological personality traits among sexual murderers and sexual aggressors.

K-means cluster analysis was carried on the MCMI data for all subjects, and two distinct personality disorder profiles were identified. The mean MCMI base-rate scores for these two profiles are presented in Table 3.5. In the first profile, no mean base-rate score reached the threshold of 75. However, notable mean elevations were apparent on the antisocial (72.4) and narcissistic (67.8) personality disorder scales. In the second profile, mean base-rate scores exceeding 75 were observed on four personality disorder scales: avoidant, dependent, schizoid and passive-aggressive. These two profiles differed significantly on all the scales except the paranoid personality scale. Finally, the prevalence of the two personality profiles was similar in sexual aggressors (profile I = 54.7%, profile II = 45.3%) and sexual murderers (profile I = 60%, profile II = 40%).

Discussion

Serious mental disorders

Our results indicate that psychotic disorders are very rare among sexual murderers. This is consistent with the results of several other studies (Dietz, 1986; Geberth, 1995; Levin and Fox, 1985; Leyton, 1986; Meloy, 2000; Myers et al., 1993). Thus, while sexual murder appears to be act of pure madness totally incomprehensible to the average person, sexual murderers are not in fact mad (psychotic). Furthermore, none of the sexual murderers in our study exhibited obsessive-compulsive disorder, consistent with the results of Myers (2002). Finally, none of the subjects was diagnosed with a mood disorder or dissociative disorder.

While it is tempting to unequivocally conclude that sexual murderers do not suffer from any serious mental problems, it must be emphasized that all of the subjects in this study were assessed while incarcerated in a penitentiary. Concretely, this means that the sexual murderers in our sample had been held criminally responsible for their crimes. Furthermore, given the dispositions of the Canadian judicial system, it is possible that other sexual murderers had been found not criminally responsible on account of a mental disorder and had subsequently been transferred to a secure psychiatric facility. Thus, a better idea of the prevalence of serious mental disorders among sexual murderers would be obtained by studying a sample that also includes sexual murderers confined to secure psychiatric facilities.

Sexual sadism was the only paraphilia diagnosed in a significant proportion (16.7%) of sexual murderers. In light of the fact that sexual sadism is considered one of the central determinants of the propensity for sexual murder (Dietz et al., 1990; Ressler, Burgess, Douglas et al., 1986), this proportion appears surprisingly low. It is possible that sampling bias is responsible for this discrepancy between our results and a model of sexual murder in which sadism plays an important role. In Dietz's and Ressler's studies, serial sexual murderers were in fact over-represented, while in our study they were completely absent.

Another possible explanation for the low prevalence of sexual sadism in our subjects is that the information used to establish the diagnoses was of questionable validity. In Canada, most sexual murderers are eligible for parole after prolonged incarceration, and consequently have no interest in divulging information likely to reveal any severe psychopathology, such as sexual sadism, that may suggest a high risk of recidivism. But to arrive at a diagnosis of sexual sadism, clinicians must rely primarily on information that sexual murderers can easily falsify, namely self-reported sadistic sexual fantasies. In the United States, in contrast, sexual murderers are incarcerated with no possibility of parole, or are executed. The extent of their psychopathology, as well as the risk of recidivism associated with it, therefore has no impact on their fate within the legal system. As a result, the information they provide on their sexual fantasies is probably more valid than that obtained from their Canadian counterparts. This second hypothesis does not exclude the possibility of the above-mentioned sampling bias.

In summary, then, the prevalence of serious mental disorders was exceedingly low, and not significantly different, in the sexual murderers of women and sexual aggressors of women in our study. Thus, psychotic, dissociative, anxiety and mood disorders, as well as paraphilias, do not appear to be psychopathological factors associated with nonserial sexual murderers or aggressors of women.

Personality disorders

The most commonly encountered personality disorders (DSM-IV criteria) among sexual murderers in our sample were antisocial, borderline and narcissistic disorder. These results are in agreement with the opinions and data that indicate that sexual murderers are either psychopaths, i.e. anti-social and narcissistic (Dietz et al., 1990; Fox & Levin, 1999; Gacono & Meloy, 1994; Langevin et al., 1988; Myers, 2002; Stone, 1998; Yarvis, 1995), or exhibit borderline personality disorder (Liebert, 1985; Meloy, 2000; Myers, 2002; Schlesinger, 2000).

This agreement between our results and those of other studies must be interpreted with caution, however. First, it should be noted that the prevalences of these three personality disorders were relatively low (anti-social: 35.7%; borderline: 28.6%; narcissistic: 25%), indeed, much lower than those reported in other studies. This discrepancy may, again, be due to sampling bias, specifically over-representation of serial sexual murderers. Furthermore, it may well be that the use of the more restrictive diagnostic criteria of the DSM-IV, rather than the more inclusive ones of the DSM-III, contributed to the lower prevalence of antisocial personality disorder in our subjects. Unfortunately, the data in the only other study to rely on the DSM-IV criteria is of doubtful validity, as it was taken from biographies of and newspaper articles on sexual murderers.

Our results indicate that there are very few significant differences between the prevalences of personality disorders in sexual murderers and sexual aggressors. Narcissistic personality disorder was observed in sig-nificantly more sexual murderers than sexual aggressors (25% vs. 9.9%), no doubt reflecting the preponderance of omnipotent and domination-oriented fantasies among sexual murderers. Although antisocial and borderline personality disorders were more prevalent among sexual murderers than among sexual aggressors, these differences were not statistically significant.

Overall, the clinical diagnoses indicate that sexual murderers are quite similar to sexual aggressors with regard to personality disorders. A cor-ollary to this finding is that personality profiles are not linked to the severity of the sexual crime (assault vs. murder). It is, however, possible that personality profiles do determine whether or not the crime is sadistic, independent of severity (see Chapter 7).

The results of the MCMI personality disorder scales also indicate that there is little difference between sexual murderers and sexual aggressors. In fact, the prevalence of personality traits and disorders was low, and did not significantly differ, in the two groups. Thus, the MCMI results and the clinical diagnoses converge. However, significant differences do emerge when we compare the personality profiles identified on the basis of the MCMI results to the profiles identified clinically.

The MCMI results indicate that the most common personality disorders (base-rate score $\geq$ 85) among sexual murderers were dependent, avoidant, passive-aggressive and schizoid disorders. These results are consistent with Brittain's (1970) model of the sadistic sexual murderer, in which sexual murderers are described as timid, anxiety-ridden, reserved men who feel inferior to others in their day-to-day relationships. Because of this relational malaise, they prefer to take refuge in an imaginary world, in which they are vengeful heroes who dominate and humiliate the women who are, in reality, inaccessible to them.

Our MCMI results with regard to personality disorders in sexual murderers also agree with those reported by Myers and Blashfield (1997). In fact, their SNAP results indicate that schizoid and schizotypal personality disorders are the most frequent personality disorders among adolescent sexual murderers. Furthermore, their SNAP personality scale results suggest that these adolescents are introverted and inhibited. This personality profile is also in very good agreement with Brittain's (1970) description of sadistic sexual murderers.

Our MCMI results also indicate that a significant proportion of sexual murderers exhibit pathological-personality traits (base-rate score of 75–84), most frequently narcissistic and antisocial. These results concord with those of Stone (1994), who also observed psychopathic personality traits (anti-social, narcissistic) and schizoid personality traits among sexual murderers. Once again, our results agree with Brittain's (1970) clinical portrait. In fact, Brittain describes the sadistic sexual murderer as a criminal predator (antisocial and narcissistic) who is bashful and timid in daily life (avoidant and schizoid).

While the scores obtained with psychometric instruments indicate a predominance of avoidant, dependent and schizoid personality disorders among sexual murderers, clinical diagnoses indicate a predominance of antisocial and narcissistic disorders. This contradiction may be a reflection of the fact that psychometric instruments evaluate the sexual murderer, while clinicians evaluate the crime itself. In fact, during forensic clinical assessment, the emphasis is on understanding the personality traits that may have contributed to the commission of the sexual murder. This leads to over-emphasis of antisocial and narcissistic features of the sexual murderer, and underemphasis of avoidant, dependent and schizoid features. In contrast, psychometric instruments evaluate the criminal's usual, day-to-day, mode of functioning, independently of the crime in question. Consequently, in forensic contexts, these tests probably provide a more accurate portrait of sexual aggressors' personality disorders than do clinical evaluations.

Typological analyses of the scores obtained on MCMI personality disorder scales offer another avenue for the exploration of the apparent contradictions between our results and those obtained by other researchers.

In fact, these analyses reveal two personality profiles among the sexual murderers in our samples: (1) avoidant, dependent, schizoid and passive-aggressive; and (2) antisocial and narcissistic. These two personality profiles are completely compatible with the two psychopathological profiles that Lee et al. (2001) identified in sexual offenders, namely: (1) social and sexual incompetence (low self-esteem, social anxiety, social withdrawal); and (2) hostility and anger (low empathy, aggressive behaviour). Finally, these two personality profiles are found in similar proportions among sexual aggressors and sexual murderers. Once again, it is possible that these personality profiles are related to the nature, rather than the severity, of the crime. We will take up this question again in Chapter 7.

Three scenarios emerge from the literature and our results concerning personality disorders in sexual murderers. In the first, sexual murderers exhibit a personality profile composed of two distinct and complementary parts: schizoid, avoidant, dependent and borderline personality disorders determine the murderers' day-to-day relationships, while antisocial and narcissistic disorders are concretized in their sexual crimes. In the second scenario, established on the basis of results obtained with psychometric instruments, sexual murderers are schizoid, avoidant and dependent. Clinical diagnosis in this case is inaccurate and provides information on the crime rather than the criminal. In the third scenario, there are two types of sexual murderers: those with schizoid, avoidant, dependent and passive-aggressive personality disorders, and those with antisocial and narcissistic disorders. The results of our typological analyses appear to favour this last scenario (see Chapter 7).

CASE STUDIES

In order to illustrate the links between the personality-disorder profiles and the modus operandi, let us consider the cases of two sexual murderers: Sylvain and Stéphane.

Sylvain

Sylvain's MCMI profile revealed evidence of schizoid (96), avoidant (115), dependent (104), passive-aggressive (107) and schizotypal (89) personality disorders. Consistent with this profile, Sylvain reported low self-esteem and difficulty making friends. He believed that people judged him, rejected him and took pleasure in mocking him. As a result, Sylvain developed feelings, albeit unexpressed, of rage and humiliation. He became withdrawn in his interpersonal relations and took refuge in a world of coercive sexual fantasies centred on the rape, torture and murder of women. In addition, he watched horror films in which women were tortured and killed. He was particular fascinated by the blood of the victims. Finally, he masturbated compulsively (three times per day), fed by deviant fantasies and horror films. These deviant sexual activities appear to have been an outlet for his unexpressed emotions of rage and humiliation.

The nature of Sylvain's actual sexual activities directly reflected his deviant sexual fantasies. He had in fact sexually assaulted several women, although they had not reported the crimes to the police. During his sexual assaults, he would restrain his victims with handcuffs, scratch them and hit them. During sexual relations with consenting partners, he usually watched horror films.

Sylvain had been unemployed for the year preceding his sexual murder, and throughout this period had consumed alcohol and drugs (marijuana, cocaine, LSD, PCP) daily. He had lived with a cousin, aged 17, for a few weeks, but rapidly developed a strong dislike for her, because she would invite her friends to his apartment. He was verbally, although not physically, abusive to her, and mentioned during interview that it had taken a great effort on his part to refrain from acting out the rape and murder fantasies he had concerning her. Finally, he asked her to leave his apartment.

A few days before the murder, he contacted his cousin, committed this time to act out his violent sexual fantasies. After an evening out to celebrate a friend's birthday, he offered to drive her home. She accepted. Once they reached a place he considered suitable, he stopped the car, grabbed her by the throat, and tried to kiss her. She fought him off and succeeded in escaping. During the interview, he admitted that had she not done so, he would have raped her and then stabbed her.

The next day, the victim's mother asked Sylvain to come over to see her. He arrived armed with a knife. The mother insulted and shoved him; he then stabbed her repeatedly. He mentioned having felt intense sexual arousal during the murder, especially when he felt the victim's hot blood on his hands. He also reported having felt powerful and in control. Despite the absence of sexual behaviour during the murder, the crime can be considered a sexual crime by virtue of the sexual arousal associated with it. Furthermore, the knife blows and victim's blood were central elements of Sylvain's sexual fantasies.

Stéphane

Stéphane was clinically diagnosed with antisocial and borderline personality disorders. His MCMI scores confirm the clinical diagnosis of antisocial personality disorder (86), but not that of borderline personality disorder. This latter result is not surprising, as the MCMI's borderline personality scale is valid for self-destructive, but not hetero-destructive, individuals. In Stéphane's case, therefore, the clinical diagnosis – antisocial and borderline personality disorders – should be retained. Stéphane had an unstable self-image and he alternated between feelings of victimization, during which he considered himself unfairly treated by society in general and women in particular, and feelings of inadequacy. He was also emotionally labile, oscillating between states of angst and intense rage. This internal chaos triggered frequent explosions of destructive violence.

Stéphane's history was marked by many crimes: his adult criminal record comprises eight convictions – three for assault, four for robbery and one for sexual assault. While incarcerated, he was the object of disciplinary measures for an attempted escape and assaults against prison staff and fellow inmates.

During the year preceding the sexual murder, Stéphane's life was marked by conflicts in several spheres. First, because of his rejection of rules and laws, he had numerous run-ins with his parole officers. In addition, he became divorced, after which he felt rejected by, and angry at, his ex-spouse. This specific conflict echoed a well-established rage against women and feminists, whom he considered overly favoured in society. Finally, his family told him that because of his criminal activities they did not want to see him any more. Once again, he felt overcome by feelings of rejection, rage and inadequacy.

In the days preceding the murder, family conflicts were particularly intense. In particular, his mother refused to let him attend a family celebration, which exacerbated his feelings of rejection and rage. He consumed significant quantities of alcohol and drugs. He did not report having had deviant sexual fantasies or having consumed pornography.

The evening of the murder, Stéphane met a woman in a bar. She went back to his apartment with him for a drink. He was looking forward to having sex with her, but when he made his feelings known, she refused and attempted to leave. Stéphane attempted to physically coerce her into having sex with him. When she fought back, he became enraged and stabbed her. To eliminate her body, he put it in the alley, sprinkled it with gasoline, and lit it. He mentioned having felt intense panic after the murder, but exhibited no empathy for his victim.

CONCLUSION

Despite the valuable contributions psychopathological variables make to the understanding of sexual murder, their interactions with developmental (Chapter 2) and situational (Chapter 4) variables should not be neglected. As Widiger and Trull (1994) indicate, psychopathy is not a sufficient condition for a recourse to violence, even if it is characterized by an absence of empathy, remorse and guilt. In fact, psychopaths must first learn violent behaviour (e.g. though physical and sexual victimization, or exposure to violent models) before they can become violent themselves. What is more, situational variables, such as anger, consumption of psychoactive substances, victim resistance and the availability of a weapon, may exacerbate the propensity for violence in individuals with personality disorders (Proulx, St-Yves et al., 1999). Chapter 5 will explore the relationships between psychopathological variables, developmental variables and situational variables in sexual murderers of women.

The main strength of our study of the psychopathology of sexual murder is the representativeness of the sample. In fact, including as it does 71% of the sexual murderers incarcerated in Quebec at the time of data collection, our sample is almost a full-fledged population. Our sample comprised 35 single-victim sexual murderers, five double-victim sexual murderers, but no serial sexual murderers. Our results highlight the limits of studies on sexual murder that rely primarily on serial sexual murderers. A comprehensive comparison of serial and nonserial murderers is presented in Chapter 6.

A further strength of our study is the homogeneity of our sample: all of the victims of the sexual murderers were post-pubescent females. In contrast, some studies of sexual murderers have included both male and female victims, both pre- and post-pubescent. And several studies of serial murderers have included both sexual and nonsexual murderers.

Our study does, however, have some limitations. First, because the data was collected during assessment in a prison setting, it is probable that some subjects lied to the clinicians responsible for their diagnosis, in order to present a positive image. In addition, some subjects may have provided false answers on the MCMI questionnaire. While the MCMI fortunately includes validation scales and correction procedures that compensate for subjects' attempts to mask their psychopathology, these measures are not infallible. A second limitation stems from the fact that our sample was composed solely of prison inmates, and comprises no sexual murderers from secure psychiatric institutions. A final limitation is that each subject was evaluated by only one clinician; consequently, it was not possible to assess inter-rater reliability.

Despite its limits, this study of the psychopathology of sexual murderers advances our understanding of sexual murder. In order to advance our understanding even further, future studies should consider the following recommendations: (1) include subjects from secure psychiatric institutions; (2) recruit subjects from several countries, in order to obtain a larger and more representative sample of sexual murderers; (3) use multiple psychometric instruments to evaluate psychopathology, in order to ensure the convergent validity of the results; and (4) obtain independent evaluations from two clinicians. These measures should provide even more reliable answers to the controversial question of the psychopathology of sexual murderers.

Chapter 4

SEXUAL MURDERERS AND SEXUAL AGGRESSORS: INTENTION AND SITUATION

Sabine Chéné and Maurice Cusson

While most studies of sexual murder emphasize explanatory personality factors (see Chapter 3), the study presented in this chapter takes a different tack, inspired by the work of Felson and Steadman (1983) and Cusson (1998a, 1998b), and focuses on situational factors. The objective of Felson and Steadman's (1983) study was to shed light on the reason some assaults end in murder. Their sample comprised criminals incarcerated for assault or murder, and the variables of primary interest were use of a weapon by the assailant, use of a weapon by the victim, alcohol and drug consumption by the assailant, alcohol and drug consumption by the victim, and the number of blows struck by the assailant. The results indicated that the victims of murder behaved differently than the victims of assault, and that this difference appeared to influence the criminal's behaviour. Victims who acted aggressively, used a weapon or were intoxicated by alcohol or drugs ran a higher risk of being killed. Felson and Steadman concluded that the victim's reaction conditioned the assailant's behaviour: aggressive resistance by victims was met by aggression on the part of assailants.

Cusson (1998a) has termed this pattern, in which criminal behaviour is determined by victim behaviour, 'negative reciprocity'. This suggests that victim behaviour has some influence on the sequence of events and outcome of the crime. We consider negative reciprocity a precipitating factor

Sexual Murderers: A Comparative Analysis and New Perspectives Edited by Jean Proulx Éric Beauregard, Maurice Cusson and Alexandre Nicole

in, rather than a sufficient cause of, the escalation of assault to murder. It is also instructive to recall that reconstruction of the escalation to murder relies solely on the account of the murderer. Nonetheless, victim behaviour is an important determinant of the sequence of events of assaults.

Gassin's (1998) definition of criminal acts provides further enlightenment on this point. In his view, criminal acts are the culmination – in a clear sequence of events – of the offender's interaction with a specific situation. Thus, the actual unfolding of the criminal act depends on the interaction between offenders and victims in specific circumstances. Throughout the crime, each person makes choices. In particular, the criminal sees his choices as rational adaptations to his situation. Although it may appear shocking to speak of rationality in the context of crimes as serious as sexual assault and sexual murder, every crime has an underlying rationale from the offender's perspective. As Cusson (1998b) puts it:

> To suggest that a crime is the instantiation of a hidden rationality is to invite researchers to go beyond appearances, beyond all that is condemnable and unreasonable in the crime, and to inquire about the reasons for, rather than the causes of, the crime. And it is not enough to simply note that a crime has a rational basis: the way it is rational must be explored. It is useful to suggest that the most varied and serious crimes proceed from choices that are not totally devoid of reason (p. 76).

This rational-choice perspective is the conceptual framework of our study of the escalation of sexual assault to sexual murder. Scene-by-scene analysis of the sequence of events of the crime sheds some light on the choices criminals make at specific moments (i.e. the rationality) during these crimes.

Criminals' choices depend not only on the situation but also on their intentions and feelings prior to the crime. These latter variables will be analysed in this study. There is interaction between the criminal as an intentional being at the moment of the crime and his environment at the time of the crime. Cohen (1966) explains this interaction with an interesting metaphor: 'The deviant act is like the reaction that occurs when we bring together two chemical substances' (p. 44). He adds:

> Some individual, in the pursuit of some interest or goal, and taking account of the situation, makes a move [...] his next move – the continuation of his course of action – is not fully determined by the state of affair at the beginning. He may, at this juncture, choose among two or more possible directions. Which it will be will depend on the state of the actor and situation at *this* point in time, and either or both may, in the meantime have undergone change (p. 44).

This quotation highlights the value of scene-by-scene analysis in the understanding of the dynamics of a crime. This type of analysis will be applied here, in an attempt to identify the elements underlying the escalation of sexual assault to sexual murder. Our situational approach requires contextualizing sexual murder and rendering it intelligible. For while sexual murder may appear irrational, by virtue of its extreme gravity, this does not mean it cannot be made intelligible. But how? Does something about the circumstances of the crime drive criminals to kill? Do criminals adapt to different circumstances and to victim behaviour? What factors could shed light on the escalation of sexual assault to sexual murder?

INTENTIONAL AND SITUATIONAL FACTORS IN SEXUAL ASSAULT

Early research on sexual assault claimed that deviant sexual arousal was the single factor that drives individuals to commit sexual assault (Bond & Evans, 1967). Barlow and Abel (1976), however, pointed out that social skills deficits, as well as deviant sexual arousal, favour sexual assault.

Yates, Barbaree and Marshall (1984) demonstrated that anger accentuates the sexual arousal response to violent sexuality during phallometric assessment. Marshall and Barbaree (1990a) observed that transitory situational factors may favour sexual assault. In this model, feelings of hostility, such as anger, could be precipitating factors of sexual assault. Groth, Burgess and Holmstrom (1977) studied the issue of power in detail. They found that for a majority of sexual aggressors, domination of their victim is a demonstration of their power. They accordingly intimidate their victim, be it with a weapon, through physical force or by threats.

Hall and Hirshman's (1991) model of sexual assault includes cognitive distortion. They pointed out that these distortions – which take the form of thoughts such as 'she wanted it', 'she deserved it', 'she consented', etc. – allow aggressors to justify their acts. Ouimet, Guay and Proulx (2000) demonstrated that the severity of sexual assaults was higher when criminals harboured the belief that 'she deserved it'. This cognitive distortion is particularly associated with a desire for vengeance, either on the victim or on women in general (Bénézech, 1995; Knight & Prentky, 1990).

Marshall et al. (1983) observed that many sexual aggressors are intoxicated by alcohol at the time of their crimes. They suggested that alcohol disinhibits sexual arousal and leads some men to ignore the social prohibitions regarding their crimes. Marshall and Barbaree (1990a) concluded that alcohol and drug consumption is a precipitating factor for sexual assault. More recently, Ouimet et al. (2000) noted that pre-crime alcohol consumption, but not pre-crime drug consumption, increases the severity of the victim's injuries.

Block and Skogan (1985, 1986) studied the role of victim resistance in the sequence of events of sexual assaults. They found that victim resistance increases the risk of injury. Thus, during sexual assaults, the more the victim resists, the more severe the physical attack of the aggressor. Felson and Krohn (1990) studied the motivations for sexual assault. Their theoretical framework was largely based on the literature on criminal violence, a choice they justified by pointing out that sexual assault is a form of criminal violence. They concluded that situational factors are important determinants of the sequence of events of sexual assaults. More specifically, they hypothesized that victim behaviour influences the sequence of events. For example, the victim's behaviour may trigger anger in the aggressor, which in turn leads to a more violent attack. And in fact, in this study, victims who resisted were more likely to have been injured.

In their study of criminal violence, Felson and Krohn (1990) also reported that the assailant's use of a weapon increased the likelihood of victim injury. Similarly, Felson and Messner (1996) reported that the likelihood of the victim suffering serious injury or death was higher when sexual aggressors used a weapon.

Felson and Krohn (1990) reported that assailants who are spouses or ex-spouses of their victims, or who know their victims well, were more likely to injure their victims. Similarly, Ouimet et al. (2000) noted that serious injury was more likely in intrafamilial assaults (assaults by spouses, ex-spouses, parents, brothers, adoptive parents) than in assaults by friends or work colleagues.

AIM OF THE STUDY

The preceding literature review suggests that the escalation of sexual assault to sexual murder is governed initially by intentional factors and subsequently by situational factors. On the one hand, the assailant's anger, desire for vengeance (a reflection of the cognitive distortion 'she deserved it') and sadistic fantasies appear to be intentional elements that underlie his violent outbreak. On the other hand, situational factors such as intoxication, use of a weapon, victim resistance, the existence of a familial or intimate assailant–victim relationship and a prolonged duration of the crime all may aggravate the sexual crime.

The impact of situational and intentional factors on the escalation of sexual assault to sexual murder will be analysed in two ways: first, by considering escalation a dichotomous variable (sexual assault vs. sexual murder); and secondly, by considering it, with Quinsey and Chaplin (1982), to be a five-level continuum (sexual assault without injury, sexual assault with minor injuries, sexual assault with serious injuries, sexual assault with murder, and sexual assault with murder and mutilation).

The two categories of variables in our analyses are the intentions of the assailant and the situation in which the assailant finds himself at the time of the crime. Thus, we will examine the role of intentional variables (variables related to the assailant) and situational variables (variables related to the context of the attack) in the process by which sexual assault escalates to sexual murder.

After a description of the study methodology, we will present the results of the multivariate statistical analyses that allow identification of the factors that precipitate the escalation of sexual assault to sexual murder. Finally, we will present decision trees and a crime narrative related to the process of escalation.

METHODS

Data

Our data source was the database of Correctional Service of Canada's Regional Reception Centre. Cases of sexual assault of children and homosexual sexual assault were excluded, but cases of intrafamilial assault of women were retained. As a result, our sample was composed of 191 men who sexually assaulted, and in some cases murdered, one or more female victims at least 14 years old. In all, we analysed 289 sexual crimes (246 sexual assaults and 43 sexual murders).

Variables

We analysed 13 independent intentional and situational variables related to the pre-crime phase, the crime phase and victim characteristics. These variables are defined in Appendix 1 of this chapter.

Two independent variables were used to capture the escalation of sexual assault to sexual murder: the outcome of the sexual crime (victim killed or not) and the severity of the sexual crime. An escalation model was developed for each of these variables (see Figure 4.1).

Statistical analyses

Our choice of variables, or specific dimensions of variables, was based on preliminary descriptive and bivariate analyses (see Chéné, 2000). The variables included in the multivariate analyses were: pre-crime anger, crime-phase anger, desire for vengeance, pre-crime alcohol consumption, verbal and physical humiliation of the victim, assailant–victim relationship (familial, intimate vs. non-intimate), verbal and physical victim resistance, use of a weapon by the assailant (blunt object vs. other) and duration of crime (less than 1 hour vs. greater than 1 hour).

Through multivariate analyses – for the outcome of the sexual crime: logistic regression; for the severity of the crime: multiple regression – the

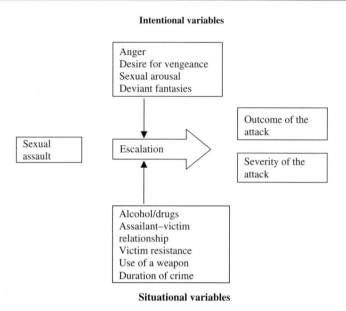

Figure 4.1   Model of the escalation process

contribution of each variable to the escalation process was measured, controlling for the other variables. The logistic regression coefficient indicates the contribution of a variable to the prediction of the outcome of the sexual crime. Logistic regression also indicates the percentage of cases correctly classified. The multiple regression coefficient expresses the contribution of a variable to the prediction of the severity of the sexual crime. The percentage of the variance explained by the model is expressed by R^2.

RESULTS AND DISCUSSION

Multivariate statistical analysis

Logistic regression analysis identified significant ($\chi^2 = 42.8$; $p < 0.001$) predictors of the outcome of sexual crimes (Table 4.1). We obtained an 87.4% correct classification. In addition, crime-phase anger, desire for vengeance, verbal and physical humiliation, verbal and physical resistance and duration of the crime did not contribute to our predictive model. In contrast, pre-crime-phase anger was significantly associated with crime outcome ($R = 0.149$; $p = 0.017$): an attack by an assailant who was angry before the crime was more likely to end in sexual murder. Sexual murder was also more likely if the assailant had consumed alcohol prior to the crime ($R = 0.114$; $p = 0.042$). On the other hand, sexual murder was much less likely if the victim and assailant were intimate or members of the same

Table 4.1 Logistic and multiple regression of the escalation process (R and β)

	Outcome of the attack	Severity of the attack
Pre-crime anger	0.149*	0.125
Crime-phase anger	0.000	0.076
Desire for vengeance	0.000	0.067
Pre-crime consumption of alcohol	0.114*	0.163**
Verbal and physical humiliation of the victim	0.000	0.143*
Assailant–victim relationship: family or intimate	−0.200**	−0.196**
Use of a weapon: blunt object	0.230**	0.244***
Verbal or physical victim resistance	0.000	0.227***
Duration of crime: less than 1 hour	0.000	−0.101

$\chi^2 = 42.8$; $p < 0.001$; percentage of correct classification $= 87.4$; $R = 0.370$; $p < 0.001$
$^*p < 0.05$; $^{**}p < 0.01$; $^{***}p < 0.001$

family ($R = -0.200$; $p = 0.003$). When a blunt object (the majority of cases in the category 'other weapons') was used, the probability of sexual murder greatly increased ($R = -0.230$; $p < 0.001$).

Multiple regression analysis identified significant ($R^2 = 0.37$; $p < 0.001$) predictors of the severity of attacks (Table 4.1). The model explained 37% of the variance of the prediction of the severity of the attack. In addition, pre-crime anger, crime-phase anger, desire for vengeance and duration of crime did not contribute to our model. On the other hand, alcohol consumption was correlated with the severity of the crime ($\beta = 0.162$; $p = 0.010$). Verbal and physical humiliation of the victim were also correlated with severity ($\beta = 0.143$; $p = 0.022$). Victims with a familial or intimate relationship with their assailant had a moderately reduced risk of injury ($\beta = -0.196$; $p = 0.002$). The severity of the crime was strongly correlated with verbal and physical resistance ($\beta = 0.227$; $p < 0.001$). Finally, severity was strongly correlated with the use of a blunt object ($\beta = 0.244$; $p < 0.001$).

In summary, the logistic and multivariate regression analyses allow us to evaluate the relevance of the two predictive models of the escalation of sexual assault to sexual murder. The three key variables to retain, for both the outcome and the severity of the attack, are alcohol consumption, the presence of a familial or intimate assailant–victim relationship and the use of a blunt object. The fact that all three exhibit a stronger statistical association with the severity of the crime than with its outcome indicates that escalation is better modelled as a continuum than as a dichotomous outcome (sexual assault vs. sexual murder). The escalation of sexual assault to sexual murder appears to be less predictable than injury level. Interestingly, pre-crime anger is associated with a fatal outcome but not with the attack severity. Verbal and physical humiliation and verbal and physical resistance are significant predictors of level of injury only. In order to better understand our two predictive models of the escalation process, and more specifically, the sequence of events of sexual crimes, we undertook the construction of decision trees.

Sequential analyses

Understanding the process by which sexual assault escalates to sexual murder requires understanding each step of the crime. One way to achieve this is by setting aside statistical reasoning and undertaking a sequential analysis of the events of the crime. The construction of sexual-assault decision trees sheds light on the choices made by sexual aggressors in different situations. Our perspective is that of an external observer of the crime, and our basic principle is that the sequence of events of a crime is not completely predetermined – choices are made as the situation progresses. The development of decision trees thus allows step-by-step analysis of the choices made by the assailant during the crime. Cohen (1966) recommends this decision-tree technique, as it provides a good representation of the theoretical model.

The decision trees for the escalation of sexual assault to sexual murder were based on four variables obtained from the multivariate analyses: pre-crime anger; the existence of a familial or intimate assailant–victim relationship; the use of a weapon; and verbal or physical victim resistance. These variables were selected on the basis of their statistical significance, theoretical value and chronological coherence. Although the use of a blunt object was statistically significant, the number of cases associated with it was small, and we instead used the generic variable 'use of a weapon'. These four variables exhibit a chronological coherence: Was the assailant angry before committing his crime? Was he close to the victim? During the crime, did he use a weapon? And, did the victim resist during the crime? Using these four dichotomous variables, we arrived at a total of 16 sexual assault scenarios.

For each variable, the frequency of sexual assaults and sexual murders was calculated (What was the percentage of sexual assaults and sexual murders perpetrated by offenders who were angry prior to the crime? What was the percentage of sexual assaults and sexual murders perpetrated by offenders who were angry prior to the crime and had familial or intimate relationships with their victims? And so on.). For level of injury, a mean severity score, rather than a frequency, was used.

Attack outcome

It should be noted that the total number of sexual assaults and sexual murders in Figure 4.2 is less than the initial 246 sexual assaults and 43 sexual murders, due to missing values for some independent variables.

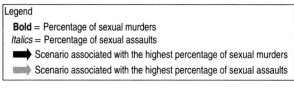

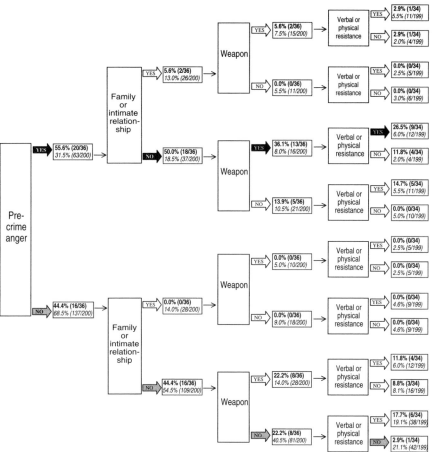

Figure 4.2 Decision tree for the outcome of the attack

Figure 4.2 presents different offending scenarios. The distribution of sexual murders and sexual assaults reveals specific scenarios for each crime. For sexual murders, the primary scenario is:

- The assailant is angry prior to the crime (55.6%).
- He has no familial or intimate relationship with the victim (50.0%).
- He uses a weapon (36.1%).
- His victim resists verbally or physically (26.5%).

This scenario clearly supports the results of our statistical analyses. The assailant's anger before he even commits the crime has repercussions on the sequence of events. Subsequently, as our statistical analyses indicate, he is more likely to kill if he has no familial or intimate relationship with the victim, if he uses a weapon, and if his victim resists.

The dominant scenario for sexual assault is:

- The assailant is not angry prior to the crime (68.5%).
- He has no familial or intimate relationship with his victim (54.5%).
- He does not use a weapon (40.5%).
- His victim does not resist verbally or physically (21.1%).

However, we also see another sexual assault scenario that, while less frequent, is nevertheless similar to the first:

- The assailant is not angry prior to the crime (68.5%).
- He has no familial or intimate relationship with his victim (54.5%).
- He does not use a weapon (40.5%).
- His victim resists verbally or physically (19.1%).

Interestingly, the only difference between the two sexual assault scenarios is the presence or absence of victim resistance. Thus, resistance to sexual assault has less decisive effects on the sequence of events under some circumstances.

The attack is most likely to end in sexual murder when the victim resists. This does not necessarily imply that victim resistance during sexual assaults triggers murder. Resistance may be the victim's adaptation to an extremely violent attack. In addition, victims of angry sexual aggressors are the most likely to resist. Anger in fact presages very violent aggression. The victim may react by exhibiting resistance congruent with the violence of the attack. Thus, victim resistance appears to be more an indicator of brutal attacks than a cause. This in no way obviates the fact that the assailant adapts to victim resistance. Depending on the adaptation chosen, the attack may or may not result in murder.

Attack severity

Figure 4.3 presents the decision tree for attack severity. In this case, the tree is derived from mean severity scores rather than outcome percentages. It should be recalled that the severity of the attack is measured on a five-point scale (from 'no injury' to 'death and mutilation'). A mean greater than 2 corresponds to a serious attack, and sexual murder is likely when the mean exceeds 3. The scenario associated with the greatest severity is:

- The assailant is angry prior to the crime (2.36).
- He has no familial or intimate relationship with the victim (2.53).

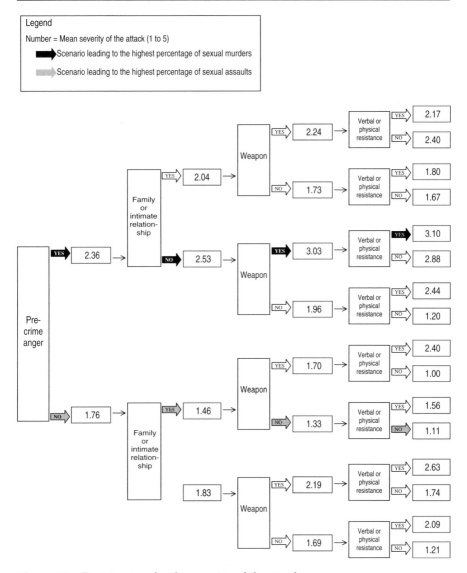

Figure 4.3 Decision tree for the severity of the attack

- He uses a weapon (3.03).
- His victim resists verbally or physically (3.10).

The scenario associated with the lowest severity is:

- The assailant is not angry prior to the crime (1.76).
- He has a familial or intimate relationship with the victim (1.46).

- He does not use a weapon (1.33).
- His victim does not resist verbally or physically (1.11).

Another low-severity scenario exists:

- The assailant is not angry prior to the crime (1.76).
- He has a familial or intimate relationship with the victim (1.46).
- He uses a weapon (1.70).
- His victim does not resist verbally or physically (1.00).

These two low-severity scenarios demonstrate that the absence of victim resistance has a significant impact on the attack. In fact, in these two cases, regardless of whether or not the assailant is armed, the absence of victim resistance is associated with a lower attack severity (1.11 and 1.00).

Taken together, the attack-severity scenarios reveal that the use of a weapon increases the severity of the crime, regardless of whether or not the assailant is angry, whether or not there is a familial or intimate assailant–victim relationship, and whether or not the victim resists (1.85 and 2.97 for unarmed and armed assailants). In addition, examination of the mean severity score of the 16 scenarios (extreme right of Figure 4.3) reveals that the mean severity scores for the eight scenarios involving angry assailants are higher than the ones for scenarios involving non-angry ones (2.21 vs. 1.72), highlighting the importance of pre-crime anger in the sequence of events.

CASE STUDIES

In order to better understand our central question, namely why some assailants go so far as to kill their victim, we analysed one sexual crime in detail. The case was selected on the basis of the logistic regression's predictions, which in this case turned out to be incorrect: the regression analysis predicted this case to be a nonfatal sexual assault, but it was in fact a sexual murder. This analysis will allow us to partially illustrate the conclusions derived from the statistical and sequential analyses. Following a brief description of the murderer, the details of the sexual murder he committed, taken from his criminal record (version of the assailant, police report, autopsy report), are presented.

Denis

Denis, age 38, was serving a life sentence for sexual assault and first-degree murder. He had a record of crimes against property stretching back to his adolescence, as well as a record of robberies (armed and unarmed) and sexual crimes. When he was two years old, his parents died in a fire, and he was placed in various foster homes. He said he had been the victim of repeated sexual abuse until he was an adolescent.

Following his divorce, when he was 29, he planned to commit suicide. He obtained the fuel necessary to set his apartment on fire, hoping to die in it. He was incapable of explaining why he did not carry out his plan. At the time of the crime, Denis had no regular sexual partner. When his girlfriend learned of his criminal record for sexual offences, she left him, fearing for the safety of her children. He said he had no drug problems and claimed to occasionally consume alcohol. At the time of the crime, Denis was unemployed, living on welfare and working under the table. He pointed out that he had no financial difficulties and that his primary problem was social isolation.

Denis left his home with the intention of 'getting laid'. Before he left, he made sure he had a vibrator, something he frequently used during sexual relations, as it compensated for his erectile dysfunction. When he arrived in the city in which he hoped to meet a woman, he wandered the streets. He went into a bar around 9:30 at night, ordered a drink and sat down. He then danced with a woman and ordered another drink. 'I felt warmed up by the drink, I'm not used to drinking.' he said. His desire to 'get laid' was steadily increasing.

Two young women entered the bar, accompanied by a man. He observed the trio for a while: 'I thought Sophie was the better looking one. I got up to ask her to dance.' At that moment, he said, he was already thinking of having sex with her. The man with the two women was an obstacle, so he sat down again and kept on watching Sophie until she left with her friends. Outside the bar, Denis saw them split up and decided to follow Sophie. The closer he got to her, the more the idea of taking her by force appealed to him. He knew that she would refuse his advances and felt incapable of coping with rejection.

The neighbourhood of the bar is particularly quiet at that time of night. 'I caught up with her on the sidewalk, I took her from behind, twisted her left arm behind her back, put my right hand on her left breast, pressed my right knee against her, bent her over and squeezed her neck. She cried out "Let me go! Let me go!" I dragged her to me, and she fell to the ground, dragging me with her. When she was on the ground, I grabbed her as best I could, wrapping my two arms around her breasts.' She resisted violently. He slapped her and punched her. She fell unconscious when her head hit a brick wall as she was falling. Denis dragged her along the wall. He undressed her upper body, caressed her breasts, took off his pants and attempted to penetrate her. Incapable of becoming erect, he grabbed the vibrator and inserted it in her vagina. He said he placed his hands around her throat and squeezed it to control her. Subsequently, he placed her on her stomach and attempted to penetrate her anally with the vibrator. He then noted that she was 'filthy' and no longer moved. He was, however, certain that she was still breathing. Denis covered her with her clothes and ran away. He was convinced that he had left the victim alive. He said he panicked when he learned that she had been found dead. The autopsy concluded that the victim had died from asphyxia from compression of the throat.

Denis had not been angry prior to the crime and had no blunt object. Because pre-crime anger and use of a blunt object are precipitating factors of sexual murder in the logistic regression, that analysis predicted Denis' crime as a sexual assault.

What elements shed light on this sequence of events? That night, Denis had been intent on having sex with a woman. He assiduously put everything in his favour. He took his vibrator. He went to a location at which there was a strong likelihood of meeting potential sexual partners. He had several drinks, which lessened his inhibitions. Denis stated that he was ill at ease around women, because he feared rejection. Alcohol increased his desire for sex. He found a woman whom he found attractive. He wanted to ask her to dance, but a friend of the woman constituted an obstacle, something that can reasonably be supposed to have frustrated Denis. He watched the woman. When he saw her exit the bar, he followed her and saw her leave her friends and find herself alone in the street. He told himself that this was his last chance. He was determined to have sex with her and nothing was going to stop him. His victim resisted verbally and physically. He overcame her by force and was probably unaware of the brutality he was capable of. He felt sexually aroused. After he had obtained what he desired, he left the scene with no concern for his victim. At no time did he think that he may have been too violent or that his acts could have been fatal. It is quite possible that Denis had no intention of killing his victim and that he simply wanted sex. The sequence of events of the crime illustrates an escalation in which the assailant does not budge from his initial idea, even if it means using excessive, and under the circumstances, fatal, force.

Examining the decision tree for attack outcome, we can see that Denis's crime corresponds to one of the two most common sexual-murder scenarios (absence of pre-crime anger, absence of familial or intimate assailant–victim relationship, absence of weapon, victim resistance). This said, this is also a scenario that closely resembles the most common sexual-assault scenario. The only difference is victim resistance, a particularly noteworthy fact that explains many sexual murders that are absolutely unpredictable and there-fore at first glance unintelligible. The first phase of the crime appears to predict that the attack will end in a sexual assault, not a sexual murder. But the victim resisted violently, and the assailant, his mind set on his plan and his body strong enough to overcome resistance, continued his attack. Some attacks end at this stage for various reasons: inadequate strength, fear of the victim's violent reaction, failure to succeed immediately, anticipation of failure, etc.

The narrative of Denis's crime highlights the elements that characterize sexual assaults that 'go wrong', and underscores the role of crime situations in determining the outcome of sexual offence. Initial intentions influence crimes, but unpredictable circumstances must also be managed as they arise.

CONCLUSION

Our multivariate analyses of the outcome and severity of sexual crimes demonstrated that alcohol consumption, the absence of a familial or intimate assailant–victim relationship and the use of a blunt object are predictors of the escalation of sexual assault to sexual murder. In addition, pre-crime anger appears to be a predictor of fatal outcomes but unrelated to attack severity. In contrast, verbal and physical humiliation, and verbal and physical resistance, are important predictors of attack severity, although they are not related to attack outcome.

One last point remains to be discussed with regard to the statistical analyses of the escalation process. As we have seen, attack severity often exhibited a stronger statistical association with intentional and situational variables than did attack outcome. Also, some variables are linked to only one of the two dimensions of escalation, indicating that different rules are at play. In addition, our analyses indicate that the outcome of sexual crimes is less predictable than their severity. In fact in some cases, our statistical analyses failed to predict that a sexual assault would culminate in sexual murder. The narrative of Denis's crime illustrates this point: Denis was not angry prior to his crime and possessed no blunt object. As pre-crime anger and use of a blunt object are factors associated with sexual murder in the logistic regression, this event was classified as a sexual assault.

The decision trees reveal that the most common sexual-murder scenario is also the scenario associated with the highest attack severity. This demonstrates a certain coherence of the characteristics associated with serious aggression (attack outcome or attack severity), regardless of analytical method. It should, however, be noted that the two dependent variables differ in that one is dichotomous, the other scalar. Thus, there are three degrees of severity for sexual assault (1: no injury; 2: slight injury; and 3: serious injury), and two levels of severity for sexual murder (4: death; 5: death and mutilation). This explains why the most common sexual-aggression scenario is not the same as the scenario for the least severe sexual assault. The lowest severity is an attack with no injuries, whereas the other two types of sexual assault involve victim injuries.

One other point should be made with regard to victim resistance: most victims of sexual murder resisted. This does not imply that victim resistance leads to escalation, but rather that serious attacks probably provoke resistance.

Finally, this study has demonstrated that murder subsequent to sexual assault is not invariably the result of the assailant's initial intentions, and that the circumstances surrounding the crime play a central role in determining the outcome of the sexual crime. As there is no consistent association between intentional variables and crime outcome, we believe that sexual attacks in which assailants clearly premeditate the murder of their victims are quite rare. Sexual murder may be the result of 'accidents' or escalation. Echoing Felson and Steadman (1983), who concluded that murders may be simple assaults that go wrong, we believe that some sexual murders are sexual assaults gone wrong.

APPENDIX I: INDEPENDENT VARIABLES

Intentional variables

- **Pre-crime/crime-phase anger:** Any sign that the assailant felt enraged, frustrated or aggressive prior to/during the crime.

- **Desire for vengeance:** Any remark indicating that the assailant resented his victim or women in general. Vengeance, in the context of our study, is best represented by the cognitive distortion 'she deserved it'.
- **Pre-crime/crime-phase sexual arousal:** Any statement by the assailant indicating that he felt sexually aroused, e.g. stating that 'I had an erection' prior to/during the crime.
- **Deviant sexual fantasies:** Sexual arousal in the 48 hours prior to the crime by thoughts of tying up a woman, whipping her or sexually assaulting her. These fantasies may or may not involve the victim.
- **Victim humiliation:** Any gesture or comment that humiliates the victim. This includes insults (verbal humiliation), anal sex followed by fellatio, and urination on the victim (physical humiliation).

Situational variables

- **Consumption of alcohol and drugs:** The consumption of alcohol or drugs by the assailant in the hours preceding the crime. This information was taken from the subject's police statement.
- **Relationship to victim:** Was the victim a stranger, a neighbour, a member of the assailant's family, someone the assailant was close to or often saw?
- **Victim resistance:** Failure of the victim to respond to the assailant's demands (passive resistance), screaming, crying (verbal resistance), hitting the assailant or trying to push him away (physical resistance).
- **Use of a weapon:** Based on information found in official documents (police reports and medical reports).
- **Duration of crime:** Calculated from the moment the assailant entered into contact with the victim. For example, if the assailant meets the victim in a bar, asks her to come home with him, talks to her and sexually assaults her, the duration of the crime is calculated from the meeting in the bar until the end of the sexual assault.

Chapter 5

THE FACTORS DISTINGUISHING SEXUAL MURDERERS FROM SEXUAL AGGRESSORS: A MULTIVARIATE ANALYSIS

Alexandre Nicole and Jean Proulx

THEORETICAL AND EMPIRICAL FRAMEWORK

In Chapter 1, the definitions, epidemiological data and theories related to sexual murder were outlined. Subsequently, in Chapters 2, 3 and 4, the potential explanatory factors for sexual murder were analysed. In this chapter, we will present a multivariate model of the gravity of sexual offences. All the analyses presented so far have revealed more similarities than differences between sexual aggressors of women and sexual murderers of women. Nevertheless, the differences that have been noted are indicators that should be taken into consideration in explanations of the escalation of sexual assault to sexual murder. It should be noted that this escalation may be better predicted by models based on the dynamic interaction, rather than simple additivity, of selected factors. For this reason, it is crucial that our analysis simultaneously take into account several potentially relevant factors.

Several authors have developed multivariate descriptive models – even 'unified' theories – of sexual aggressors (Bard et al., 1987; Hall & Hirschman, 1991; Knight & Prentky, 1990; Malamuth, 1986; Malamuth et al., 1993; Marshall & Barbaree, 1990a). In all these models, several factors are related to a proclivity for sexual assault. In addition, integrated models specific to

Sexual Murderers: A Comparative Analysis and New Perspectives Edited by Jean Proulx Éric Beauregard, Maurice Cusson and Alexandre Nicole
© 2007 John Wiley & Sons, Ltd.

sexual murderers have also been developed (see Chapters 1 and 2): the FBI's motivational model (Burgess et al., 1986; Ressler et al., 1988), the trauma-control model (Hickey, 1997, 2002) and Arrigo and Purcell's (2001) model. While these integrated models are of a great interest from a theoretical viewpoint, they have not been extensively verified empirically.

Careful consideration of all these models of sexual offenders and of the results presented in Chapters 2, 3 and 4, make the need for integrated analyses clear. This chapter will present the results of a single analysis based on the principal significant results reported in the preceding chapters and on selected variables of theoretical interest. This analysis was undertaken to develop a predictive model of the escalation of sexual assault to sexual murder. To this end, the analysis will include developmental, psychopathological, situational and intentional variables, as well as variables related to criminal career.

METHODS

The basic analytical strategy was to include variables of particular theoretical interest and variables from the analyses presented in Chapters 2, 3 and 4 that distinguished between sexual aggressors and sexual murderers of women. First, we will present the results of statistically significant bivariate analyses from previous chapters, and a correlation matrix of the variables in question. This will be followed by a three-block hierarchical logistic regression analysis that will assess the predictive value of different types of factors. The first block (B1) comprises developmental variables, namely victimization scale (integrating physical, psychological and sexual victimization), and the sum of problematic childhood and adolescent behaviours (e.g. social isolation, low self-esteem). The second block (B2) comprises structural variables, namely personality profile (antisocial and narcissistic vs. schizoid, avoidant and dependent) and deviant sexual fantasies, as well as two variables related to criminal career – the severity of previous crimes against property and against persons. The last block (B3) comprises situational and intentional variables: pre-crime anger, pre-crime consumption of alcohol, verbal and physical victim resistance and use of a weapon.

RESULTS

The results of the bivariate analyses of the variables included in the logistic regression are presented in Table 5.1. The correlation matrix for all the variables is presented in Table 5.2. Scores in this matrix indicate the strength of the association between the type of crime (sexual aggression or sexual murder) and the independent variables; this evaluation is expressed in terms of Pearson's r, phi or a point biserial correlation, depending on the

Table 5.1 Bivariate comparison (percentage or mean) of the variables included in the multivariate analysis

Variables			Sexual aggressors ($N = 101$)	Sexual murderers ($N = 40$)
B1	n.s.	Victimization scale	37.86	49.80
	**	Inappropriate behaviours	5.87	10.29
B2	n.s.	Personality profile (profile 2: schizoid, avoidant and dependent)	45.3%	40.0%
	*	Deviant sexual fantasies	22.7%	40.0%
	*	Severity of crimes against property	112.74	49.51
	*	Severity of crimes against persons	33.51	64.73
B3	**	Pre-crime anger	24.7	52.9
	*	Pre-crime consumption of alcohol	62.4%	84.2%
	*	Verbal and physical resistance	56.0%	78.4%
	**	Use of a weapon	34.7%	65.0%

n.s.: not significant; * $p < 0.05$; ** $p < 0.01$

specific variable. The variable with the strongest association with the type of crime (sexual aggression vs. sexual murder) was the sum of inappropriate behaviours (biserial $= 0.380$; $p < 0.01$). This was followed by the use of a weapon (phi $= 0.276$; $p < 0.01$), pre-crime anger (phi $= 0.272$; $p < 0.01$), pre-crime consumption of alcohol (phi $= 0.209$; $p < 0.05$), verbal or physical victim resistance (phi $= 0.205$; $p < 0.05$), mean severity of crimes against property (biserial $= -0.190$; $p < 0.05$), mean severity of crimes against persons (biserial $= 0.186$; $p < 0.05$) and presence of deviant sexual fantasies (phi $= 0.169$; $p < 0.05$).

Furthermore, as Table 5.2 indicates, there were significant associations between developmental variables (block 1), structural variables and criminal career (block 2), and situational/intentional variables (block 3). The two block-1 variables, i.e. victimization score and sum of inappropriate behaviours, were very strongly associated with each other ($r = 0.465$; $p < 0.01$). In addition, there were significant associations between some developmental variables and variables in other blocks. Thus, victimization score was associated with a schizoid, avoidant and dependent personality profile (biserial $= 0.271$; $p < 0.01$) and the use of a weapon (biserial $= 0.195$; $p < 0.05$). The sum of inappropriate behaviours was associated with the schizoid, avoidant and dependent personality profile (biserial $= 0.235$; $p < 0.05$), the presence of deviant sexual fantasies (biserial $= 0.230$; $p < 0.01$), pre-crime angry affect (biserial $= 0.254$; $p < 0.01$) and the use of a weapon (biserial $= 0.270$; $p < 0.01$).

Similarly, some block-2 variables were associated with each other. The presence of deviant sexual fantasies was associated with a schizoid, avoidant and dependent personality profile (phi $= 0.397$; $p < 0.01$) and with the

Table 5.2 Correlation matrix of the variables included in the multivariate analyses (Pearson's r, phi, point biserial)

Variable	(1)	(2)	(3)	(4)	(5)	(6)	(7)	(8)	(9)	(10)	(11)
B1 (1) Crime (sexual assault / sexual murder)	–										
(2) Victimization scale	0.121	–									
(3) Inappropriate behaviours	0.380*	0.465**	–								
(4) Personality profile	–0.047	0.271**	0.235*	–							
B2 (5) Deviant sexual fantasies	0.169*	0.163	0.230**	0.397**	–						
(6) Severity of crimes against property	–0.190	0.076	0.023	0.058	0.080	–					
(7) Severity of crimes against persons	0.186*	0.112	0.096	0.185	0.188*	0.285**	–				
B3 (8) Pre-crime anger	0.272**	0.159	0.254**	0.125	0.037	–0.093	–0.147	–			
(9) Pre-crime consumption of alcohol	0.209*	0.003	0.003	–0.053	–0.013	–0.120	–0.044	–0.043	–		
(10) Verbal and physical resistance	0.205*	–0.078	0.061	–0.071	0.007	0.079	–0.083	0.080	0.213*	–	
(11) Use of a weapon	0.276**	0.195*	0.270**	0.099	0.114	0.066	0.109	0.252**	–0.041	0.012	–

* $p < 0.05$; ** $p < 0.01$

severity of previous crimes against persons (biserial $= 0.188$; $p < 0.05$). The severity of crimes against property was correlated with the severity of crimes against persons ($r = 0.285$; $p < 0.01$). However, no associations were observed between variables in block 2 and those in block 3. Two significant associations were observed between the situational/intentional variables in block 3. Pre-crime affect of anger was associated with the use of a weapon (phi $= 0.252$; $p < 0.01$), and pre-crime consumption of alcohol was asso- ciated with verbal and physical victim resistance (phi $= 0.213$; $p < 0.05$).

Finally, the results of the hierarchical logistic regression can be found in Table 5.3. This type of analysis evaluates the contribution of each block and each of the variables (exp(B)) to the prediction of the type of crime committed (sexual assault or sexual murder). Developmental variables alone were sufficient to obtain a 74.9% correct classification ($\chi^2 = 12.84$; $p < 0.001$). After introduction of block-2 variables, the model remained significant ($\chi^2 = 18.39$; $p < 0.001$) and the percentage of correct classification increased slightly (77.2%). However, block-2 variables were not significantly associated with the type of crime. After introduction of the third block, comprising situational and intentional variables, the model remained significant ($\chi^2 = 38.84$; $p < 0.001$) and the percentage of correct classification increased to 87.1%. When all the variables were included in the model, five variables were observed to be significantly related to the type of crime: the sum of inappropriate behaviours, the severity of previous crimes against persons, pre-crime anger, pre-crime consumption of alcohol and the use of a weapon.

Table 5.3 Hierarchical logistic regression analysis of the type of crime committed (sexual assault/sexual murder)

Variables		[exp(B)/p]	[exp(B)/p]	[exp(B)/p]
B1	Victimization scale	n.s.	n.s.	n.s.
	Inappropriate behaviours	1.289/0.000	1.287/0.001	1.302/0.001
B2	Personality profile			
	(profile 2)		n.s.	n.s.
	Deviant sexual fantasies		n.s.	n.s.
	Severity of crimes against			
	property		n.s.	n.s.
	Severity of crimes against			
	persons		n.s.	1.020/0.048
B3	Pre-crime anger			1.782/0.047
	Pre-crime consumption of			
	alcohol			3.217/0.016
	Verbal and physical resistance			n.s.
	Use of a weapon			2.861/0.029
χ^2		12.84	18.39	38.84
P		0.000	0.000	0.000
% correct classification		74.9	77.2	87.1

n.s.: not significant

DISCUSSION

We carried out multivariate statistical analyses in order to distinguish between sexual aggressors and sexual murderers, using data described in Chapters 2, 3 and 4. Those results indicate that while sexual aggressors and sexual murderers resemble each other, the differences between them are statistical predictors of the escalation of the former crime to the latter. Through the use of force coefficients, it was possible to identify the variables most strongly associated with the type of crime. The variable most strongly associated with sexual murder was the sum of inappropriate childhood and adolescent behaviours. This result agrees with current models of sexual murder, in which the propensity for lethal violence is seen primarily as the result of disturbed development (Arrigo & Purcell, 2001; Hickey 2002; Ressler et al., 1988). Our results also indicate that situational and intentional variables (alcohol, anger, resistance, weapon) are strongly associated with the type of crime. According to Marshall and Barbaree (1990), anger and pre-crime consumption of alcohol are precipitating factors for sexual crimes. Ouimet et al. (2000) noted, and our results here confirm, that pre-crime consumption of alcohol is associated with more serious injuries. The use of a weapon in sexual assault has been reported to increase the risk of the victim dying (Felson & Krohn, 1990; Felson & Messner, 1996), and Block and Skogan (1985, 1986) reported that victim resistance increases the risk of injuries.

The correlation matrix revealed significant associations between the variables in the multivariate analysis. The victimization-scale score was strongly associated with the sum of inappropriate behaviours, and was associated with a schizoid, avoidant and dependent personality profile. Thus, our results are consistent with the hypothesis so often invoked in studies and theories of sexual assault (Hall & Hirschman, 1991; Malamuth et al., 1993; Marshall & Barbaree, 1990), namely that most sexual aggressors grew up in inadequate environments, which causes various inappropriate behaviours and the development of a pathological personality.

Other significant associations in our study are also consistent with general theories of sexual assault. For example, subjects who exhibited a greater number of inappropriate behaviours in their developing years had a greater tendency to exhibit schizoid, avoidant or dependent personality profiles. Furthermore, the presence of deviant fantasies was strongly associated with inappropriate behaviours and with schizoid, avoidant or dependent personality profiles.

A large number of inappropriate childhood and adolescent behaviours were associated with a greater likelihood of pre-crime anger and use of a weapon during the crime. It should be recalled that the variable describing inappropriate behaviours is the sum of variables such as angry temperament, rebellious attitudes and dangerous behaviours. Thus, a propensity for violence can be observed as early as childhood, and continues in adulthood.

In Chapter 2, it was observed that a very strong majority of sexual offenders of both types (sexual aggressors and sexual murderers) had had previous convictions. Furthermore, the results indicated that sexual offenders were, generally speaking, polymorphic criminals, a finding consistent with other published reports (Boutin, 1999; Hazelwood & Warren, 1989; Heritage, 1992; Soothill et al., 2000). Such polymorphism is supported by the strong association found between the severity of previous crimes against property and the severity of previous crimes against persons.

The correlation matrix reveals that victims were more likely to verbally or physically resist assailants who had consumed alcohol prior to the crime. Does intoxication promote violence on the part of the assailant, which in turn triggers a stronger defence reaction from the victim? This scenario merits further study.

Turning now to our multivariate predictive model of the escalation of sexual assault to sexual murder, we can see that the hierarchical logistic regression yielded a high percentage of correct classification (87.7%). The complementary analysis of the area under the ROC curve (0.92) provides yet another demonstration of the predictive validity of our model. In addition to these global results, other observations stand out. Thus, the introduction of structural variables and variables related to criminal pathways (block 2) only marginally improves the percentage of correct classification. However, this percentage significantly increases when situational/intentional variables (block 3) are introduced. When all three blocks of variables are introduced, the effect of each variable, controlling for the other variables, can be evaluated. Half the variables (5 of 10) of the model were significantly associated with the type of crime. These variables are the sum of inappropriate behaviours, the severity of prior crimes against persons, pre-crime anger, pre-crime consumption of alcohol and the use of a weapon. Victimization scores and the presence of deviant sexual fantasies were no longer related to the type of crime.

According to Meloy (2000), the presence of deviant sexual fantasies is the best predictor of sexual murder and a central element of specific models of sexual murder (Arrigo & Purcell, 2001; Hickey, 1997, 2002; Ressler et al., 1988). The bivariate results reported in Chapter 2 – deviant sexual fantasies having been reported by twice as many sexual murderers as sexual aggressors – tend to support this conclusion. Once included in the multivariate model, this variable does not significantly improve the prediction of the type of crime. It thus appears that the statistical impact of deviant sexual fantasies is attenuated by the presence of other variables. In fact, an association between developmental variables and deviant sexual fantasies has been demonstrated (Beauregard, Lussier & Proulx, 2004), and this association may explain why the inclusion of deviant sexual fantasies adds almost nothing to a predictive model that already includes developmental variables. A similar situation prevails with regard to the severity of previous crimes against property and verbal and physical victim resistance, two variables which, in the bivariate analysis, differed significantly in the two groups of sexual offenders but which had no additional significant impact on predictive power after controlling for other variables.

In Chapter 3, it was mentioned that although psychopathological factors are generally considered useful in understanding sexual murderers, no differences in psychopathology were observed between sexual murderers and sexual aggressors. Furthermore, the heterogeneity of diagnoses associated with sexual murderers was noted. Despite these findings, these variables were included in the analyses described here, in an attempt to identify any significant interactions with either developmental or situational/intentional variables. Once again, psychopathological variables did not significantly improve the ability to predict the type of crime. Although personality disorders did not distinguish between sexual aggressors and sexual murderers, they do distinguish between sadistic and nonsadistic sexual offenders, as will be discussed in Chapter 7.

To some extent, our results agree with previously published integrative models of sexual murder. It should, however, be recalled that the samples upon which these integrative models (Arrigo & Purcell, 2001; Hickey, 1997, 2002; Ressler et al., 1988) were biased, as serial murderers were over-represented and the victims were variously men, women and children. Chapter 6 will discuss the differences between nonserial and serial murderers. Despite the differences in samples, however, parallels with these studies merit discussion.

The FBI's motivational model (Ressler et al., 1988) posits that sexual murderers are the product of inadequate environments and of victimizing experiences (Chapters 1, 2). In fact, according to Ressler et al. (1988) these factors lead to social isolation, deviant fantasies and negative personality traits (rebellion, aggressivity, feelings of injustice, a desire for vengeance) that interfere with the development of gratifying social networks, pro-social values and empathy. Our data partially supports this conclusion, although the inclusion of neither inadequate environments nor victimizing experiences improved our multivariate model's ability to predict the type of crime. On the other hand, the sum of inappropriate childhood and adolescent behaviours was a significant predictor of the type of crime. As this variable integrates social isolation, low self-esteem, habitual lying, dangerous behaviours and rebellious attitudes, our results support those of Ressler et al. (1988). Ressler et al. also claim that inappropriate behaviours are expressed in destructive acts. Our finding that a criminal record of violence (severity of prior crimes against persons) is a significant predictor of sexual murder supports this hypothesis.

According to the motivational model, a sexual murderer's first murder is precipitated by a stressor, e.g. financial difficulties or a conflict with a woman or a parent. The analyses presented in this chapter are insufficient for us to draw any conclusions about this point. The fact that pre-crime anger is a significant predictor of sexual murder could, however, support this element of the motivational model, since conflicts with women may provoke anger in sex offenders. Both pre-crime consumption of alcohol and the use of a weapon were mentioned in the FBI study, but in the typology distinguishing between organized and disorganized murderers, rather than in the integrative model. For methodological reasons, therefore, our study cannot be easily compared to that of the FBI. However, our results do allow us to conclude that situational/intentional variables exert a considerable impact on the type of sexual crime, a phenomenon not taken into account by the motivational model.

Hickey's trauma-control model (Hickey, 1997, 2002) is strongly inspired by the FBI's model (Ressler et al., 1988), and leads to essentially the same conclusions. However, the trauma-control model includes precipitating elements such as pre-crime consumption of alcohol and drugs, and the consumption of pornography. Our results provide partial empirical valida-tion of this model: sexual aggressors who consumed alcohol prior to their crimes were more likely to kill their victims, presumably because of the disinhibitory effect of alcohol.

The model of Arrigo and Purcell (2001) implies a cyclical process that includes interaction among deviant fantasies, paraphilias and orgasmic con-ditioning. Our results do not agree with this model. In fact, in Chapter 3 we noted a very low prevalence of paraphilias among sexual murderers, and that the presence of deviant sexual fantasies did not predict the outcome of the attack. However, we should bear in mind that the deviant sexual fantasies variable was introduced into the multivariate analysis after the sum of problematic behaviours, with which it is correlated. Thus, the absence of an association between deviant sexual fantasies and the outcome of the crime is a consequence of our multivariate analytical strategy.

What emerges from all the comparative studies of sexual aggressors and sexual murderers presented in Chapter 1 is that the principal distinctions between the two types of criminals are related to social isolation, pre-crime anger, deviant sexual fantasies and paraphilias, all of which were more prevalent among sexual murderers. Our predictive model supports the role of social isolation and pre-crime anger, but the presence of deviant sexual fantasies was only found to be significant by the bivariate analysis. It is difficult to directly compare the results presented in this chapter with those presented in Chapter 1, as the latter were taken from studies that used samples that were biased (over-representation of serial sexual murderers) and small. It is nevertheless possible to state that our results partially agree with those reported in previous comparative studies.

The objective in this chapter was to present the results of a single multivariate analysis of the variables in several groups of factors, in order to determine the statistical associations that remain after appropriate controlling. This analysis identified variables with a unique significant association with the type of crime. The bivariate analysis revealed statisti-cally significant associations for eight of the 10 predictors retained. In the hierarchical logistic regression, five of the 10 variables (some of which were scales themselves based on several dichotomous variables) were sufficient to obtain a high percentage of correct classification. This reduction of the number of predictors retained for multivariate analysis is not surprising, since the variables are correlated with each other. A noteworthy finding in our study was that inappropriate behaviours in childhood or adolescence, the nature of the adult criminal record (presence of violence), and situational and intentional variables all have a major impact on the type of crime. Thus, developmental factors, as well as the circumstances surrounding a sexual crime, are determinants of the escalation of a sexual assault to sexual murder.

APPENDIX I

Study variables

- **Type of crime** (dependent variable): Dichotomous variable representing the outcome of the attack; distinguishes between sexual aggressors and sexual murderers.
- **Victimization scale:** A score calculated on the basis of victimization experiences prior to age 18 (psychological violence, physical violence, incest, sexual assault, parental abandonment). Each experience is weighted on the basis of its duration (years) and exact frequency. The scale thus is a summation of weighted variables.
- **Inappropriate behaviours:** Variable representing the sum of inappropriate behaviours occurring during childhood and adolescence: daydreams, social isolation, habitual lying, enuresis, rebellious attitudes, nightmares, cruelty towards animals, low self-esteem, angry temperament, sleep disorders, phobias, running away from home, school discipline problems, dangerous behaviours, migraines, self-mutilation and somatic complaints.
- **Personality profile:** (1) antisocial and narcissistic; (2) schizoid, avoidant and dependent (obtained through K-means cluster analysis of the 11 scales of the MCMI personality disorder scale).
- **Deviant sexual fantasies:** The offender admits having had deviant sexual fantasies during the year preceding the crime. These fantasies may or may not involve his victim.
- **Severity of crimes against property/persons:** Each criminal charge for crimes against property or person was multiplied by a severity score (Wolfgang et al., 1985). These products were then summed.
- **Pre-crime anger:** Any indication that the offender felt enraged, frustrated or aggressive in the hours preceding the sexual assault or sexual murder.
- **Pre-crime consumption of alcohol:** Any consumption of alcohol by the offender in the hours preceding the crime.

- **Physical or verbal resistance:** Verbal (screaming, crying) or physical (hitting, pushing) resistance to the offender's demands.
- **Use of a weapon:** Use of a weapon in the commission of the crime. This weapon may have been brought to the crime scene or found there. All types of weapons were considered (knives, firearms, blunt object, other).

Chapter 6
SERIAL KILLERS AND SEXUAL MURDERERS

Élisabeth Campos and Maurice Cusson

Serial killers and sexual murderers are often considered equivalent in the criminological literature. Indeed, this is often considered so self-evident that no proof of it is deemed necessary. However, such an equivalence presupposes two things: first, that serial killers are all sexual murderers; and secondly, that most sexual murderers kill repeatedly. As we shall see, however, neither of these assertions has any scientific basis.

The equation of serial killers with sexual murderers no doubt has its origins in the best known and frequently cited study on the subject, namely the 1988 study by Ressler, Burgess and Douglas described in the book tellingly titled *Sexual Homicide*. The book asserts that most serial killers are sexual murderers and suggests that sexual murderers have a strong tendency to commit multiple, similar, murders. While these statements are valid for the very specific sample described in that book, it is far from certain that they can be generalized to all serial killers and sexual murderers. In fact, it must be borne in mind – as the authors themselves point out – that their sample of 36 incarcerated sexual murderers from across the United States was not representative, because the recruitment process had a selection bias in favour of murderers who had killed multiple victims. These criminals had claimed a total of 118 victims, and only seven of them had killed only one victim. Given the authors' interest in profiling, there was a natural tendency to select sexual murderers having killed more than once, as this technique is particularly applied to the apprehension of this type of criminal. Thus, the very nature of

Sexual Murderers: A Comparative Analysis and New Perspectives Edited by Jean Proulx Éric Beauregard, Maurice Cusson and Alexandre Nicole
© 2007 John Wiley & Sons, Ltd.

the selection process led to a blurring of the distinction between serial killers and sexual murderers.

The samples used by subsequent authors have been even more limited (rarely more than 30 subjects) and, above all, of questionable representativity. The over-representation of serial killers is a recurring problem. Dietz et al. (1990) studied 17 serial killers and five nonserial killers. Almost half (20 of 42) of the subjects studied by Gratzer and Bradford (1995) were serial killers. And Warren et al. (1996) studied 20 sadistic serial sexual murderers. Our sample, the result of a systematic attempt to include all the sexual murderers in Quebec, yielded markedly different results.

Previous studies have also had definitional weaknesses. In most studies, a killer has been classified as a serial killer if he satisfied two criteria: he committed murder on at least three different occasions; and his murders comprised some sexual element. The difficulties with this type of definition are glaring: basing a definition of serial killer on both the number of victims and the sexual nature of the crime not only eliminates any possibility of distinguishing between serial sexual murderers and nonserial, nonsexual murderers, but also suggests that repetitive murder can only be motivated by sexual drive. It strikes us that definitions that *distinguish* among types of murderers rather than *combine* them are more useful for scientific purposes.

Our starting point is the definition of *sexual murderer* presented in Chapter 1: a murderer whose crime is accompanied by sexual assault or mutilation of sexual organs, or who left his victim naked or in a sexually explicit position. The *serial sexual murderer* is an individual who has committed sexual murders on three different occasions. To these basic definitions we now add the following definitions of other, related, types of murderers. *Serial killers* (when not otherwise qualified) are individuals who have killed at least three people on three different occasions. It should be noted that this definition does not require the murders to have comprised a sexual element – a hit man with three 'contracts' to his credit would be considered a serial murderer, for example. *Mass murderers* are murderers who have killed at least three people at the same place and in a relatively short period (e.g. Timothy McVeigh). *Compulsive or spree murderers* (e.g. Michael Ryan, Richard Speck) resemble serial killers to the extent that they commit repeated murders in different places, but differ fundamentally from serial killers by virtue of the very narrow timeframe in which they act.

The first objective of our analysis was to determine the number of serial sexual murderers in the province of Quebec. A second objective was to compare nonserial and serial sexual murderers. Are their profiles similar or significantly different? For the purposes of this comparison, which will verify whether the common equation of serial sexual killers and sexual murderers is valid, we will compare Ressler et al.'s American serial sexual killers to 41 Quebec nonserial sexual murderers. Specifically, we will compare life histories, deviant sexual fantasies, aggressor–victim relationships and premeditation in serial sexual killers and nonserial sexual murderers.

HOW MANY SERIAL KILLERS AND SERIAL SEXUAL MURDERERS ARE THERE IN QUEBEC?

The database we used to determine the number of serial killers and serial sexual murderers in Quebec was constructed by Fabienne Cusson (1996, 1999) for the purposes of establishing the number of murderers having killed more than once in Quebec between 1956 and 1995. Over this period, 3854 individuals had committed at least one murder. Of these, 100 had killed twice and 31 had killed at least three times. It is the last group that is of interest here. In this group of 31 serial murderers:

- three had committed at least three sexual murders
- 16 had only committed murders that were settling of accounts (murders committed by a member of the criminal world following a conflict related to criminal activities)
- 12 had committed multiple types of murder (settling of accounts, conjugal murder, murder associated with robbery, murder as a result of a quarrel, murder during an escape from prison).

From these figures, we must conclude that serial killers are a very rare species: over a 40-year period, only 31 of 3854 murderers had committed at least three murders, and among these 31, only three were serial sexual murderers. Furthermore, the greatest number of serial killers belong to the 'settling of accounts' category. The 16 murderers specializing in this type of murder are probably hit men. Cusson (1996) also found that that highest rates of recidivism (committing a second murder) and specialization (committing a murder similar to the first) were among murderers who committed settling of accounts and murderers who committed sexual murders.

DO THE LIFE HISTORIES OF NONSERIAL SEXUAL MURDERERS IN QUEBEC RESEMBLE THOSE OF SERIAL SEXUAL KILLERS IN THE UNITED STATES?

Given the rarity of serial sexual murder, it is natural to ask whether Ressler et al.'s serial sexual killers are similar to nonserial sexual murderers in Quebec. It is possible to answer this question because it so happens that the questionnaire used in Quebec to collect information was partially derived from the questionnaire used by Ressler et al., and we therefore have comparable information for both samples. On the one hand, there is the information from Ressler et al.'s studies (Ressler et al. 1988; Ressler, Burgess, Douglas et al., 1986; Ressler, Burgess, Hartman et al., 1986) of 21–28 serial sexual murderers (the exact number depended on the specific variable studied). On the other hand, the Quebec study provides information on 41 individuals having committed a single murder. The only

Table 6.1 Childhood characteristics

Behaviours	Serial murderers* (Ressler, USA)	Nonserial sexual murderers** (Quebec)
Daydreams	82%	28.9%
Compulsive masturbation	82%	2.2%
Social isolation	71%	44.4%
Habitual lying	71%	31.1%
Nightmares	67%	24.4%
Low self-esteem	52%	48.9%
Sleep disorders	48%	13.3%
Phobias	38%	37.8%
Cruelty to animals	36%	13.3%
Migraines	29%	8.9%
Self-mutilation	19%	2.2%

*Number of subjects: 21–28, depending on the variable
**Number of subjects: 41

selection criterion for this sample was the commission of nonserial sexual homicide; neither the sex of the victim, the age of the victim, nor any other variable were used to select participants. The sample comprised 35 sexual murderers of women, four sexual murderers of children and two sexual murderers of men. Supplemental information on the construction of the Quebec sample can be found at the end of Chapter 1.

As Tables 6.1 to 6.3 indicate, the profiles of the murderers are remarkably stable from childhood through adolescence all the way to adulthood. We may therefore conclude that the murderers' psychological problems neither

Table 6.2 Adolescence characteristics

Behaviours	Serial murderers* (Ressler, USA)	Nonserial sexual murderers** (Quebec)
Daydreams	81%	31.1%
Compulsive masturbation	82%	11.1%
Social isolation	77%	46.7%
Habitual lying	75%	44.4%
Nightmares	68%	20.0%
Low self-esteem	63%	66.7%
Sleep disorders	50%	17.8%
Phobias	43%	40.0%
Cruelty to animals	46%	8.9%
Migraines	33%	13.3%
Self-mutilation	21%	2.2%

*Number of subjects: 21–28, depending on the variable
**Number of subjects: 41

Table 6.3   Adulthood characteristics

Behaviours	Serial murderers* (Ressler, USA)	Nonserial sexual murderers** (Quebec)
Daydreams	81%	31.1%
Compulsive masturbation	81%	8.9%
Social isolation	73%	46.7%
Habitual lying	68%	44.4%
Nightmares	52%	20.0%
Low self-esteem	62%	66.7%
Sleep disorders	50%	20.0%
Phobias	50%	37.8%
Cruelty to animals	36%	11.1%
Migraines	45%	22.2%
Self-mutilation	32%	8.9%

*Number of subjects: 21–28, depending on the variable
**Number of subjects: 41

resolved nor became accentuated over time. An even more important finding is that, for almost all characteristics, the differences between American serial killers and Quebec nonserial murderers are considerable during childhood and persist throughout life. As early as childhood, American serial sexual killers are much more likely than Quebec nonserial sexual murderers to suffer from social isolation (71% for American serial killers vs. 44% for Quebec sexual murderers), sleep disorders (48% vs. 13%), nightmares (67% vs. 24%), migraines (29% vs. 9%) and self-mutilation (19% vs. 2%) (Table 6.1). There is also some evidence that American serial sexual killers are more likely than Quebec sexual murderers to live in a world of violence and deviant sexuality: compulsive masturbation (72% vs. 2%), daydreams (82% vs. 29%) and cruelty towards animals (36% vs. 13%) were all more frequent in the former group (Table 6.1). Only two variables exhibited no or only minor differences: low self-esteem (52% vs. 49%) and phobias (38% vs. 38%). These patterns remain essentially the same in adolescence and adulthood. Nonserial sexual murderers were clearly less disturbed, less isolated and less distressed than were serial sexual killers.

SEXUAL MURDERERS VS. SERIAL SEXUAL KILLERS: DEVIANT SEXUAL FANTASIES, PREMEDITATION AND RELATIONSHIP TO THE VICTIM

Deviant sexual fantasies

Several authors have suggested that it is in childhood that sexual murderers become daydreamers and acquire the habit of building a sexualized fantasy world in which they dominate others, and that these fantasy activities provide imaginary rehearsals for the murders to come. Deviant sexual fantasies are thus thought to play a decisive role in the aetiology of sexual murder, and, especially, in its repetition (Brittain, 1970; Ressler et al., 1988; Revitch & Schlesinger, 1981). If this is indeed the case, serial sexual killers should be more likely than nonserial sexual murders to nourish deviant sexual fantasies. This hypothesis can be tested by comparing the data from our sample with those of Prentky at al. (1989). Fantasies of murder or sexual assault were reported by:

- 86% of Prentky et al.'s sample of 25 serial sexual murders
- 23% of Prentky et al.'s sample of 17 nonserial sexual murders
- 36% of the Quebec sample of 41 nonserial sexual murderers.

Thus, serial sexual murderers were the only group in which at least half the subjects had fantasies of murder or sexual assault. In particular, such fantasies were reported by only one third of Quebec nonserial sexual murderers, and one quarter of the subjects in Prentky et al.'s study. These results suggest that deviant sexual fantasies are extremely important determinants of serial sexual murder and are much less important in the aetiology of nonserial sexual murder. This conclusion is consistent with Ressler's (1993) observation:

> They [serial killers] are obsessed by their fantasy, and their unsuccessful attempt to act out their fantasies, drives them to repeat their crime until it perfectly matches their fantasy. This is the true meaning of the term serial killer (p. 41).

Relationship to the victim and premeditation

Serial sexual killers and nonserial sexual murderers differ in two other respects. The first concerns the presence or absence of a relationship between murderer and victim. In more than 80% of all murders of all types, the murderer knows his victim beforehand, as these latter are either a colleague, friend, neighbour or family member (Cusson, Beaulieu & Cusson, 2003). Sexual murders, particularly those committed by serial murderers, are different. In fact, 81% of Ressler's serial killers did not know their victim beforehand. Among our sample of nonserial sexual murderers, the figure was only 40%. These results are not unrelated to the second difference, namely premeditation. In 36% of the sexual murders in the Quebec sample, the crime was clearly premeditated, compared to 50% in Ressler's sample. Thus, serial sexual murderers nurture fantasies of sexual assault and murder; they premeditate their crimes and usually attack strangers. On the other hand, such a pattern could only be observed in approximately one third of sexual murders with only one victim.

Taken in their entirety, our results exhibit considerable consistency. Serial sexual murders have characteristics that distinguish them from nonserial sexual murderers. Specifically, Ressler et al.'s American serial sexual murderers were clearly different from the nonserial sexual murderers in the Quebec study. They more frequently suffered from social isolation, migraines and sleep disorders, and were more likely to take refuge in violent fantasy worlds, masturbate compulsively, premeditate their crimes and attack strangers. This portrait is not valid for nonserial sexual murderers. In addition, it would be an error to equate sexual and serial murderers, especially since serial murderers, in the strictest sense of the term, are much more likely to be hit men than sexual murderers.

The fact that 86% of the serial sexual murderers in Ressler et al.'s sample nurtured fantasies of murder or sexual assault, compared to 36% in the Quebec sample, seems to conclusively suggest that there are many more sadists among serial sexual murderers than among nonserial ones. The repetition of their crimes is yet another element supporting this conclusion. In fact, everything we know about sadists suggests that they are prone to repeatedly commit the same type of sexual assault. This question of sexual sadism will be discussed in Chapter 7.

Chapter 7
SADISTIC SEXUAL OFFENDERS

Jean Proulx, Etienne Blais and Éric Beauregard

The origin of the term sadism is found in the literary works of the French writer the Marquis de Sade (1740–1814), which describe scenes of torture, cruelty and murder that are committed in order to derive sexual pleasure. It was after the publication of Krafft-Ebing's *Psychopathia Sexualis* (1886) that the term sadism was recognized as a diagnostic category. Krafft-Ebing defined sadism as 'the experience of sexual, pleasurable sensations (including orgasm) produced by acts of cruelty...It may also consist of an innate desire to humiliate, hurt, wound or even destroy others thereby to create sexual pleasure in one's self' (p. 53).

The definition of sadism in the *Diagnostic and Statistical Manual of Mental Disorders* (DSM-IV, American Psychiatric Association, 1994) largely coincides with that offered by Krafft-Ebing over a century ago. The DSM-IV definition includes the following criteria:

> Over a period of at least 6 months, recurrent, intense sexually arousing fantasies, sexual urges, or behaviors involving acts (real, not simulated) in which the psychological or physical suffering (including humiliation) of the victim is sexually exciting to the person (p. 530).

This definition of sexual sadism indicates that the origins of sexual pleasure and sexual arousal are found in fantasies or acts in which physical or psychological torture causes the victim to suffer. However, for several authors, the essence of sadism is not the victim's suffering, but

Sexual Murderers: A Comparative Analysis and New Perspectives   Edited by Jean Proulx Éric Beauregard, Maurice Cusson and Alexandre Nicole

rather the absolute power exerted over them (Dietz et al. 1990; Gratzer & Bradford, 1995; Johnson & Becker, 1997; MacCulloch et al., 1983).

Even if the debate about the essence of sadism is not over, there is nonetheless a certain consensus about this paraphilia's manifestations. After reviewing studies on sadism, Marshall and Kennedy (2003) identified elements frequently associated with this sexual disorder. First, they noted the following characteristics of the crime scene: the use of a weapon, kidnapping, unlawful confinement, torture, humiliation, mutilation of the victim, anal sex, penetration with an object, bizarre sexual acts, murder and postmortem mutilation. Second, fantasies reported by sadists revolved around themes of control, sexual violence and sadism. Finally, during phallometric assessment, sadists manifested a sexual preference for scenarios which involved sexual violence.

In order to clarify the scope of the manifestations of sadism, Hazelwood, Dietz and Warren (1992) stressed that the victim has to be conscious, must be able to suffer or be enslaved. Moreover, they mentioned that postmortem mutilations are not necessarily manifestations of sexual sadism. In fact, these mutilations can have a purely instrumental purpose, such as eliminating elements that might allow the identification of the victim.

AETIOLOGICAL AND DEVELOPMENTAL FACTORS OF SADISM

Krafft-Ebing (1886) believed that sexual sadism constitutes an atavistic expression engraved in our genes. Contemporary authors such as Chessick (1997) have defended a similar position: that 'all humans are born with a primal biological archaic aggressive-destructive drive, the gratification of which gives satisfaction just like the sexual drive' (p. 612). However, the predominant point of view in recent studies stipulates that this innate capacity to destroy others only expresses itself if specific developmental factors favour its emergence (Marmor & Gorney, 1999).

As for the biological causes of sexual sadism, the study of neurologically impaired patients seems to be a promising avenue of research. In fact, physiopathologies of the right frontal lobe are frequent in sadistic sexual offenders (Hucker, 1999; Hucker et al., 1988; Langevin et al., 1985; Money, 1990). However, it has not been confirmed that brain damage causes sexual sadism. The role of such damage, whether genetic or traumatic, requires further investigation.

In addition to the biological causes of sexual sadism, developmental factors appear to contribute to the emergence of this paraphilia in sexual offenders. Based on his clinical experience, Brittain (1970) concluded that the early childhood of sexual sadists was characterized by overprotective and controlling behaviours on the part of the mother, and acts of violence by an authoritarian father. In response to these inadequate parental relationships, sexual sadists develop an insecure attachment style which expresses itself through attitudes of withdrawal. These conclusions, however, were based on Brittain's clinical observations rather than systematically collected evidence.

The results of a study by MacCulloch et al. (1983) indicate that all 13 sadistic sexual offenders studied said they had experienced difficulties in their interpersonal relationships and sociosexual interactions during adolescence. MacCulloch et al. considered these relational failures to be responsible for the development of low self-esteem and the aggravation of social isolation among sexual sadists. In such conditions, sadistic sexual fantasies and paraphilic behaviours (voyeurism, exhibitionism, fetishism) establish themselves as a surrogate source of emotional and sexual gratification in these offenders. For a majority of MacCulloch et al.'s subjects (79%), deviant sexual fantasies became increasingly violent, presumably as a result of habituation. Finally, certain sadists (54%) conducted behavioural try-outs of their fantasies in order to further enhance them. For example, one sadistic sexual offender in the making broke into a woman's apartment and watched her while she slept.

PORTRAIT OF AN ADULT SADISTIC SEXUAL OFFENDER'S DAILY LIFE

Brittain's (1970) profile of sadistic sexual offenders indicates that their adult life is an extension of their childhood. He described them as shy, anxious, introverted and socially isolated, and of superior intelligence. They are also studious, punctual, meticulous, prudish and teetotallers. They have little sexual experience and have difficulty achieving an erection with a partner. It is, therefore, not surprising that they consider themselves sexually inferior to other men. The only aspect of their lives in which they are triumphant is their secret worlds, which are dominated by sadistic sexual fantasies, paraphilic behaviours, the torture of animals, and ultimately, the commission of sexual assaults and sexual murder. Furthermore, their secret worlds reflect their interest in books or films with themes of enslavement and the suffering of others (e.g. Nazism, witchcraft, sadomasochistic pornography). Sadists are well mannered, which sometimes leads them to be seen as effeminate and pedantic. Moreover, they never openly express their anger. Finally, they rarely have previous convictions; the few that were seen were for sexual nuisance offences (e.g. exhibitionism, voyeurism, obscene phone calls).

While some aspects of Brittain's clinical portrait of the sadistic sexual offender were confirmed by empirical studies conducted by Dietz and his colleagues (Dietz et al., 1986; Dietz et al., 1990; Hazelwood & Douglas, 1980; Warren, Hazelwood & Dietz, 1996), others have not. These studies were based on a sample of 34 sexual sadists in which sexual murderers were over-represented (20/34). In the two most recent studies, diagnostic criteria from the DSM-III-R (American Psychiatric Association, 1987) were used to identify sexually sadistic subjects. These subjects differentiated themselves from Brittain's prototypical sadist by their abuse of alcohol and drugs (50%) and their criminal records (35%). These additional attributes are congruent with the severity of their sexual deviance (i.e., serial sexual murder).

The majority of subjects (80%) studied by Dietz and his colleagues reported having sadistic sexual fantasies, whereas other paraphilias were infrequent (between 20% and 45%); these results differ from Brittain's sadistic prototype. Among the other characteristics of sadistic sexual offenders observed by Dietz and his collaborators was an interest in police activities (30%), as well as aimless car rides (40%). Dietz and his colleagues also found that some of their subjects had a reputation for being good citizens, as a result of their volunteer work and their involvement in charity events (30%). Finally, a majority of subjects were employed (75%) and married at the time of their offence (50%).

PHALLOMETRIC PROFILE

Some phallometric studies of sadists have indicated that they have a preference for sexually coercive activities (Barbaree et al., 1994; Fedora et al., 1992; Proulx, 2001). For example, in Proulx's (2001) study, sadistic sexual aggressors of women – identified using the MTC-R-3 sadism scale (Knight & Prentky, 1990) – exhibited a higher mean physical-rape index (arousal to physically abusive rape divided by arousal to consensual sex) than did nonsadistic sexual aggressors (1.6 vs. 0.7). For the humiliation rape index (i.e. arousal to a humiliation rape divided by arousal to consensual sex), the mean was 1.6 for sadists and 0.6 for nonsadists. However, results of a study by Marshall, Kennedy and Yates (2002) indicated that nonsadists had a more pronounced sexual preference for rape than did sadists. Finally, offenders identified as sadists and nonsadists did not exhibit any significant differences in the studies conducted by Seto and Kuban (1996) and by Langevin et al. (1985). These divergent results may be due to discrepancies in the definitions of sexual sadism or may result from differences in the samples used.

PSYCHOPATHOLOGICAL PROFILES

Some authors have concluded that sexual sadists are psychopathic and narcissistic (Dietz, 1986; Dietz et al., 1990; Smith & Braun, 1977). However, these authors did not collect data to support their hypotheses concerning the personality disorders they attributed to sadistic sexual offenders. It appears that personality disorders were assessed based on the characteristics of the offences and not on the basis of any careful evaluation of the sexual sadists.

The results of a study by Holt, Meloy and Strack (1999) contradict the conclusions of Dietz et al. These authors observed no significant association between psychopathy, evaluated using the PCL-R (Hare, 1991), and sexual sadism, established using the diagnostic criteria of the DSM-IV. This was the case for both sexual aggressors ($N = 19$) and nonsexual offenders ($N = 22$).

The different opinions about the personality disorders of sadistic sexual offenders presented above can be interpreted in several ways. First, Dietz et al.'s (1990) opinion is unfounded, since they did not evaluate the personality disorders of their subjects. Secondly, it may be that in their everyday interpersonal relationships, sexual sadists present a functioning mode characterized by avoidant (introversion, low self-esteem) and schizoid (solitary) personality features, but adopt a psychopathic functioning mode (lack of empathy) in their sexual fantasies and sexual offences. Finally, it is possible that two types of sadistic sexual offenders exist, one with avoidant and schizoid personality disorders, the other with psychopathic traits (Knight, 2002, personal communication). In fact, Siomopoulos and Goldsmith (1976) suggest the existence of five types of sadists. Due to the lack of studies on the subject, it is not possible to decide in favour of one hypothesis. Nevertheless, Millon and Davis's (1996) studies on personality disorders help us weigh the respective value of these hypotheses.

In their theoretical model of psychological functioning, Millon and Davis (1996) stipulate that individuals with an avoidant personality disorder have several features in common with those presenting an antisocial-sadistic disorder. Both types are said to have suffered at the hands of violent parents and to have been exposed to models of violence during childhood. While adult antisocial-sadists and individuals with avoidant personalities exhibit the same mistrust and hostility, their coping strategies differ:

> At first glance, one might be inclined to note that the polarity focus [in antisocial-sadists] is essentially the same as seen in the avoidant personality, where both pain and active polarities are preeminent as well. However, the avoidant actively anticipates and escapes from abuse, whereas the [antisocial] sadist actively assaults and degrades others (Millon & Davis, 1996, p. 482).

Extrapolating from Millon and Davis's account, it might be expected that both avoidant and antisocial-sadistic sexual aggressors of women have the same propensity for violence. According to this view, the avoidant aggressor, however, will only express this propensity in his sexual fantasies and offences, whereas the antisocial aggressor expresses it daily in his interpersonal relationships, including his sexual activities. Consequently, Millon and Davis's model (1996) is compatible with both a psychopathic mode of functioning, as well as an avoidant personality disorder, in sadistic sexual aggressors. Choosing a victim he sees as weak (i.e. a woman) suits the avoidant because of his lack of self-confidence. The antisocial-sadist, however, adopts a predatory mode with everyone he meets, whom he considers inferior to him (Feister & Gay, 1991; Spitzer et al., 1991).

PRE-CRIME AND CRIME PHASES

Over the course of the pre-crime phase, the sadistic sexual offender is overcome by sadistic sexual fantasies (MacCulloch et al., 1983; Ressler et al., 1988), which results in a state of intense sexual arousal (Brittain, 1970; Podolsky, 1965). According to Brittain, deviant sexual fantasies become overwhelming due to a decline in sadists' self-esteem. MacCulloch et al. believe that sadistic sexual fantasies are stable in the sadist and are not precipitated by external events.

As for the modus operandi of sadistic sexual offenders in the crime phase, the most complete study on this issue was conducted by Dietz et al. (1990). It included 30 sadistic offenders, 17 of whom were serial murderers. The victims were of both sexes and of all ages. In most of the cases, the offences were planned (93.3%), and the victim was usually previously unknown to the offender (83%). The victim was tortured (100%), and tied up and gagged (87%). Sexual acts were diverse and included sodomy (73%), fellatio (71%) and vaginal intercourse (57%). If the victim was killed, it was often by asphyxia (58%). In cases where the victim was stabbed (10%), the blows were multiple and more abundant than those necessary to kill the victim (overkill). Finally, in addition to recording the crime (53.3%), some sadists kept souvenirs (40%). These could be the victim's belongings (e.g. jewellery, clothes) (Hazelwood et al., 1992) or even body parts (Hazelwood & Douglas, 1980).

COMPARISON OF SADISTIC AND NONSADISTIC SEXUAL OFFENDERS

Langevin et al. (1985)

Langevin et al. (1985) examined the sexological, psychological and developmental characteristics of 20 sexual aggressors of women (9 sadists and 11 nonsadists), and compared them to 20 nonsexual and nonviolent offenders. The criteria used to consider a sexual offender sadistic were the admission of sadistic sexual fantasies ($N = 7$) or the commission of an offence that included presumed elements of sadism ($N = 2$).

The three groups did not differ in their phallometric responses (i.e. rape index) or in their scores on the Derogatis Sexual Functioning Inventory. However, sadists tended to have less sexual experience, knowledge and drive than did nonsadists. Scores on the Clarke Sex History scales confirmed that fewer sadists (75%) had nondeviant heterosexual experiences than did nonsadists (82%). However, only sadists threatened and intentionally frightened their victims (25%). Sadists perceived themselves as sexually inadequate (63%), and reported low sexual desire (38%), as well as a fear of being homosexual (38%). Finally, sadists found it difficult to speak to a woman (75%) and felt anger towards women (38%).

With regard to psychological characteristics, sadists differed from non-sadists in some aspects. Many presented brain pathologies, namely impairments to the right frontal lobe (56%) and nonspecific neurological impairments (33%) (see also Langevin et al., 1988). Sadists rarely consumed drugs, but did consume alcohol (75%), although rarely prior to their offences (25%). Finally, none of the sadistic sexual aggressors showed a psychopathic profile (4–9) on the MMPI.

On a developmental level, Langevin et al. (1985) found that sadists suffered punishment for temper tantrums and enuresis more often than the subjects in the two other groups. They were also more likely to collect weapons. However, they were, in daily life, less violent towards others than the subjects in the other two groups.

Gratzer and Bradford (1995)

Gratzer and Bradford (1995), using DSM-III-R (American Psychiatric Association, 1987) criteria, conducted a study of the developmental, social and criminological characteristics of sexual offenders. Their study included 28 sadists (20 sexual murderers and 8 sexual aggressors) and 29 nonsadists (14 sexual murderers and 15 sexual aggressors). Although this study included 34 sexual murderers, only four were serial murderers (3 sadists and 1 nonsadist). The sadists were more likely than nonsadists to have been physically abused during childhood (42.9% vs. 12.9%). Sadists reported indulging in sexually deviant activities (transvestism, voyeurism, exhibitionism) as adults more frequently than did nonsadists.

Gratzer and Bradford (1995) found that the characteristics of sadists' sexual offences differed from those of nonsadists. Sadists usually planned their offences well (82.1%), and performed a variety of coercive acts such as torture (78.6%) and blows resulting in injuries (64.3%). Their offences also included sexual acts that included vaginal intercourse (39.3%), sodomy (21.4%) and fellatio (17.9%). Sexual sadists reported having experienced emotional detachment during the crime (82.1%). In many cases (50%), they suffered from a sexual dysfunction. There was no significant difference in the way sadists and nonsadists killed their victims. Finally, 86% of sadists were diagnosed as having an antisocial personality disorder (DSM-III-R criteria) and 55% had neurological anomalies.

Marshall, Kennedy and Yates (2002)

Marshall, Kennedy and Yates (2002) conducted a study of the psychological and criminological characteristics of incarcerated sexual offenders who had been diagnosed by psychiatrists as either sadistic ($N = 41$) or nonsadistic ($N = 18$), using DSM-III-R or DSM-IV. The proportion of sexual murderers was similar in both groups (sadists: 29.3%; nonsadists: 27.8%). All of the nonsadists' victims, and the majority of the sadists' victims, were women. It is important to recognize that the subjects of this study were not representative of incarcerated sadistic and nonsadistic sexual offenders. In fact, this sample only included subjects for whom a psychiatric assessment was conducted in order to determine the danger they posed.

The proportion of subjects diagnosed with an antisocial personality disorder was similar in the two groups of sexual offenders (sadists: 51.2%; nonsadists: 66.7%). However, more nonsadists were diagnosed with an additional personality disorder (50% vs. 17.1%). At phallometric assessment, more nonsadists exhibited sexual arousal to violent rapes (44.4% vs. 17.1%). Nevertheless, only the sadists reported a high frequency of murderous fantasies (41.5%).

The two groups of sexual offenders differed only slightly in their criminological characteristics. Their criminal records for sexual and nonsexual offences were very similar. Only two characteristics of their current offences differed significantly: torture and blows to the victim. Both of these two coercive acts were more prevalent among nonsadists than among sadists (torture: 38.9% vs. 9.8%; blows to the victim: 61.1% vs. 24.4%). It is also important to note that the sadistic subjects in this study committed less-coercive offences than has been generally reported in studies on sexual sadism.

AIM OF THE STUDY

There have been relatively few empirical studies of sexual sadism, and the existing ones have had some limitations. The studies by both Langevin et al. (1985) and MacCulloch et al. (1983) had limited numbers of subjects. Moreover, the samples used in other studies (Dietz et al., 1990; Warren et al., 1996) were biased, having been composed in large part of serial sexual murderers. Finally, several samples were composed of mixed groups of sexual aggressors (both sexual aggressors of women and sexual aggressors of children) (Dietz et al., 1990; Marshall et al., 2002). The aim of our study was to compare the developmental, psychological, sexological and criminological characteristics of large unbiased samples of sadistic and nonsadistic sexual aggressors of women.

METHODS

Subjects

Two sadism scales of the MTC-R-3 (Knight & Prentky, 1990) were used to classify subjects as sexual sadists or not. The five items from the sadism scale A were: (1) presence of intense and recurring sexual and aggressive fantasies; (2) torture of the victim prior to death; (3) ritualized violence; (4) postmortem intercourse; and (5) postmortem mutilation. The three items from the sadism scale B were: (1) marks of violence on erogenous zones (anus, vagina, breasts); (2) burns inflicted prior to or after the murder; and (3) insertion of objects into body cavities. To be classified a sadist, a subject had to present at least one of the five criteria of scale A or at least two criteria of scale B. In total, 43 subjects were classified as sadists (18 sexual murderers and 25 sexual aggressors of women) and 98 as nonsadists (22 sexual murderers and 76 sexual aggressors of women).

A French version of the MCMI-I (Millon Clinical Multiaxial Inventory; Millon, 1983) was completed by 30 sadists and 70 nonsadists; 13 sadists and 28 nonsadists either refused to complete the questionnaire or were unable to do so because of reading deficits.

Instruments

Phallometric assessments used French translations of the stimuli reported by Abel et al. (1978). Satisfactory discriminant validity of the French translations has been demonstrated in two studies (Earls & Proulx, 1986; Proulx et al., 1994). For each sexual aggressor whose phallometric data were valid, three deviance indexes were calculated: (1) physical violence rape index; (2) humiliation rape index; and (3) nonsexual physical violence index.

RESULTS

The exposure of the two groups to inadequate models in childhood or adolescence did not differ significantly. Nevertheless, a large proportion of both sadists and nonsadists had been exposed to displays of physical (51.2% and 42.3%, respectively) and psychological (51.2% and 47.4%) violence. Psychological victimisation, i.e. humiliation, was more prevalent among sadists than among nonsadists (62.8% vs. 43.3%). Furthermore, both sadistic and nonsadistic offenders were often physically abused (55.8% and 44.3%). Finally, a nonnegligible proportion of sadists and nonsadists were abandoned by their parents (51.2% and 39.2%).

Sadists were found to differ from nonsadists with regard to the following inappropriate behaviours prior to age 18: consumption of pornographic videos (35.7% vs. 14.7%), consumption of pornographic magazines (35.7% vs. 18.1%), visiting strip clubs (31.0% vs. 10.5%), compulsive masturbation (25.0% vs. 11.7%) and deviant sexual fantasies (48.8% vs. 18.6%). Sadists reported lower self-esteem, as well as nightmares more often than did nonsadists (46.3% vs. 28.4% and 25.0% vs. 9.5%, respectively). Subjects from both groups showed high levels of social isolation during childhood (sadists: 45.0%; nonsadists: 33.7%). Finally, during adolescence, sadists were more likely than nonsadists to suffer social isolation (52.5% vs. 34.7%) and frequent temper tantrums (47.5% vs. 25.5%). It is important to note that a large proportion of both sadists and nonsadists had low self-esteem (56.1% and 42.1%).

There was no statistically significant difference between sadists and nonsadists with regard to criminal career parameters. The criminal activity of both groups was diversified and intense, resulting in several convictions. Neither sadists nor nonsadists specialized in sexual crime, which accounted for only about 20% of their criminal activities.

During phallometric assessment, sadists exhibited a higher mean humiliation rape index than did nonsadists (1.7 vs. 0.6). Also, the mean physical violence rape index was higher for sadists (1.7 vs. 0.7). However, the two groups did not differ in terms of their nonsexual physical violence index.

The mean scores and percentages of sadistic and nonsadistic subjects on the MCMI personality scales are shown in Table 7.1. On average, sadistic sexual aggressors of women scored higher than nonsadists on the following scales: avoidant, schizoid and schizotypal. Nonsadists presented a higher average score than did sadists on the histrionic personality scale. Finally, a larger proportion of sadists scored above 84 on the schizoid scale.

We carried out complementary analyses in order to clarify the relationship between the nature of the personality disorders and sexual sadism. Specifically, we were interested in determining whether the types of personality profiles identified through cluster analysis were associated with sexual sadism. The most frequent personality profile among sadistic sexual offenders (58.3%) was a combination of avoidant, schizoid, dependent and

Table 7.1 Mean scores and percentages of sadistic and nonsadistic sexual aggressors of women on the MCMI personality scales

Personality disorders	Score (MCMI)		Percentage score > 84	
	Sadists (N = 30)	Nonsadists (N = 70)	Sadists (N = 30)	Nonsadists (N = 70)
Schizoid	66.0*	54.6	44.0**	14.3
Avoidant	71.0*	58.2	33.3	18.6
Dependent	69.9	70.2	46.7	38.6
Histrionic	45.6*	54.1	0.0	2.9
Narcissistic	55.8	61.9	10.0	11.4
Antisocial	56.9	58.8	6.7	7.1
Obsessive-compulsive	57.0	59.4	3.3	2.9
Passive-aggressive	57.5	48.0	26.7	17.1
Schizotypal	62.0*	56.5	6.7	0.0
Borderline	58.3	58.6	6.7	1.4
Paranoid	62.2	63.8	6.7	5.7

*p < 0.05; ** p < 0.01

passive-aggressive elements, whereas the most frequent personality profile among nonsadistic sexual aggressors (62.0%) was a combination of narcissistic and antisocial elements. The association ($p = 0.08$) between sexual sadism and personality disorder profiles, however, did not reach the standard level of significance ($p < .05$).

Table 7.2 shows the proportion of pre-crime characteristics (48 hours prior to the offence) among sadistic and nonsadistic sexual aggressors of women. As can be seen, generalized conflict with women was observed more often among sadists than among nonsadists, as was anger. Deviant sexual fantasies were also more common among sadists than in nonsadists. Even though there was no significant difference between the two groups, alcohol and drugs were frequently consumed in the hours leading up to the sexual offence.

Table 7.3 shows the proportion of offence characteristics in sadistic and nonsadistic sexual aggressors of women. The level of organization of the crime was higher for sadists than for nonsadists. Sadists planned their crimes more often than did nonsadists. Moreover, a higher proportion of sadists selected their victim on the basis of specific criteria. The level of coercion during the offence was higher for sadists than for nonsadists, due

Table 7.2 Characteristics of the pre-crime phase of sadistic and nonsadistic sexual aggressors of women during the 48 hours prior to the offence

Characteristics	Percentage of sadists (N = 43)	Percentage of nonsadists (N = 98)
Sexual dissatisfaction	12.2	6.3
Perceived rejection	35.0	25.0
Low self-esteem	39.0	32.6
Specific conflicts with:		
Partner	4.8	9.5
Other woman	11.9*	2.1
Victim	7.1	3.1
A man	4.8	3.1
Generalized conflicts with:		
Women	58.5***	21.1
Men	0.0	0.0
The system (police, judge, laws)	31.7	20.0
Emotional state		
Anger	65.8**	39.0
Sexual arousal	13.5*	32.5
Alcohol	64.3	70.1
Drugs	53.7	38.1
Pornography	2.4	2.1
Strip club	20.0	15.4
Deviant sexual fantasies	46.5***	17.3

*$p < 0.05$; ** $p < 0.01$; *** $p < 0.001$

Table 7.3 Offence characteristics of sadistic and nonsadistic sexual aggressors of women

Characteristics	Percentage of sadists (N = 43)	Percentage of nonsadists (N = 98)
Planned offence	86.0**	60.8
Selected victim	52.5**	28.7
Unknown victim	83.8	80.6
Accomplice	14.0	16.3
Coercive contact strategies	15.0	18.5
Kidnapping and unlawful confinement	18.6*	6.1
Victim tied up	23.8*	8.2
Enslavement of the victim (bondage)	16.3***	0.0
Use of a weapon	55.8*	37.8
Expressive violence	90.7***	58.2
Psychological torture (humiliation)	53.7**	26.7
Physical torture (mutilation)	30.2***	1.1
Mutilation of erogenous zones	25.6	1.1
Insertion of objects		
Vagina	9.3*	1.1
Anus	7.0	1.1
Anal intercourse	14.3	6.5
Fellatio	27.9	30.8
Vaginal intercourse	67.4	62.8
Insertion of fingers		
Vagina	26.2	22.0
Anus	7.1	5.4
Cunnilingus	9.3	12.1
Recording of the offence	4.7	1.0
Sexual murder	37.2	22.4
Serial sexual murder	0.0	0.0

$^*p < 0.05$; $^{**}p < 0.01$; $^{***}p < 0.001$

to the higher prevalence of the following elements: kidnapping and unlawful confinement; tying up the victim; enslavement of the victim (bondage); expressive violence; use of a weapon; psychological torture (humiliation); physical torture (mutilation); mutilation of erogenous zones; and insertion of objects into vagina. Although the difference was not statistically significant, the percentage of sexual murderers was higher among sadists than among nonsadists. Finally, the diversity of sexual acts (intercourse, fellatio, cunnilingus, sodomy) was considerable for both sadists and nonsadists.

Table 7.4 shows the crime scene characteristics for 18 sadistic and 22 nonsadistic sexual murderers. Asphyxia by strangulation was the most

Table 7.4 Crime scene characteristics of sadistic and nonsadistic sexual murderers

Characteristics	Percentage of sadists (N = 18)	Percentage of nonsadists (N = 22)
Cause of death		
Blows to the head	12.5	22.7
Asphyxia		
Strangulation	50.0*	27.3
Suffocation	12.5	9.1
Bullet wound	0.0	0.0
Knife wound	25.0	22.7
Drowning	0.0	9.1
Other	0.0	9.1
Body hidden	33.3	36.3
Body completely naked	88.2***	11.8
Postmortem intercourse	31.3**	0.0
Postmortem mutilation	44.4***	0.0
Dismemberment of the body	5.6	4.5
Object in body cavity	16.7	0.0
Writings or drawings at the crime scene	5.6	0.0
Symbolic artefact (e.g. crucifix, dead animals)	5.6	0.0

$p < 0.05$; ** $p < 0.01$; *** $p < 0.001$

frequent cause of death among victims of sadists, and was far less prevalent among the victims of nonsadists. Nonsadists did not appear to have a preferred method of killing their victims. The victims of the sadists were found completely naked more often than were those of the nonsadists. Moreover, only the sadists engaged in postmortem intercourse and mutilation. Finally, we should note that a third of all sexual murderers hid the body of their victims.

DISCUSSION

Our study was based on a sample of 141 extrafamilial sexual aggressors of women. The sample included 94% of the sexual aggressors assessed at Correctional Service Canada's Regional Reception Centre between 1995 and 2000. The sample also included 71% of the sexual murderers of women serving a sentence in Quebec in 1999. The sample of sexual murderers did not include offenders whose victims were male or juvenile. Consequently, the portrait of the sexual sadist that emerges from these results is probably clearer than portraits from previous studies.

Our results indicate that sadistic sexual offenders grew up in inadequate environments. They were exposed to physical and psychological violence, as well as alcohol abuse during childhood and adolescence. A large proportion were also victims of physical and sexual violence. These results are similar to those obtained in previous studies (Gratzer & Bradford, 1995; Langevin et al., 1985) and are compatible with the clinical portrait of the sexual sadist presented by Brittain (1970). Sadists were more likely than nonsadists to have suffered psychological violence (e.g. humiliation) during their childhood and adolescence years. This form of victimization is compatible with the development of an avoidant personality disorder, which is characterized by a fear of being humiliated, criticized or rejected by others.

The sadistic sexual offenders in our sample distinguished themselves from the nonsadistic ones by their low self-esteem and pronounced social isolation during childhood and adolescence. These results agree with those of MacCulloch et al. (1983), as well as Brittain's (1970) description of the sexual sadist. It should be noted that these characteristics of the sexual sadist constitute crucial clinical manifestations of an avoidant personality disorder. However, the sexual sadist's temper tantrums in adolescence do not fit this personality disorder. A typological approach to sexual sadism may shed light on the reasons for this inconsistency. The first type of sadist, socially isolated and devalued, presents an avoidant personality disorder, whereas the second type of sadist, short-tempered and violent with his next of kin, presents an antisocial personality disorder.

Sadists' adolescence is dominated by sexual activities that set them apart from nonsadists. They consume pornography and turn to violent sexual fantasies during their masturbatory activities. This overwhelming sexuality in the everyday lives of sexual sadists was also observed by MacCulloch et al. (1983), who believed that, after the failure of a relationship, sexual sadists resorted to sexuality as a surrogate for emotional gratification.

The results of the phallometric assessments indicate that the sadistic aggressors had a sexual preference for rape (humiliation, physical violence). These sexual preferences reflected their pervasive sadistic sexual fantasies (reported by 35/43 subjects). These results coincide with those of other phallometric studies (Barbaree et al., 1994; Fedora et al., 1992; Proulx, 2001). Thus, the violence exhibited by sadists during their sexual crimes appears to be an extension of their sadistic sexual fantasies and their preference for coercive sexual activities. Unfortunately, these results do not appear to be universal, since others have reported that sadists do not have deviant sexual preferences (Langevin et al., 1985; Marshall et al., 2002; Seto & Kuban, 1996). It is possible that this discrepancy reflects differences in sample construction, and the validity of some of the stimulus sets used to evaluate sexual preferences may be debatable. Nevertheless, the most plausible explanation is a problem in the diagnosis of sexual sadism. For example, Seto and Kuban (1996) identified subjects as sadistic if, during the commission of their offences, they used expressive violence and physically injured their victim. None of the sexual aggressors in their study admitted having recurrent sadistic sexual fantasies. Thus, it is probable that their sample of sadists was composed of several types of sexual offenders – not only sadists, but also the angry type of sexual aggressors (Proulx, Perreault & Ouimet, 1999). In fact, while both types of sexual aggressors use expressive violence and injure their victims, the angry type does not exhibit a sexual preference for rape.

In our study, sadists and nonsadists exhibited different psychopathological profiles. The sadists were characterized by avoidant and schizoid personality disorders. Individuals with this personality profile have low self-esteem and isolate themselves in order to avoid being criticized and rejected. Their inner world is dominated by humiliation, suffering, anxiety and anger. This personality profile is compatible with the portrait of a sexual sadist who is dominated by low self-esteem, and social isolation, and who withdraws into a world of sadistic fantasies. The likely function of both the fantasies and the sadistic sexual offences is to compensate for the suffering, humiliation and anger that is felt but left unexpressed by the sexual sadist in his everyday life. Thus, the physical and psychological (humiliation) suffering of the victim seems to provide the sexual sadist with catharsis, temporarily releasing him from his own internal distress. However, due to the inflexible and inappropriate nature of his coping strategies, the sexual sadist remains devoted to sexual violence.

During the pre-crime phase, sadistic sexual offenders in our study displayed anger and generalized conflict with women, and had coercive sexual fantasies. Results from other studies also highlighted the presence of such fantasies in the hours leading up to the crime (MacCulloch et al., 1983; Ressler et al., 1988). The explanation for the activation of sadistic fantasies may lie in the personality profile of this type of sexual offender. Due to his avoidant and schizoid personality, the sadist feels inferior to others and believes that people he meets, especially women, reject and humiliate him. These distorted perceptions trigger unexpressed feelings of rage, humiliation and suffering. The sadist thus retreats from relationships, and flees into a world of sexually coercive fantasies. Due to the amount of time he dedicates to his sexual fantasies, these fantasies become elaborate and become an outlet for his unexpressed emotional states (rage, humiliation and suffering) (Proulx, McKibben & Lusignan, 1996; Proulx, Perreault & Ouimet, 1999). However, recourse to coercive sexual fantasies may prove to be an insufficient coping strategy in the face of unusually intense stressful events. Such stresses could take the form of intense conflicts with women, rejection or low self-esteem. Actualizing his fantasies through a sadistic sexual offence constitutes another coping strategy, which the sadist resorts to in order to deal with his internal distress. Moreover, anger and intoxication may be disinhibiting factors, which accentuate the intensity of his deviant sexual arousal, thereby facilitating the commission of the offence.

The actual sexual offence constitutes a continuation of the sexual sadist's coercive sexual fantasies. Consequently, it is not surprising to find that the offence is usually planned down to the smallest detail. The offences of the sadists in this study included elements of physical and psychological violence, which distinguished them from those of nonsadists. However, the sadists in our study humiliated their victims more frequently than they indulged in physical cruelty, whereas the opposite was true in the Gratzer and Bradford study. This divergence is probably due to the higher percentage of sexual murderers in Gratzer and Bradford's study (71.4%) compared to Proulx et al.'s (28.3%). Indeed, a lethal sexual crime necessarily involves high levels of physical violence.

The crime scene elements of sexual murderers in our study were similar to those reported in the Gratzer and Bradford (1995) study, but differ from those reported by Dietz et al. (1990). A larger proportion of Dietz et al.'s subjects hid the bodies of their victims and inserted objects into body cavities. These characteristics indicate a high level of organization and ritualization of the offence, which may be construed as an indicator of the severity of sexual deviance in Dietz et al.'s subjects. This is consistent with the high proportion of serial sexual murderers in their study (56.7%), a proportion that is in fact much higher than that observed in the Gratzer and Bradford study (10.7%) or our study (0%).

Overall, our results are in agreement with those of Gratzer and Bradford (1995), and indicate that sadistic sexual offenders differ from nonsadistic ones on several levels. In both studies, sexual sadists were differentiated from nonsadists on the basis of the diagnostic criteria of the American Psychiatric Association (DSM-III-R, DSM-IV). In spite of the high discriminant validity of some studies that had used the diagnostic criteria of the American Psychiatric Association, Marshall and Yates (2004) expressed reservations about this method of identifying sexual sadism. In addition, Marshall, Kennedy, Yates and Serran's (2002) study showed that internationally renowned forensic psychiatrists, all of whom were known for their work on sexual sadists, could not agree on who was and was not a sadist. Consequently, the validity of studies on sexual sadism is limited by the absence of a consensus on the definition of sexual sadism. In order to better delimit the specificities of sexual sadists, a new sadism scale should be developed, or a firm consensus should be established about the diagnostic criteria to be used.

Chapter 8

ANGRY OR SADISTIC: TWO TYPES OF SEXUAL MURDERERS

Éric Beauregard, Jean Proulx and Michel St-Yves

To our knowledge, seven typological studies of sexual murderers have been conducted; the number of subjects, types of subjects, sources of data, variables and methodology of these studies are presented in Table 8.1. Only the studies by the FBI (Ressler et al., 1988), Clarke and Carter (1999), Kocsis (1999) and Beech, Robertson and Clarke (2001) provide information on the number of subjects. The FBI developed its typology on the basis of 36 subjects, Clarke and Carter 32, Kocsis 85 and Beech et al. 50. Neither Revitch and Schlesinger (1981) nor Meloy (2000) provide information on the number of subjects, and Keppel and Walter (1999) had no subjects. The FBI and Kocsis used heterogeneous samples, i.e. their samples comprised both serial and nonserial sexual murderers, and the victims of the murders were of either sex and all ages. The other studies provided no information on the composition of their samples.

The data used to develop the typologies came from a variety of sources. Revitch and Schlesinger, as well as Meloy, based their typologies on clinical observations. The FBI, Clark and Carter, and Beech et al. relied upon self-reported information and on data from official sources (court and police files). Kocsis used official police data only. The variables used to construct the typologies include the characteristics of the victims, murderers and crime scenes, the modus operandi, the interactions between victims and murderers, and some inferences related to the personality of the murderers.

Sexual Murderers: A Comparative Analysis and New Perspectives Edited by Jean Proulx Éric Beauregard, Maurice Cusson and Alexandre Nicole

Table 8.1 Characteristics of typological studies of sexual murderers

Study	Number of subjects	Type of subjects	Data sources	Variables used	Construction method
Revitch and Schlesinger (1981)	Not specified	Not specified	Clinical observation	Not specified	Clinical judgement
Ressler et al. (1988)	36	Mixed (murderers of women, men, children, serial and non-serial murderers)	Self-reported information; data from official sources	Characteristics of the aggressors; modus operandi; inferences regarding personality	Qualitative judgement
Keppel and Walter (1999)	0	Not applicable	Not applicable	Characteristics of the aggressors; modus operandi; inferences regarding personality	Typology of Groth and Birnbaum (1979), adapted on the basis of the police experience of the principal author
Clarke and Carter (1999)	32	Not specified	Self-reported information; data from official sources	Modus operandi; inferences regarding motivation	Clinical judgement
Kocsis (1999)	85	Mixed (serial and nonserial), sex and age of victims not specified	Official police data	Characteristics of the crime scene, aggressors, victims, and aggressors–victim interactions	Statistical method: multidimensional scaling
Meloy (2000)	Not specified	Not specified	Clinical observations	Modus operandi; variables related to personality (Rorschach test)	Clinical judgement
Beech et al. (2001)	50	Not specified	Self-reported information; data from official sources	Modus operandi; inferences regarding motivation	Statistical method: cluster analysis

Finally, it should be noted that the typologies of Revitch and Schlesinger, Ressler et al., Clarke and Carter, and Meloy were constructed on the basis of clinical judgement, while those of Kocsis and Beech et al. were derived from multivariate analyses.

These typological studies reveal four types of sexual murderers, with each study describing between two and four types. Two types of sexual murderer are consistently reported in the various studies: angry and sadistic. In addition, we also find the sexual murderer who kills to eliminate witnesses. Finally, some studies include a residual category ('other'). A summary of these types of sexual murderers is presented in Table 8.2.

Revitch and Schlesinger (1981) and Meloy (2000) use the term 'catathymic murderer' (displacement of intense matricentric rage towards another woman) to describe the angry murderer, while Ressler et al. (1988) use the term 'disorganized murderer'. Keppel and Walter prefer the term 'anger-retaliatory rape murderer', taken from the typology of Groth and Birnbaum (1979), while Kocsis (1999) uses the term 'fury murderer'. Clarke and Carter (1999) opt for 'aggressive dyscontrol murderer', and Beech et al. (2001) for 'grievance murderer'.

The sadistic sexual murderer is termed a 'compulsive murderer' by Revitch and Schlesinger (1981) and Meloy (2000). The FBI researchers (Ressler, Burgess, Douglas et al., 1986; Ressler et al. 1988) use the term 'organized murderer', while Kocsis (1999) defines two categories of sadistic sexual

Table 8.2 Summary of the types of sexual murderers in the typological studies corresponding to the angry, sadistic and witness-elimination types

Typology	Angry	Sadistic	Witness elimination	Other
Revitch and Schlesinger (1981)	Cathatymic	Compulsive	Not applicable	Not applicable
Ressler et al. (1988)	Disorganized	Organized	Not applicable	Mixed
Keppel and Walter (1999)	Angry-Retaliatory	Angry-Excitation	Not applicable	Power-assertive; power-reassurance
Clarke and Carter (1999)	Anger dyscontrol	Sexually motivated	Aggressive control	Neuropsychological dysfunction
Kocsis (1999)	Fury	Predator/Pervert	Rape	Not applicable
Meloy (2000)	Cathatymic	Compulsive	Not applicable	Not applicable
Beech et al. (2001)	Grievance motivation	Sexually motivated	Motivation to sexually offend	Not applicable

murderer, namely the predator and the pervert. Keppel and Walter (1999) prefer the expression 'anger-excitation rape murderer', while Clarke and Carter (1999) and Beech et al. (2001) speak of sexually motivated murder.

Clarke and Carter (1999), Kocsis (1999) and Beech et al. (2001) identified a type of sexual murderer who kills in order to eliminate witnesses or escape justice, known variously as the 'sexually triggered – aggressive control murderer', 'rape murderer', or 'motivation to sexually offend murderer' type. It should be noted that some typologies include an 'other' category, under which we find 'mixed murderer' (Ressler et al., 1988), 'power-assertive rape murderer', 'power-reassurance rape murderer' (Keppel & Walter, 1999), and 'neuropsychological dysfunction murderer' (Clarke & Carter, 1999).

Despite terminological variations from study to study, sadistic and angry murderers present a number of consistent characteristics. To illustrate this point, we have grouped in Tables 8.3 and 8.4 the primary characteristics of sadistic and angry sexual murderers.

The primary intent of sexual murderers who kill a victim to eliminate any witnesses is sexual assault; the murder is merely instrumental. This type of murderer is often described as less likely to have had long-term emotional relationships, and to exhibit a deviant phallometric profile. His victims are unknown to him and often younger than 30, and his sexual assault is characterized by coitus and some sadistic elements. The murder may or may not be premeditated, and is panicky or cold-blooded, depending on his criminal experience. Usually, the victim's wounds are restricted to a single site on the body, and the victim is found lying on her back. Often, the crime is committed, and the victim's corpse found, at the site at which first contact between the murderer and the victim occurred.

The typological studies of sexual murder conducted to date suffer from several limitations. First, most of the samples comprise a wide spectrum of sexual murderers (serial and nonserial murderers, sexual murderers of women, of men, and of children), completely ignoring the specific characteristics of each group. It should also be noted that some studies have limited themselves to a single source of data (e.g. clinical observations, self-reported information or data from official sources), which precludes the possibility of using multiple sources of data to draw up a complete and detailed profile of the sexual murderer and his crimes. Additionally, while some studies have proposed models in which the murderer's motivation and personality have been inferred, none propose a standardized method that permits adequate assessment of these elements. Furthermore, most of the studies – regardless of whether their approach is rooted in clinical psychology or law enforcement – pay little attention to pre-crime phase variables, such as situational factors that may have precipitated the sexual murder. Finally, several authors have constructed their typology on the basis of clinical judgement, which precludes any verification of the validity of their analyses. In light of these limitations, the primary aim of the study

Table 8.3   Summary of the sadistic sexual murderer

Characteristics of the murderer	Pre-crime phase	Modus operandi	Post-crime phase
• mobility • high intelligence • post-secondary education • preference for work placing him in contact with authority or death • cruelty towards animals • enuresis during childhood • fire setting • tendency to be isolated • antisocial, narcissistic, schizoid, and obsessive-compulsive personality disorders • severe psychopathy • lack of empathy • history of breaking and entering • history of sexual crimes • fascination for objects related to police work • possession of violent pornography and detective magazines • paraphilias: cannibalism, vampirism, necrophilia, fetishism, masochism, transvestism, voyeurism, exhibitionism, obscene telephone calls • sexual sadism • serial sexual crimes	• impressive amounts of unexpressed anger • very elaborate sadistic fantasies • fantasy world more important to him than reality • situational stress • often murders after a blow to his self-esteem • 'hunts' his prey • selection of a specific victim following surveillance • premeditation of crime • consumption of alcohol prior to the crime	• ruse and manipulation to approach the victim • victim unknown to him • isolated crime scene, chosen in advance, far from his residence • vehicle used in commission of crime • presence of instruments of torture or of a rape kit • reflects sadistic fantasies • victim held captive for several hours, with recording of aggression • consumption of alcohol during the crime • submission of victim demanded • victim tied up and gagged • fellatio by victim • anal or vaginal penetration of victim • possible sexual dysfunction • insertion of objects into various body cavities • prolonged and ritualized torture • mutilation of genital organs • non-random pattern of wounds on the victim's body • premortem mutilation • death by strangulation • sexual arousal elicited by violent acts committed on the victim, culminating in the murder • dismembering • retention of souvenirs belonging to the victim or taken from her	• moving of the corpse • hiding of the corpse • crime scene reflects control • absence of weapons or evidence at the crime scene • interest in media coverage of the crime • possible change of job or city after the crime • may volunteer to help during the investigation • relatively normal behaviour between crimes • absence of remorse for his acts • pleasure in describing the horror of his acts • low profile during incarceration

Table 8.4 Summary of the angry sexual murderer

Characteristics of the murderer	Pre-crime phase	Modus operandi	Post-crime phase
• mid-20s • residence and workplace near crime scene • average intelligence • married or in a stable relationship • little work experience • socially incompetent • not socially isolated • difficulties with authority • impulsive • anger • selfish • various nonspecific personality disorders • low to moderate psychopathy • severe mental disorders such as mood disorders • history of violence towards women • history of substance abuse • no consumption of pornography • sexual dysfunctions • absence of sadistic sexual fantasies	• depressive mood • suicidal ideation • feelings of anger • low alcohol consumption prior to the crime • victim selected on the basis of murderer's daily activities • victim selected on the basis of a familiar setting • victim stance • rage displaced towards victim • desire to kill • absence of premeditation	• access to crime scene on foot • victim is known to murderer • victim older than murderer • crime scene outdoors • crime scene known to murderer • use of a weapon found at the crime scene • minimal use of physical restraints • low consumption of alcohol during the crime • anxiety during crime • explosive and violent attack • vengeance is displaced to a specific victim • blows specifically directed towards victim's face • wounds on several areas of the bodies • humiliation and extreme violence • possible sexual assault of the victim • insertion of objects into various body cavities of the victim • absence of sperm at the crime scene • murder provoked by the victim's words or actions • murder by strangulation • postmortem sexual acts and mutilation • overkill	• feelings of relief • corpse of victim left at the crime scene • corpse left in view • body found on its back • crime scene reflects lack of organization • no interest in media coverage of the crime

described in this chapter was to develop a typology of sexual murderers of adult women, based on objective crime-scene criteria and multivariate statistical analyses. A secondary goal was to determine whether any pre-crime factors are specific to either type of sexual murderer.

METHODS

Subjects

The participation rate in this study was 71% (40/57 sexual murderers). It should be noted that the results discussed below are taken from analyses of 36, not 40, sexual murderers, as data for four subjects was not available at the time of statistical analysis. The marked resistance of some sexual murderers to participate in the study can be attributed, at least in part, to the fact that sexual crimes are as poorly tolerated by inmates as by the general population, and for reasons of personal safety sexual murderers therefore wish to avoid calling attention to themselves. The explicit reasons for refusal are, however, of interest as well. In most cases of refusal, inmates attempted to convince us that the murder they were convicted of contained no sexual component per se: they were, they said, guilty of murder – but not of sexual assault. Others simply saw no benefit in participating in this type of research and would not participate unless they were paid, received special privileges or had a favourable report added to their file. Yet others did not want to recount their lives and crimes one more time, as this brought up unpleasant memories. Finally, a few rare cases stated that they were not guilty and had been the object of a judicial error.

Procedure

A semi-structured interview based on the Computerized Sex Offenders Questionnaire was conducted with each participant. The interviews took place in a closed room, and the participant was encouraged to talk freely. In general, the interviews lasted 3–5 hours, although when interviewees wished to talk about subjects not part of the interview protocol they sometimes took more than 5 hours.

We conducted a complete study of each participant's institutional file. The institutional file contained the results of psychological evaluations, psychiatric evaluations and specialized tests (psychometric tests, phallo-metric assessments, etc.), disciplinary reports, information on programmes taken while incarcerated, criminal record, court transcripts and police reports. In cases of discrepancies between self-reported information and information in official documents, the latter were considered authoritative.

As the study of offending processes requires police information, we also consulted each participant's complete police file; in some cases, we also had access to crime scene photographs. These files were provided by the homicide unit of the Montreal Urban Community Police Service (now the City of Montreal Police Service), the major crime unit of the Sûreté du Québec and the homicide unit of the City of Quebec Police Service.

RESULTS

As characteristics present or absent in almost all subjects have no discriminatory power, they were not retained; concretely, only crime-phase variables whose frequency was above 10% or below 90% were retained. This yielded 24 variables. Categorical analyses (χ^2 tests) were performed to determine the relationships between the 24 variables and to identify the key variables for the construction of a typology. Nine variables were found to be related to several others, and these were subjected to a K-means cluster analysis. This analysis yielded two subgroups of sexual murderers, namely sadistic and angry, based on similarities in the nine crime-phase variables retained (Table 8.5).

Sadistic murderers accounted for 44.4% (16/36) of our sample. These murderers premeditated their crime and selected a victim previously unknown to them. During the crime, these murderers humiliated their victims and in many cases physically restrained them and mutilated them. The crime lasted more than 30 minutes, which increases the risk of being caught by police. This type of murderer tends to move or hide the victim's corpse, in order to avoid its detection.

Angry murderers accounted for 55.6% (20/36) of our sample. They did not premeditate their crimes and their victims were circumstantial. They did not usually humiliate, physically restrain or mutilate their victims. In

Table 8.5 Distribution of subjects in the two profiles of offending process: crime phase

	Angry ($N = 20$)	Sadistic ($N = 16$)
** Crime premeditated	5%	81%
n.s. Victim previously known to murderer	30%	6%
** Victim is explicitly selected	0%	79%
** Victim is humiliated	11%	82%
* Victim is mutilated	10%	44%
* Physical constraints during crime	5%	38%
* Crime lasts more than 30 minutes	53%	87%
* Victim's corpse is left at crime scene	84%	44%
** High risk of being caught	35%	80%

* $p < 0.05$;
** $p < 0.01$; n.s.: not significant

Table 8.6 Distribution of subjects in the two profiles of offending process: supplemental crime-phase variables

	Angry (N = 20)	Sadistic (N = 16)	Total (N = 36)	Phi
Searches for specific characteristics in the victim	25.0%	41.7%	31.3%	0.174
Murder occurs in the evening	70.0%	56.3%	63.9%	−0.142
Victim had consumed alcohol or drugs at the time of the murder	38.9%	20.0%	32.1%	−0.194
Kidnapping and confinement of the victim	10.0%	25.0%	16.7%	0.200
Victim resists	80.0%	92.3%	84.8%	0.168
Weapon used	42.1%	53.3%	47.1%	0.112
Victim obliged to commit sexual acts	5.6%	23.1%	12.9%	0.258
Coitus	80.0%	76.9%	78.6%	−0.037
Torture	10.5%	33.3%	20.6%	0.280
Postmortem mutilation	15.8%	33.3%	23.5%	0.205
Dismembering of corpse	0.0%	18.8%	8.8%	0.334*
Victim found on her back	76.9%	33.3%	63.2%	−0.420
Corpse hidden	0.0%	18.8%	8.8%	0.330

* $p < 0.05$

approximately half the cases, the crime lasted less than 30 minutes; a short duration which decreases the risk of being caught by the police. The victim's corpse was often left at the crime scene.

We also compared sadistic and angry murderers in terms of the crime-scene variables not retained for typological analysis (Table 8.6). Some sadistic sexual murderers dismembered their victim's corpse, something that angry murderers never did (18% vs. 0%, phi = 0.334; $p < 0.05$). Other, albeit nonsignificant comparisons, are also noteworthy. Sadistic murderers were more likely than angry murderers to select victims with specific characteristics (41.7% vs. 25%, phi = 0.174), oblige their victims to commit sexual acts (23.1% vs. 5.6%, phi = 0.258), torture their victims (33.3% vs. 10.5%, phi = 0.280) and use a weapon (53.3% vs. 42.1, phi = 0.112). On the other hand, sadistic murderers were less likely to leave their victims on their back (33.3% vs. 76.9%; phi = −0.420) than angry murderers. Finally, both sadistic and angry offenders committed murders that were characterized by coitus (76.9% vs. 80%) and victim resistance (92.3% vs. 80%). Some relatively high phi values were not statistically signficant, due to missing values.

Not surprisingly, anger was more characteristic of the pre-crime phase of angry murderers than of sadistic murderers (83.3% vs. 33.3%; phi = −0.508; $p < 0.01$) (Table 8.7). Sadistic murderers were more likely than angry murderers to present a positive affect in the pre-crime phase (41.7% vs.

Table 8.7 Distribution of subjects in the two profiles of offending process: affect prior to crime, precipitating factors (48 hours prior to crime) and predisposing factors (1 year prior to crime)

	Angry (N = 20)	Sadistic (N = 16)	Total (N = 36)	Phi
Angry affect in pre-crime phase	83.3%	33.3%	63.3%	−0.508**
Positive affect during pre-crime phase	11.1%	41.7%	23.3%	0.354*
48 hours prior to crime				
Loneliness	22.2%	0.0%	12.1%	−0.339*
Separation	0.0%	26.7%	12.1%	0.407*
Marital difficulties	16.7%	0.0%	9.1%	−0.289
Idleness	38.9%	0.0%	21.2%	−0.474**
1 year prior to crime				
Loneliness	27.8%	0.0%	15.2%	−0.386**
Separation	22.2%	26.7%	24.2%	0.052
Marital difficulties	27.8%	13.3%	21.2%	−0.176
Idleness	38.9%	26.7%	33.3%	−0.129

* $p < 0.05$; ** $p < 0.01$

11.1%; phi $= 0.354$, $p < 0.05$). This positive affect may take the form of sexual arousal, calmness or feelings of well being. Angry murderers reported having experienced significantly more problems of loneliness (22.2% vs. 0%; phi $= -0.339$, $p < 0.05$) and idleness (38.9% vs. 0%; phi $= -0.474$, $p < 0.01$) in the 48 hours preceding their crime than did sadistic murderers, as well as more problems of loneliness during the year preceding the murder (27.8% vs. 0%; phi $= -0.386$, $p < 0.05$). On the other hand, sadistic murderers more often reported breaking up with partners during the 48 hours preceding their crimes (26.7% vs. 0%; phi $= 0.407$, $p < 0.05$).

The two types of sexual murderers exhibited no statistically significant differences with regard to disinhibitory factors. However, more sadistic murderers than angry murderers reported having had deviant sexual fantasies in the 48 hours prior to their crime (50% vs. 21.1%; phi $= 0.303$). Furthermore, almost all (82.4%) the sexual murderers reported having consumed alcohol, and slightly more than half (51.5%) reported having consumed drugs, in the hours preceding their crimes.

The attitudes of the two types of sexual murderers towards their crimes are summarized in Table 8.8. Angry sexual murderers turned themselves in more frequently than did sadistic murderers (85.7% vs. 25%; phi $= -0.607$, $p < 0.05$). During intake interviews in prison, all the angry murderers (100%) admitted to all the acts they had committed against the victims, compared to 81.3% of the sadistic murderers (phi $= -0.337$, $p < 0.05$). In

Table 8.8 Distribution of subjects in the two profiles of offending process: crime-related attitudes

	Angry (N = 20)	Sadistic (N = 16)	Total (N = 36)	Phi
Turns himself in after committing murder	85.7%	25.0%	53.3%	−0.607*
Admits the crime when arrested	61.1%	33.3%	48.5%	−0.277
During the entry interview in penitentiary, admits to all the acts committed	100.0%	81.3%	91.7%	−0.337*
Admits the negative consequences of his acts on the victim	95.0%	75.0%	86.1%	−0.287
Admits his responsibility in the murder	100.0%	73.3%	88.6%	−0.415*
Admits having a problem of a sexual nature	27.8%	50.0%	38.2%	0.228
Admits having other personal problems	61.1%	86.7%	72.7%	0.286

* $p < 0.05$

addition, all the angry murderers (100%) accepted responsibility for their acts, compared to 73.3% of sadistic murderers (phi = −0.415, $p < 0.05$). Despite the absence of a statistically significant relation, we note that angry murders admitted their crime upon being arrested more often than did sadistic murderers (61.1% vs. 33.3%; phi = 0.277).

DISCUSSION

The crime phase

Our analysis of the modus operandi and crime scenes allowed us to identify two types of nonserial sexual murderers of women: sadistic and angry. Interestingly, the FBI also identified two types of sexual murderers in their analysis of the modus operandi and crime scene of serial sexual murderers (Ressler et al., 1988). Because the FBI study shared many features with our own (self-reported data and data from official sources such as police reports and court transcripts, objectively defined variables), it is instructive to contrast its results with ours, despite the differences with regard to the number of victims.

The modus operandi of the FBI's 'organized' sexual murderer is similar to this study's sadistic sexual murderer. The crime is premeditated, involves a previously unknown victim, physical restraint and mutilation of the victim prior to the murder, and the moving or hiding of the victim's corpse at a site away from the crime scene (Ressler, Burgess, Douglas et al., 1986; Ressler et al. 1988). The modus operandi scenario of the FBI's 'disorganized' sexual murderer is similar to that of the angry sexual murderer in our study: there is no premeditàtion, no physical constraints and the corpse is left at the crime scene.

The profiles of the sexual murderers in our study do, however, diverge from the FBI profiles in three ways. Firstly, acts of mutilation were characteristic of the sadistic murderers in our sample, but not of the organized sexual murderers in the FBI sample. Secondly, our results indicate that it is sadistic murderers who run the highest risk of being caught, while the FBI results indicate that it is disorganized murderers, equivalent to the angry murderers in our study, who are most likely to be arrested (primarily because of the numerous leads left at the crime scene). Finally, the FBI's disorganized murderer positions the victim's corpse in a way designed to shock those who find it; this often entails placing it in a sexually explicit position. This practice was not seen with the angry murderers in our sample, who usually simply left the victim on her back at the crime scene. Unfortunately, we have no explanation for these differences.

The two types of sexual murderers in our study can also be distinguished in terms of their modus operandi. Sadistic murderers were more likely than angry murderers to seek out victims with specific characteristics, torture victims, and mutilate, even dismember, the corpses of their victims. We believe that these differences are related both to premeditation and to deviant sexual fantasies, which are more prevalent among sadistic murderers. These two elements favour the execution of certain acts (e.g. torture) that instantiate the imagined crime scenario.

The pre-crime phase

Our results indicate that angry sexual murderers possess an angry affect in the pre-crime phase, while sadistic murderers possess positive affects that may include happiness, pleasure, feelings of well-being and sexual arousal. These positive affects may be the thrill of the hunt and may be associated with deviant sexual fantasies.

The FBI study is the only study in the literature to mention pre-crime-phase elements. Ressler, Burgess, Douglas et al. (1986) evaluated the emotional state of sexual murderers in their sample on a scale of 1 to 5. Their results indicate that organized murderers were more depressed, more calm, less nervous, less frightened and less confused than were disorganized murderers.

The pre-crime phase emotional state of sexual murderers in our sample differed from that of the murderers in the FBI study. There are two possible explanations for this difference. Firstly, there may be methodological differences in the way emotional state was studied, e.g. the FBI researchers may not have investigated positive affects. Secondly, the observed differences in affect may simply reflect the more pathological nature of the serial murderers in the FBI sample, as well as differences in motivation.

In the 48 hours and the year preceding the murder, angry murderers experienced more problems of loneliness than did sadistic murderers (who in fact reported no such problems). We suggest that the differences in the relational problems of the two types of sexual murderers reflect differences in personality disorders. In Beauregard and Proulx's (2002) study, angry murderers exhibited a borderline personality disorder, which is indicative of a simultaneous desire for contact with other people and an inability to obtain and maintain intimacy (Beck & Freeman, 1990). On the other hand, sadistic murderers exhibited schizoid and avoidant personality disorders (as assessed by the MCMI), suggesting that they have renounced contact with other people in favour of fantasy worlds. This being so, it is understandable that no sadistic murderer reported experiencing problems of loneliness prior to committing his murder.

Nevertheless, sadistic murderers reported having experienced significantly more problems related to separation from their intimate partners in the 48 hours preceding their crime than did angry murderers. It is possible that sadistic murderers become increasingly invested in their deviant fantasies in the days preceding their crime, which may accelerate the separation of a couple. But it is also possible that sadistic murderers are more competent in their interpersonal relationships than are angry murderers, and are therefore simply more successful at finding and keeping partners.

Our results also indicate that it is possible to distinguish between the two types of sexual murderers on the basis of their occupational problems. In fact, in the 48 hours preceding their crimes, 38.9% of angry murderers, but none of the sadistic murderers, experienced problems of idleness. These problems favoured the consumption of alcohol and drugs. We believe that this constellation of behaviours is primarily attributable to differences in the personality disorders of the two types of murderers, sadistic murderers typically exhibiting schizoid and avoidant personality disorders, and angry murderers typically exhibiting borderline personality disorder. Angry murderers' abuse of psychoactive substances in the 48 hours preceding the crime is also due to unstable and disorganized lifestyles related to their personality disorders. Sadistic murderers, on the other hand, spend the hours preceding their crime consuming pornographic material, indulging in deviant sexual fantasies and planning their crimes.

The studies by Ressler et al. (1986, 1988) and others appear to have neglected the pre-crime phase. This is somewhat surprising, as this phase is crucial to an understanding of the motivations of the murder. One of the most noteworthy types of pre-crime phase factors are disinhibitory factors. The majority of sexual murderers in our sample reported consuming alcohol in the hours preceding their crime. We believe that this high frequency is not surprising for this type of crime. In fact, others have reported that sexual aggressors often blamed alcohol consumption for their acts (Amir, 1971; Bartol, 1999; Groth & Birnbaum, 1979). However, Groth and Birnbaum (1979) noted that prior to their crime, sexual aggressors of adult women rarely consumed more than their usual amount of alcohol. Despite the fact that sexual offenders may exaggerate their statements, we suspect that alcohol has an effect on the commission of sexual murder. Groth and Birnbaum have suggested that alcohol only acts as a disinhibitor in individuals predisposed to sexual assault. We hypothesize that alcohol may also favour the emergence of deviant sexual fantasies, by removing sexual murderers' inhibitions. Langevin et al. (1988), noting that the rate of alcohol abuse among sexual aggressors and sexual murderers greatly exceeds the rate of abuse in the general population, suggest that alcohol contributes to criminal behaviour by disinhibiting anger and sexual arousal.

Furthermore, while organized and disorganized murderers in the FBI study differed in the prevalence of pre-crime alcohol consumption (56% vs. 19%) (Ressler, Burgess, Douglas et al., 1986), the angry and sadistic murderers in our sample exhibited no such difference (85% vs. 79%). In addition, pre-crime alcohol consumption was lower among the serial sexual murderers of the FBI study than among the nonserial sexual murderers in our sample. This may be due, at least in part, to the fact that deviant sexual fantasies are so overwhelming in serial sexual murderers that they are capable of triggering an offence by themselves, whereas in some nonserial sexual murderers alcohol may play a necessary facilitating role. Despite these differences, the consumption of alcohol seems an important facilitator of acting out in both types of sexual murderers.

More than half of the subjects in our study reported having consumed drugs in the hours prior to the murder, and a large proportion of the murderers interviewed reported having taken more than one psychoactive substance prior to committing their crime. Thus, drugs, like alcohol, appear to play a disinhibitory role, diminishing self-control over sexual arousal to rape cues. It is nevertheless interesting to note that drug consumption is much higher among sexual murderers than among sexual aggressors of adult women. For example, Pithers and Cummings (1996) reported that 42% of their sample of sexual aggressors had consumed alcohol, while only 14% had taken drugs. There are two possible explanations for this difference. Firstly, individuals who commit serious crimes (e.g. murder) may be more likely to report alcohol and drug consumption, in an attempt to justify their acts. But it is also possible that the more disinhibited an individual becomes as a result of psychoactive substances, the more serious his crimes will be.

A significant proportion of the subjects in our study reported having had deviant sexual fantasies, which are important disinhibitory factors, in the 48 hours prior to their sexual crime (sadistic murderers: 50%; angry murderers: 21%). According to Ressler et al. (1988), it is sexual murderers' fantasies that motivate them to kill. It has often been pointed out that these individuals consider themselves unjustly treated by society or lacking control over others; it is therefore conceivable that their deviant sexual fantasies provide an outlet for their negative emotions and their desire to control others. Only one third of our sample stated having had such fantasies in the 48 hours preceding their murder. It is, however, possible that murderers who denied having any sexual problems also denied having had this type of fantasy prior to their crime. Such a denial may hide the existence of sexual problems and of premeditation of their crime. However, sadistic murderers were more likely than angry murderers to admit to having had deviant sexual fantasies in the 48 hours prior to their crime (50% vs. 21%). Our results are comparable to those obtained by Proulx et al. (1999) for sadistic and angry sexual aggressors of women (58.3% vs. 21%).

Post-crime attitudes of sexual murderers

Our results indicate that angry sexual murderers differed significantly from sadistic murderers with regard to their post-murder behaviours. Angry murderers turned themselves in more often, were more cooperative during interrogation and were more likely to completely admit their responsibility for their sexual murder. It is possible to explain these features of angry murderers in terms of the organization of their personality. As we have already pointed out, these individuals suffer from borderline personality disorder (Beauregard & Proulx, 2002), a personality disorder characterized, among other things, by impulsive acts and disproportionate reactions. These behaviours are followed by guilt, as individuals realize the horror of their acts (Beck & Freeman, 1990). Angry murderers, once they have realized the seriousness and irreparable nature of their acts, are afflicted with remorse and admit their crimes to authorities. In a study in which violent offending processes were compared in borderline and narcissistic personalities, Bernard and Proulx (2002) demonstrated that violent narcissists tend to try to avoid being caught and do not admit their guilt, whereas offenders with borderline personality disorder more frequently admit their responsibility. Similarly, St-Yves (2002), in his study of suspects' attitudes during police interrogation, mentioned that sexual criminals who report after-the-fact feelings of guilt were more inclined to cooperate with police.

These results allow us to draw up two profiles of sexual murderers' attitudes, and identify the best specific approaches to interrogation for each profile. Our results indicate that angry murderers are prone to guilt. Furthermore, the impulsive nature of their acts suggests that they had not taken care to check whether they had left any evidence at the crime scene that could link them to their victims. Investigators who take into consideration these two personality traits of angry murderers increase the chances of obtaining a confession. With sadistic murderers, investigators must provide solid evidence and conduct a tightly controlled interrogation, applying pressure to the suspect (fear of prison/sentence, persuasive interview techniques) in order to obtain a confession (St-Yves, 2002).

CASE STUDIES

In order to illustrate the two types of sexual murderer identified in our sample, we have selected two subjects on the basis of their short distance from the centre of their cluster. The subjects selected to illustrate the sadistic and angry profiles had distances from the centre of 0.750 and 0.700, respectively, and were the most representative subjects in their respective cluster. These case studies allow us to identify the choice-structuring properties of a sexual murderer and to understand the logic underlying the variables constituting the crime scenario.

Frank: A sadistic murderer

Frank's fantasy scenario consisted of establishing contact with a woman, having sex with her, torturing her, killing her and, finally, dismembering her. However, he started by acting out his less violent fantasies, such as voyeurism and fetishism (involving masturbation with women's underwear).

Even after two or three years of marriage, Frank continued to act out some of his fantasies. He would contact women by telephone and offer them lucrative jobs in the fashion or restaurant sectors, or in upscale prostitution. He would ask them to dress in a specific way (which would always involve nylon stockings) and made an appointment to meet them at a public place. Frank would go to the appointed place, but remained hidden and observe the unsuspecting woman. He described these practices as 'providing enormous mental satisfaction', and 'control over women', and 'good manipulation'. This excited him and gave him a thrill. This game corresponds to MacCulloch et al.'s (1983) 'behavioural try-outs'. Furthermore, in order to feed his fantasies and test his power over women, he even picked up female hitchhikers – for him, this was a hunting trip. Frank continued these behavioural try-outs for seven years, each time wondering whether he should take the final step and actually kill. It is important to note that neither his marital relations nor his work ever suffered from his deviant sexual fantasies or his behavioural try-outs. Frank also adopted avoidance and withdrawal behaviours. He spent much of his leisure time developing his fantasies, which appear to have constituted a sort of outlet for all his unexpressed affects, such as rage towards women, and humiliation.

There is nothing in Frank's account of events of the 48 hours preceding his crime that explains his transition to concrete action, unless it be his generalized conflict with women and a certain degree of self-loathing. It appears that this conflict with women had led to hostility towards them and had even weakened his inhibitions against actually committing violent acts, Furthermore, several hours before the crime he was overwhelmed by fantasies of sexual murder.

This time, he contacted a 17-year-old girl whom he had closely watched in the past, and made an appointment to see her near his place of work. He always chose young girls who appeared to be on the fringes of society or who consumed drugs, and who therefore, in his view, would agree to be prostitutes; however, if he judged that they would not be amenable, he merely offered them jobs in the fashion or restaurant sector. Towards 7 o'clock in the morning, the site at which they were to meet was deserted. Frank had made sure that no one had seen him with her. He brought her to his workplace and talked to her about the work she would do (i.e. prostitution). He asked for a demonstration of her talents and they began to have sex, which consisted of vaginal penetration, initially with the fingers and subsequently with the penis, and rubbing of the genital areas. Experiencing problems maintaining an erection, he demanded that she masturbate him. After ejaculating, Frank asked her to get on her hands and knees.

He continued to penetrate her with his fingers, and, with the other hand, he grabbed a hammer he had hidden and struck her violently on the head while verbally humiliating her. Finally, to ensure that his victim was truly dead, he stabbed her through the heart seven times with a screwdriver. His meticulous planning allowed him to commit his crime without any resistance from his victim. In addition, the modus operandi allowed him to express his rage towards women. During his interview with us, he stated that he had been extremely sexually aroused prior to committing the murder and that he had never experienced anything as powerful as when he took the life of the young girl. The crime scenario thus corresponded to the deviant sexual fantasies Frank had been harbouring for years. In fact, the crime was so well planned that it went off almost exactly as he had planned.

One week after the murder, realizing that he had to get rid of the body, he decided to act out another important element of his fantasies, namely the dismembering of a woman's body. He took care to bring with him garbage bags and an electric knife; he also used a hacksaw that was at the crime scene. He began by cutting off one foot, but when this proved too demanding he decided to settle for more simple measures, namely cutting off the legs, the head and the arms. He took pains to point out to us that he had cut the limbs at the joints in order to facilitate the job. He put the arms and the head in one bag, the legs in another and the trunk in yet another. While he did not find the act of dismembering the victim's body sexually arousing, he did greatly enjoy the feelings of total control over a woman it gave him.

The next morning, he put the bag containing the head and the arms in a garbage container and threw the bag containing the trunk in a vacant lot, hoping that waste collectors would pick it up. The legs were placed near a garbage container. A passer-by discovered the trunk, and another discovered the legs. The head and arms were never recovered. The total duration of the crime phase was thus one week, which considerably increased Frank's risk of getting caught.

After disposing of the body, Frank felt at ease. He participated in discussions about the disappearance of the victim, even suggesting possible suspects, and followed media coverage of the case. He told us that the day he disposed of the body, he returned to his normal activities without feeling at all disturbed.

He did not admit to his crimes during his interrogation. In fact, he mentioned to us that he felt to some extent superior for having eluded the police for so long. But after a few hours of interrogation, he provided incriminating evidence to the police, which led to his conviction.

Paul: An angry murderer

Paul fell in love with a nurse who worked with him. He started studying to become a nurse himself, in order to be the young woman's equal. But his hopes rapidly disappeared, and his self-esteem plummeted, when she fell in love with a physician. Subsequently, Paul increasingly adopted a marginal and hedonistic lifestyle centred on sexual promiscuity. Because of his lifestyle, Paul spiralled downwards into ever-increasing isolation. He felt intensely lonely and believed that others rejected him. His self-esteem was low, and his problems with women got even worse. With regard to women, he told us, during an interview, that 'women are nothing more than objects, objects which, to give me pleasure, must be mastered, controlled'. Such was his mental state immediately prior to his crime.

The night of his first murder, Paul met a prostitute and decided to have sex with her. He had consumed drugs and alcohol. Towards 2 o'clock in the morning, they left together in a taxi to go to a hotel room. Paul described the prostitute he chose as very pretty. During their taxi ride, he believed that the woman was making fun of him to the taxi driver. According to Paul, the prostitute told the driver that he was 'an easy client'. This simple phrase was enough to trigger intense rage towards her.

As soon as they entered the hotel room, Paul grabbed the victim from behind and strangled her to death. When she no longer resisted, he completely undressed her, turned her on her back and had sex with her corpse. According to him, he had vaginal penetration with his fingers and penis (without ejaculating), touched her and masturbated to ejaculation. After the murder, he said, he became totally calm. He left the hotel room without attracting attention. In all, the crime took less than 30 minutes.

Approximately two weeks later, Paul contacted a prostitute he had previously been with on several occasions. He had no murderous intent. This woman worked from her home, and made an appointment to see Paul. That evening, Paul arrived a bit early. When he knocked on the door, the prostitute told him to wait, as she was already with a client. Paul told us, during the interview, that he did not like this turn of events, or rather the position of power the prostitute held. He was frustrated to be treated as just a client. From his point of view, the prostitute didn't see his beauty, his qualities and the fact that he wasn't like the others. It was in this state of rage that Paul entered the room when the other client had left. He replayed essentially the same scenario as with the previous victim, grabbing the prostitute from behind and strangling her with his arm. He then had sex with her corpse. Finally, he fled, leaving the corpse at the crime scene.

The two murders had taken less than 30 minutes each. Several months later, unable to live with his guilt, Paul confessed to the two murders to the police, who in fact had no leads in the cases. He described everything he had done, including the postmortem sexual acts.

CONCLUSION

This study has identified two crime profiles in a sample of 36 sexual murderers of women at least 14 years old. Our study does, however, have some limitations. First, there is the problem of missing data. In studies of crime scenarios of sexual offenders it is predictable that these criminals will refuse to reveal information that they alone can provide. And even when they do cooperate, the veracity of the information provided is open to debate. Self-reported information that is false or merely minimized may have had repercussions on the results of our analyses.

We are also aware of the limited scope of our analyses. Although a small number of subjects is an important limitation in quantitative analyses, we must recall that sexual murderers are a rare type of sexual offender and that other studies of these offenders were conducted on similarly small samples. However, the small sample size did limit the statistical power of our analyses.

Despite the precautions taken to avoid sampling bias, our research is not completely free of such biases. The characteristics and motivations of the sexual murderers who agreed to participate must be considered, and compared to those of the sexual murderers who declined. Perhaps these latter murderers are different in some way from those who participated.

As the study progressed, we were struck by the rarity of empirical studies of sexual murder. As there are few Canadian studies on the subject, we had to rely on studies undertaken in the United States. However, the subjects in these latter studies had usually committed more than two sexual murders, i.e. were serial murderers. We must therefore be prudent in comparing the results of those studies to our results, obtained in Quebec with nonserial sexual murderers.

We hope that police officers responsible for investigating this type of violent crime find our typology useful. More specifically, we believe that our typology may be useful in criminal investigative analysis (criminal profiling) (Douglas & Burgess, 1986; Geberth, 1996; Holmes & Holmes, 1996; Homant & Kennedy, 1998; Jackson & Bekerian, 1997; Knight et al., 1998; Kocsis, 2006; McCann, 1992; Pinizzotto, 1984; Pinizzotto & Finkel, 1990). Criminal investigative analysis is a technique for generating hypotheses about criminals, based on the analysis of the crime scene and the victim. Thus, a typology based primarily on crime scenarios may provide useful information on the characteristics of unknown sexual murderers (for more information, see Chapter 12).

In the future, approaches inspired by the rational-choice perspective (Cusson & Cordeau, 1994) may shed light on the decision-making process associated with the commission of sexual murder. Moreover, given the difficulty in constituting samples large enough to support sophisticated statistical analyses, researchers may wish to follow the approach taken by Ward, Louden, Hudson and Marshall (1995) in their study of 26 paedophiles' offending processes. In that study, an approach derived from grounded theory was used to gather the qualitative information necessary for the description of the transition to concrete action.

Chapter 9

THE MOTIVATION AND CRIMINAL CAREER OF SEXUAL MURDERERS

Maurice Cusson and Jean Proulx

The monstrous nature of sexual murder should not overshadow the fact that its authors are human beings, and, accordingly, have motivations for their actions. This chapter takes two approaches to understanding these motivations. The first approach focuses on elucidating the murderer's goals at the moment of the murder – what was he actually trying to do at that precise time and place? Answering this question requires situating the crime in the context of immediately preceding events, detailing the facts related to, and the actions of, the murderer and his victim, and, finally, analysing the criminal's own statements about his motivation. The second approach focuses on establishing the relationship between the murderer's criminal career and a specific sexual murder. Was the sexual murder the logical extension of past behaviour, or did it mark a new direction? Was it the culmination of a long series of sexual assaults that share a common pathway?

This chapter will address these questions, and will describe the criminal career of sexual murderers, including, of course, the murder itself. The approach will be narrative, rather than statistical, and the establishment of these personal histories will be based on the murderer's own account of his life and latest crime, the murderer's criminal record, police reports (including descriptions of crime scenes, confessions and autopsy reports) and the murderer's answers to questions about his past criminal activities

Sexual Murderers: A Comparative Analysis and New Perspectives Edited by Jean Proulx Éric Beauregard, Maurice Cusson and Alexandre Nicole
© 2007 John Wiley & Sons, Ltd.

(including those unknown to police). The validity of this approach stems from the fact that there is after all such a thing as historical causality. When events do not simply follow each chronologically but are interrelated, a causal relationship exists between successive events.

The chapter is divided into two sections. The first is concerned with the crime itself and addresses the murderer's motivations in committing his crime. The second attempts to identify the relationships between the criminal career of sexual murderers and the specific sexual murders whose meanings we are attempting to understand.

WHAT WAS THE POINT OF THE MURDER?

Grubin (1994), Bénézech (1997) and Beech (2003) investigated the specific motivations for sexual murder. Grubin interviewed 21 sexual murderers incarcerated in British prisons. A specific motive could be identified in 18 cases: anger at victim resistance in eight cases; the desire to silence a potential accuser in four cases; the quest for sexual satisfaction in three cases; and panic in two cases.

In a short article published in 1997, Bénézech listed five potential reasons for sexual murder:

1. Violent efforts to overcome the victim's resistance during a sexual assault; death in these cases may be accidental.
2. Attempts by a sexual aggressor to stifle his victim's cries or kill the only person who could accuse, identify or convict him.
3. Fury at victim resistance.
4. The premeditated acting out of a script, with sexual assault and murder concretizing fantasies and providing the murderer with sexual pleasure.
5. Delusional ideation; for example, a psychotic may be delusional and harbour hostile feelings towards women or be in a state of panic.

Further, Bénézech observed that sexual murder, in the strictest sense of the term, must be distinguished from murder accompanied by sexual assault (for example, breaking and entering followed by sexual assault and murder), and false sexual murder (for example, murder in which the sexual element is simulated in order to throw the police off the trail). While Bénézech's analysis is of interest, he neither provides supporting figures nor describes the data on which his classification system is based.

Finally, Beech (2003) identifies three distinct motivations for sexual murder. Type I murder is primarily sexually motivated: the murderer lives out his masturbatory fantasies revolving around murder, and the act of killing is sexually arousing. Type II murder is motivated by the desire of a sexual offender to eliminate the person who could accuse or identify him. Type III murder is motivated by anger: an already angry offender becomes enraged in the face of victim resistance, loses control and ultimately kills.

Our own analysis is based on the descriptions of 26 sexual murders committed in the province of Quebec by 21 murderers (five of whom had committed two murders). These descriptions are primarily based on the murderers' versions of events, and are complemented by autopsy and police reports. A close reading of the narratives allows identification of four typical scenarios:

1. The murderer kills out of rage at the victim's actions.
2. The murderer kills in a quest for sexual pleasure.
3. The murder occurs during an attempt to subdue a woman during a sexual assault.
4. The murderer kills the woman he has just sexually assaulted, in order to eliminate a witness.

Rage and vengeance

In our sample of 26 murders, 12 were primarily motivated by rage. The following scenarios summarize these murders:

1. A woman rejects the murderer's sexual advances. The murderer becomes infuriated and murders her, either immediately or soon after (four cases).
2. A man and a woman have an argument with no sexual overtones. The man feels offended, becomes enraged and strikes the woman with such force that she dies. The corpse exhibits signs of sexual assault (five cases; see the case report for Philippe, below).
3. A waitress is murdered because she refuses to serve alcohol to a customer who is too drunk (one case; see the case report for Thomas, below).
4. A man kills his spouse when she informs him that she is a prostitute (one case).
5. A woman is sexually assaulted and murdered because the murderer has hated her for a long time (one case).

When rage, not sexual arousal, is the primary motivation, is it still reasonable to classify the crime as sexual murder? It must be pointed out that all the murders described above comprised a sexual component, albeit one present before or after, rather than concurrent with, the actual murder. The existence of a few murders of a pseudo-sexual nature or in which the sexual component was secondary does not alter the overall picture. Quite frequently, the murderer hit his victim when rebuffed in his quest for a consensual sexual relationship, his sexual desire replaced by rage. In other cases, the murderer was driven to murder by rage at an offence that had no sexual overtones whatsoever, and committed necrophilia.

The role of sadism in sexual murder

Since Krafft-Ebing (1886), sexual murderers have often been presented as sadists. Typically, in this paradigm, an individual seeks refuge in an imaginary world in which, omnipotent, he subjugates, humiliates, terrorizes, sexually assaults, tortures and kills. These fantasies provide him with sexual pleasure. One day, he decides to act out a scenario that he has imagined hundreds of times: he plans the operation with care (weapon, vehicle, restraints), chooses a victim who corresponds to his fantasies, confines her in a safe place and lives out the details of his fantasy. The act of killing, preferably by strangulation, is eroticized.

This scenario was unambiguously present in only one case ('Frank' – see Chapter 8). In addition, a few murders initially motivated by rage appear to have become eroticized as they were being committed. Michel (see below) had committed several clearly sadistic sexual assaults prior to the murder he committed, in which his victim, confined, strangled to death on a gag that was too tight.

In summary, then, murder committed with the intent to secure sexual pleasure is the exception rather than the rule. What is much more common, at least in our sample, is a sadistic sexual assault followed by a nonsadistic murder or an eroticized angry murder. The presence in Ressler's sample of many cases of sexually gratifying murder may be due to the marked overrepresentation in his sample of serial sexual murderers, who are motivated by sadistic fantasies to repeat the offence.

Neutralization of victim resistance

Five murders resulted from sexual aggressors' excessive use of force to subdue their victims. In these cases, the murderer apparently would have preferred consensual sex but met with strong resistance, and in the resulting scuffle killed the victim. It should be noted that the only source for this version of events is the murderer, who may have found it in his interests to explain the murder in this way.

Elimination of a witness

Six murders were cold-blooded affairs committed by sexual aggressors who decided to kill their victim to avoid being accused of sexual assault (see, for example, the case report for François, below).

Comments

As we saw in Chapter 1, a murder is classified as a sexual murder on the basis of the sexual context in which it occurs. The murder is not necessarily sexually gratifying in itself, and in fact is usually motivated by rage. Sexual gratification typically is provided by a sexual assault concomitant with or subsequent to the murder. In some cases, the murderer's initial intention is sexual assault, and the murder is committed to eliminate a witness, whereas in others, it occurs accidentally during the struggle between the sexual murderer and his victim. It should be noted that more often than not, the murder is a reaction to a rebuff, offence or quarrel.

Like Grubin, Bénézech and Beech, we observed three primary types of sexual murder: murders in which anger, rage and the desire for vengeance predominate; murders with sadistic elements; and murders in which the murderer's intention was a sexual relationship, with the murder occurring during a struggle or committed after the assault in order to silence the victim. Using different methods and data we thus arrive at convergent results.

THE LINK BETWEEN CRIMINAL CAREER AND SEXUAL MURDER

What is the role of criminal activity in the life of the sexual murderers? What relationships can be established between their criminal careers and the murders they commit?

In answer to these questions, two hypotheses have been suggested. The first is implicit in the very concept of the sexual offender: namely that one group of criminals can be distinguished from others by the fact that they commit primarily sexual crimes. The literature on serial sexual killers and sadistic sexual murderers supports this concept, and suggests that sexual murder lies on a continuous spectrum with the murderer's past crimes.

According to the second hypothesis, the majority of sexual murderers are essentially polymorphic criminals. In this view, murder is the culmination of a series of crimes of various types, all of which can be explained in the same way. Because they are impulsive, caught in the moment and without scruple, these murderers commit crimes of all types. Because they put their immediate gratification before everything else, they steal and may even commit sexual assault. Because they cannot cope with frustration, they go as far as killing women who will not submit to their whims. If this hypothesis is valid, sexual criminals, including sexual murderers, will have a polymorphic criminal career similar to most incarcerated criminals (Simon, 2002; Tedeschi & Felson, 1994; West, 1983).

The statistics support the second hypothesis: sexual aggressors and sexual murderers (but not paedophiles) are, for the most part, criminals like any other, and commit many nonsexual crimes. Nicole (2002) observed that 74% of the sexual aggressors and 72% of the sexual murderers in his sample had committed at least one crime against property. Among sexual aggressors, 46% had committed nonsexual crimes against persons, compared to 62% of sexual murderers. In addition, only 29% of sexual aggressors and 26% of sexual murderers had previously committed at least one sexual crime. As noted in Chapter 2, sexual aggressors and sexual murderers committed several crimes against property (mean: 4.71 and 3.05, respectively). In other words, most of these 'sexual offenders' had committed markedly more nonsexual crimes (robbery and violent crimes with no sexual component at all) than sexual crimes.

Furthermore, Nicole and Proulx (see Chapter 2) reported that only 17% of sexual aggressors and 22% of sexual murderers in their sample had a Wilkstrom index above 0.67 (sexual crimes/total crimes). These results are consistent with those of Boutin (1999), who made a strong case for polymorphism among sexual aggressors. Two results taken from her thesis support this position: 86% of sexual aggressors in her sample had committed at least one nonsexual violent crime (for example, robbery) and 92% had committed at least one nonsexual crime. Recently, Proulx et al. (2003) reported that sexual aggressors of women did not tend to specialize in sexual offences.

In 2001, Henriette Haas published a study on self-reported offending in an entire population of army recruits in Switzerland, where military service is obligatory. Of the 21,347 subjects, 30 admitted having committed sexual assault with coitus. Among these sexual aggressors, 80% had committed a nonviolent crime (theft, breaking and entering, sale of drugs, etc.) in the year preceding the sexual assault (Haas, 2001). Their choice of victims was eclectic, and included strangers, partners, neighbours and sisters. This research, conducted in a non-incarcerated population, corroborates the conclusions of studies conducted with incarcerated samples, namely that sexual aggressors are polymorphic criminals.

In summary, sexual murderers, like sexual aggressors, exhibit a polymorphic criminal activity that is strikingly similar to that of chronic nonsexual offenders. From this, we can conclude that these sexual murderers, like sexual aggressors and chronic nonsexual offenders, possess well-recognized features that drive them to impulsively transgress all types of rules: they are caught in the present and take no account of the long-term consequences of their decisions; they have little, if any, cognitive control of their behaviour; they are egocentric and convinced that they have always been the victims of injustices (Cusson, 1998c). A plausible conclusion is that many sexual murderers are first and foremost criminals who are unstoppable in their pursuit of immediate gratification and who react explosively to frustration. But could there be other explanations? Is it possible, for example, that behind the apparent polymorphism indicated by statistics lies a true sexual offender? For example, consider a sexual aggressor previously convicted for breaking and entering: if the burglary was committed with the intent of committing sexual assault, the criminal is not truly polymorphic. To get at the heart of question, it is thus necessary to go beyond mere figures and scrutinize the motivation of the apparently nonsexual crimes of sexual murderers.

We analysed the criminal career of 37 sexual murderers for whom complete, convergent and credible information was available. There were three distinct sources of data: (1) the official criminal record; (2) self-reported juvenile and adult criminality; and (3) case reports, largely based on interviews with the murderers. Our use of both qualitative and quantitative data ensured that we obtained as complete portraits as possible of the criminal career of the sexual murderers up to the murder for which they were incarcerated. Four criminal pathways were identifiable from this data: (1) violent polymorphism; (2) sexual aggression; (3) marginality; and (4) overcontrol.

Violent Polymorphism: François

François was serving a sentence for double homicide, sexual assault and unlawful confinement. In school, François was considered an aggressive child and a fighter. He began his criminal career when he was 13 years old. He admitted having committed approximately 50 robberies and 20 assaults during his adolescence. In addition, he had several convictions as an adult for possession of drugs, assault (including an assault causing bodily harm involving three police officers), mischief, armed robbery, auto theft and possession of sawed-off firearms. He also admitted to having committed, as an adult, a great many (he could not count them all) robberies, assaults, armed robberies and confinements for which he had not been charged.

Towards 4 p.m. on the day of his crime, he went, alone, to the home of his victims. He rang the doorbell, and when the husband, 58 years old, opened the door he immediately stunned him and tied him up. He then went through the house looking for valuables. When the husband regained consciousness, François smothered him to death.

At around 4:30, the wife, a 52-year-old woman who had been François's grade-school teacher, came home. He let her in, overpowered her and tied her to a bed. He cut off her clothes with a pair of scissors and sexually assaulted her. The autopsy revealed the presence of a large amount of sperm in her vagina.

François then buried the man and stole the victims' credit cards and hunting rifles, as well as the microwave oven and a television, both of which he needed. When night fell, he forced the woman into the trunk of his car, drove to a quarry approximately 20 kilometres from the victims' home, made the woman get out and killed her with a blow to the head with a rock.

François used the stolen credit card three times. The cashier of one of the stores at which he used the card was able to provide a valuable description of him, and the police were able to produce a sketch. Their investigations led them to François, already well known to them.

Of the 37 murderers, 15 (41%) had, like François, a criminal record full of crimes of all sorts. Among these 15, assault and robberies involving violence were well represented, although they did not predominate. In many cases the subjects had committed so many adolescent and adult robberies that they were unable to estimate their number. Quite often, they had consumed and sold drugs. Some had committed fraud or arson. Astonishingly, few had committed sexual assault.

How does a polymorphic criminal become a killer of women? In François' case, the motivation was to kill a woman he had just sexually assaulted so that she could not accuse him. Others were driven to kill out of anger: as a result of an argument with a woman or rejection by a woman, they became enraged, sexually assaulted the woman and killed her. Yet others attempted to sexually assault a woman and used excessive force to subdue her. None of these criminals reported that they killed to act out sadistic fantasies. In light of the fact that they had each committed few or no sexual crimes, it is reasonable to conclude that their murders were not sexual in nature.

Why did these men given to robbery and with no compunctions about violence finally kill in a sexual context? The answer may lie in their background. Like all chronic offenders, they were motivated by immediate gratification, violent reaction to any and all sources of frustration and hatred for everyone around them. They were capable of killing because they had become inured to pursuing pleasure by any means, reacting violently to frustration and resolving conflicts through violence. When faced with a woman who refused their advances, some became overcome with rage and hate. Others went as far as sexual assault and then decided that the best way to ensure that they never returned to prison was to eliminate their victim. Yet others decided to break the woman's resistance by any means necessary.

Sexual aggression: Michel

Michel had been convicted for second-degree murder. Ten years earlier, he had been convicted of robbery of less than $200 and of sexual assault.

Abandoned by his mother, he was adopted at six months. He complained that his adoptive mother was overbearing and dominant, and exerted a sort of emotional blackmail over him by threatening to put him in foster care. He never forgot his abandonment as an infant, was deeply resentful of his biological mother – whom he came to hate – and devalued his adoptive mother. His hatred extended to all women, which drove him to seek control over them. 'Control, power, humiliation', he pointed out. When he felt frustrated, he was overwhelmed by sadistic sexual fantasies.

He had worked in a factory for 15 years. His work colleagues found him odd and disliked him a great deal. His locker was covered with posters of naked women over whose breasts he drew bars and circles. He would later draw these same designs on one of his victims, using a white-hot spoon. Conflicts with work colleagues drove him into depression, and he eventually lost his job and could find no other.

Over a period of 10 years, Michel indulged in a series of sexual assaults. His first sexual assault was particularly brutal: he broke into his victim's apartment, assaulted her for three hours and burned her breasts with a small white-hot spoon.

This assault was followed by five others over the following years. The features of his assaults demonstrate his desire for domination and humiliation: insults, drawings on the victims' bodies, shaving of the victims' pubic areas, forced fellatio, sodomy. In every case, he managed to elude the police.

The day of the murder, Michel, still unemployed, went to the employment office to check on help-wanted ads. His fantasies that day had turned towards the humiliation of women. At the employment office, he met a young woman. He pretended to be an employer and offered to drive her to his house. She accepted. He drove her to the home of his girlfriend's parents (which was empty). There, he tied her hands and feet with stockings and suspended her by the arms from a ceiling beam. He told her that she was his mother and whipped her with an electric wire. To prevent her from screaming, he stuffed a rag into her mouth. He shaved her pubic area and had intercourse with her. After three days of torment, his victim finally died, smothered by a gag that he had stuffed in her mouth. Michel indulged in postmortem mutilation of the corpse. He took the corpse and disposed of it on the side of the road, in fact wanting her body to be found so that everyone would know that his victim had received 'her punishment'. He had drawn, with a red marker, a circle with bars (like a cage) on her breasts and a star of David on her stomach. One week later, he was arrested. Although he denied everything he was convicted.

Of the 37 murderers, 10 (27%) had had a history of sexual crimes prior to the murders for which they were incarcerated. Michel had committed several sexual assaults. Another murderer was a compulsive voyeur and stole women's clothing. The eight others had interspersed their sexual assaults with numerous thefts and assaults. Among the sexual crimes of which they had been found guilty, voyeurism was particularly prevalent. Other sexual crimes include frottage, exhibitionism and sexual assault.

It is in this category that we find the true sexual criminal, one whose dominant criminal motivation is inherently sexual. These individuals engaged in voyeurism, sexual assault and even murder because they had eroticized the domination, humiliation and terrorization of women. Of the 10 murders which emerged from this pathway, two were frankly sadistic. In the other cases, the murder was preceded by a sadistic sexual assault (as was the case with Michel, whose initial sexual assault culminated in murder when his victim was smothered by a gag). In other cases, the murders were initially motivated by rage, but nevertheless gave the murderers sexual pleasure.

Marginality: Philippe

Philippe was serving a life sentence for second-degree murder. He had no criminal record before the murder and denied having committing any crimes during his adolescence or adulthood.

Philippe is the youngest of three children (he has one brother and one sister). The family unit appears to have been strong. His father is a farmer. He described his mother as generous and helpful. Philippe says he has fond memories of family life, even if the household was very strict.

At a young age, he started working on his parents' farm. He frequently fought with his father, especially during summer haying. His mother would mediate between the two. Philippe has very bad memories of his school years, as his peers considered him stupid and 'thick', and made fun of him. He feels bad about not having had girlfriends like other boys in his class, and is convinced that people would not have made fun of him had he gone out with a girl. Upon leaving school, he worked as a mechanic and farm worker. At the time of the murder and his arrest, he was working as a truck driver. Philippe began drinking occasionally when he was 12 years old, and started consuming hard drugs regularly when he was 13. He later became a drug addict.

One summer day, Philippe, then 20, spent the night at a bar with friends. He had some drinks and consumed cocaine. Later, the group went to a restaurant to end the night. There they met Louis, who had just met a young girl, Claire, 16. Claire had had many strong drinks and had consumed drugs. By the end of the evening, she had fallen asleep and Philippe and his friend had trouble waking her. Philippe wanted to drive her home, but she no longer remembered where she lived, as she was too 'stoned'. He drove through the city with the windows open, to try to clear her thoughts, but this was unsuccessful. He drove to a wooded lane and parked. She woke up and asked him if he had any drugs. She got out of the truck, sat on the hood and asked again for drugs, punctuating her requests with kicks to the truck. Philippe said he wanted to slap her to calm her down, but in fact ended up punching her, causing her to fall to the ground. He then picked up an iron bar from his trunk and hit her twice, killing her.

Philippe then took some rope and wrapped it around the victim's neck, to drag her to the woods. He searched her and took her identification. He undid her pants and took them off. At the time of interview, he recalled that she had been wearing black leotard-like underwear; the autopsy revealed that the crotch of the underwear was ripped.

During a fishing trip approximately one year later, he decided to tell a friend what had happened. As he was telling the story, he threw his victim's identification papers into the campfire. His friend reported all this to the police.

To verify this information, the police went to the lake at which Philippe and his friend had gone fishing. There, they found the victim's identification card; because it had been laminated, it had not been completely consumed, and the victim's name was still legible. Philippe was arrested, and immediately admitted his crime. He showed investigators where to find the body. The autopsy revealed a skull fracture behind the ear on the left.

In our sample, eight of the 37 (22%) murderers had either substance abuse problems or a long history of nonviolent crimes. Substance abuse was a dominant feature of the lives of six of the 37, Two others had committed countless robberies, but no violent crimes, no sexual crimes and no drug-related crimes.

These murderers had been driven to murder by rage. Philippe struck a drug-intoxicated woman, with whom he was fighting, with an iron bar. Others had killed prostitutes whom they perceived to have been humiliating them. One killed a woman whom he had long hated. The lives of these murderers were marked by failure and marginality. Chronically intoxicated, their lives stalled and they drifted into solitude and boredom. Despising themselves – with some reason – they saw despisal in the eyes of women. Too deviant, too intoxicated, too unpredictable to interest a woman for long, they frequented prostitutes and drug-intoxicated women.

Overcontrol: Thomas

Thomas was serving a life sentence for involuntary homicide, kidnapping and unlawful confinement, and sexual assault of a 24-year-old woman. Remarkably, he had no previous criminal record. What is more, he appeared to be telling the truth when he said that he had committed no sexual assaults or acts of violence as an adolescent or adult.

Thomas described his mother in negative terms: authoritarian, aggressive, degrading and humiliating. He saw himself as the scapegoat of the family. When he contradicted his mother, she would use force to correct him. She would tell him that he was good for nothing. When he was 10 years old, his brother sodomized him and told his mother in detail. His mother's reaction was to laugh at Thomas and recount this episode, ridiculing him, for two weeks.

When he was 12 or 13, Thomas sodomized a goat. His brother saw him and ran to tell his mother, who took advantage of the occasion to humiliate Thomas once again. She told Thomas that he may have gotten the goat pregnant. She also threatened to tell his eventual first girlfriend that his first love had been a goat. This made Thomas think of killing her.

Around the time of the murder, Thomas was employed at a job at which he was much appreciated. He worked so hard that he neglected his social life and no longer saw his friends. His life revolved around his work, his girlfriend, and hunting and fishing. For six-and-a-half years, Thomas had been living with his girlfriend, who was the daughter of his boss. Gnawed by jealousy, he had sexual relations an average of two or three times a day: he believed that if he gave his girlfriend great sexual satisfaction, she would not be tempted to seek satisfaction elsewhere. Thomas hid many things from his girlfriend. He lied about their financial situation, and led her to believe that they would soon be able to buy a house. Thomas wanted to preserve the image of a responsible man.

Thomas had deviant sexual fantasies in which he would pick up a young hitchhiker in his pickup truck, take her to a deserted location, tie her, naked, to a tree, and have sex with her. Although the victim would resist at first, she would eventually enjoy herself.

The day of the murder, Thomas's girlfriend was out of town on a school trip, and he felt he was losing her. His jealousy was triggered by the memory of having seen his girlfriend kiss a friend on the cheek almost one month before. Thomas went out to a bar for a drink. He drank quite a lot of beer and 'screwdrivers'. Towards midnight, he attempted to pick a fight with another customer, but was unsuccessful. Thomas then went to a little 24-hour restaurant. After ordering some French fries, he was told by the waitress that her boss didn't allow 'drunk guys' in the restaurant. Deeply stung by this remark, Thomas left the restaurant, got a knife out of his truck and returned to the restaurant.

Once back in the restaurant, he threatened the waitress with the knife, and made her get in his truck. On the road, they got stuck in the snow and he had to get out to push. He even asked the victim to drive the truck while he pushed. Realizing his efforts were in vain, he went in search of help. According to him, the victim was adamant in wanting to go with him, going so far as to grab his arm. This enraged him, and he punched her hard. According to Thomas, she then said to him 'I know what you want' and then took off her pants. They had intercourse with no physical violence or humiliation.

Afterwards, Thomas went in search of help but came back empty-handed. At first he didn't see the victim, but then she came out from the bushes, knife in hand. In his attempts to grab the knife, Thomas hurt himself, which made him explode with rage. He managed to get hold of the knife and stab the victim seven times in the throat and chest. Thomas said that he felt rage during the murder, but that this rage was directed at his mother, who was the one he saw during the murder, not the victim.

Among the 37 sexual murders in our sample, four, like Thomas, had virtually no criminal record prior to the murder they committed. Search as we might through their past, we could find no trace of robbery, assault or breaking and entering. One had been convicted of a few cases of indecent assault, and one had committed a sexual assault. The family and occupational life of these four murderers was, mirroring their personal history, relatively crime-free. They all had stable jobs and appeared to have been dedicated workers. They all had markers of overconformity: absence of criminal record, heavy investment in their work, marked submission to a woman. All this is to say that their murders were clear discontinuities with their previous respect for the law.

How to explain these murders? Thomas beat to death a waitress who had refused to serve him a drink. Others killed women who had rebuffed their advances. How did these innocuous men – good workers, conformists – commit one of the worst crimes imaginable? Given the absence of a criminal record, we seek the key to this enigma in these men's relationships with their mothers or girlfriends. Thomas's girlfriend was a woman whom he was jealous of and from whom he hid things; in addition, he wanted to kill his mother. Two other murderers, although in their 30s, lived with their mothers, whose yoke they could never throw off; in one case (Serge, Chapter 2), the mother systematically opposed his going out with women. In these men, the offending process may correspond to that of the 'chronically overcontrolled personalities' described by Megargee (1970). The men in this latter group were mild, polite, unassuming individuals who had suffered a long succession of bullying and insults without replying, and who suddenly exploded one day and killed their persecutors in an unprecedented flurry of violence. The problem faced by the sexual murders in our study was different, even if their reaction was essentially the same. Thomas is a case of displaced aggression: tyranized and humiliated by his mother and jealous of his girlfriend, he became deeply resentful. This resentment was eventually discharged on a woman who was made to pay the price for the others. His crime was the culmination of a backlash that is even more absurd for having been directed at an innocent victim.

CONCLUSION

The sexual murderers in our sample, with the exception of the four overcontrolled murderers, had a well-established criminal history prior to the murders they committed. Most had committed robbery. Almost half had committed violent crimes. Many had substance abuse problems. A quarter of them had been convicted of sexual crimes. These lost men drifted at the margins of the law, with no direction, no goals and no hope. Incapable of attaching themselves to anything or anyone, slaves to immediate gratification, deviant sexual fantasies or drugs, too intoxicated, too criminal, too irresponsible, they gradually became capable of the worst, and lost the ability to form long-lasting relationships with women. Possessed by hate or sadistic fantasies, frustrated, they could only treat women as either prey or enemies.

PART II
THE BIRMINGHAM STUDY

Chapter 10

A COMPARISON OF RAPISTS AND SEXUAL MURDERERS ON DEMOGRAPHIC AND SELECTED PSYCHOMETRIC MEASURES

Caroline J. Oliver, Anthony R. Beech, Dawn Fisher and Richard Beckett

INTRODUCTION

Home Office figures for 2001–3 report that around 9% of the prison population in England and Wales are sexual offenders.[1] Roughly half of all these sexual offenders are men who have offended against adults, resulting in a conviction for rape or, in the most extreme cases, murder. In fact, current estimates would suggest that there are around 200 men within the prison system in the UK who have committed a murder with an apparent, or admitted, sexual motivation (Adam Carter, Lifer Unit, HM Prison Service, UK, personal communication, May 2003). For the most part, such individuals have, up until only recently, been managed within the prison system in the same way as other, nonsexual, violent offenders because of their status as a 'murderer' rather than a 'sex offender' (given that currently no offence of 'sexual murder' exists). It is only relatively recently that the sexual element of their crime has been formally recognized in terms of treatment provisions, with men who have killed their victims (where it is suspected or known that there was a sexual component to the killing) now accounting for approximately 5% of all men going through sex

---

[1]Source: *HO Statistical Bulletin, 15/04*, Table 8.2 Available from www.homeoffice.gov.uk/rds/hosb2004.html.

Sexual Murderers: A Comparative Analysis and New Perspectives   Edited by Jean Proulx Éric Beauregard, Maurice Cusson and Alexandre Nicole
© 2007 John Wiley & Sons, Ltd.

offender treatment. In fact, to date, it is estimated that between 50% and 60% of identified sexual murderers have now undertaken treatment for the sexual component of their offence (information obtained from the Prison Service Lifer Unit and the Offending Behaviour Programmes Unit[2] of the English and Welsh Prison Service).

Although sexual murderers have increasingly been included in sex offender treatment programmes in prison, empirical research to support the inclusion of this type of offender in such programmes has, unfortunately, lagged behind. Sexual murderers and rapists (sexual aggressors of women) currently receive the same package of treatment as men who have offended against children and yet, due to the paucity of research into sexual murder, it is difficult to determine how well such treatment actually maps on to the criminogenic needs of this offender group. As Grubin (1994) points out, little is known about men who kill in a sexual context. What literature does exist has tended to focus on case studies, usually providing a descriptive account of sadistic, serial sexual murderers (Revitch, 1965; Brittain, 1970; Swigert, Farnell & Yoels 1976; Dietz, Hazelwood & Warren, 1990), as these are the cases that have generally attracted the greatest media attention. However, such cases where an individual has been driven by sadistic fantasy to claim multiple victims are, fortunately, comparatively rare; e.g. Jenkins (1988) showed that serial killers accounted for only 1.7% of all murders in England and Wales between the years 1940 and 1985. Further, Levin and Fox (1985) suggest that sexually sadistic serial killers constitute only 28% of all serial murderers and yet such a relatively (and thankfully) tiny subgroup of offenders, perhaps because of their tendency to attract such media attention, has generally monopolized any research into sexual murder. More often than not, there is a single victim, and the murderer's motivation is less than clearly established, although the offence contains some evidence of sexual activity. It is this less clearly defined group of sexual murderers that has, to a large extent, been neglected in the literature, although Prentky and his colleagues (Prentky, Burgess et al., 1989) did compare a group of serial sexual murderers to a group of sexual murderers with only one victim in terms of the role of sexual fantasy. However, apart from the fate of the victim, the question as to how they differ from other sexual offenders who do not kill remains unclear, and findings from the small number of comparative studies of rapists and sexual murderers that have been carried out (Langevin et al., 1988; Grubin, 1994; Gratzer & Bradford, 1995; Milsom, Beech & Webster, 2003; Proulx, Beauregard & Nicole, 2002; Langevin, 2003) are somewhat equivocal.

Grubin (1994) compared 21 men who had murdered in the course of a sexual attack to 121 rapists. He found that his two offender samples differed most in terms of their personal history, including childhood and more

---

[2]This unit is a section of the English and Welsh Prison Service that was set up to develop and support the delivery of high-intensity programmes designed to reduce reoffending.

recent social circumstances. The sexual murderers reported much higher levels of social isolation compared to the rapists, both childhood (a finding replicated by Milsom et al., 2003) and adulthood. Most notably, the sexual murderers were comparatively sexually inexperienced, with well over half (62%) of the sample reporting having had 'few sexual relationships' in their lifetime, compared to 19% of the rapists. This was in spite of the fact that the sexual murderer sample was generally older when they committed their index offence (mean age for sexual murderers: 30 (s.d. 8.7); mean age for rapists: 25.9 (s.d. 6.9)).

Proulx et al. (2002), in their study of 40 sexual murderers, also found greater levels of social isolation in this group and showed that they were also more likely to have been single at the time of their index offence compared to the rapists, although Milsom at al. (2003) found the opposite to be true. However, curiously, despite their relative social isolation, Grubin (1994) found that the sexual murderers reported a more stable upbringing compared to the rapists, in terms of family structure at least, with 66% of the latter experiencing a change in primary caretaker during their formative years compared to 43% of the sexual murderers. In addition, the sexual murderers were more likely to report a 'present' and 'stable' father prior to the age of 10 compared to the rapists, although Langevin et al. (1988) had found the opposite to be true, in that their sexual murderers reported more disturbed relationships with their father. Proulx et al. (2002) did not find any real differences between the two groups in terms of dysfunctional family background (parental alcoholism, domestic violence, etc.). Other findings included: a difference in ethnic origin, with all of the sexual murderers in Grubin's study being white, whereas 40% of the rapists were from a minority ethnic background; and a higher mean age of victim for the sexual murderers.[3]

No difference was found in terms of relationship to victim, with just under half of the offenders in both samples knowing their victims prior to the offences, although the study does not define what is meant by 'knowing' (e.g. being in a relationship with the victim or just knowing the victim by sight). Interestingly, despite what has been cited in the past as being characteristic of sadistic killers (Brittain, 1970), Grubin found that factors such as an interest in aggressive pursuits, sexual deviation and a rich fantasy life were equally likely to be present in rapists. Proulx et al. (2002), on the other hand, found that sexual murderers reported more sexually deviant fantasies compared to rapists. Langevin et al. (1988) found more evidence of transvestism and sadism in his sexual murderer group compared to a group of men who had raped but not killed.

Findings relating to childhood behavioural problems are also equivocal, with Grubin finding that rapists and sexual murderers did not differ in

---

[3]Although this was skewed by the fact that five out of the 21 had killed women who were over the age of 60.

terms of incidence of conduct disorder in childhood, whereas Proulx et al. found that the sexual murderers reported more indiscipline in childhood compared to the rapists. Similarly, Langevin (2003) reported that, compared to other types of sex offenders, sexual murderers started their criminal careers earlier, and more often had been to reform school, were members of criminal gangs, set fires and were cruel to animals. Proulx et al. (2002) also found that his cohort of sexual murderers were more likely to have been victims of incest compared to the rapists, whereas Grubin found no differences between the two groups in terms of their own victimization, sexual or otherwise.

AIM OF THE STUDY

The aim of the present study was to further investigate similarities and differences between rapists and sexual murderers in terms of various factors, including family background, personality, offence and victim characteristics. Hence, the study compares a group of men convicted of murder or manslaughter where there is either clear forensic evidence of a sexual element to the killing, or a sexual component is admitted or suspected, with a group of rapists, which includes men who have committed a penetrative sexual assault (vaginal or anal), against a victim of at least 16 years of age[4] as well as men who have been convicted of a serious sexual assault that probably would have resulted in penetration had they not been disturbed or fought off by the victim. Therefore, this definition is wider than the legal definition of rape.

METHODS

Participants

Participants were drawn from a total of 55 different sex offender treatment programmes running at seven different prison establishments in England between 1998 and 2002. Information was obtained through a combination of interview and case file analysis for 112 rapists and 58 sexual murderers who were waiting to undergo treatment. Of note here is that men scoring 25 or more on the Hare (1991) Psychopathy Checklist – Revised (PCL-R) are generally excluded from the Prison Service treatment programme. Therefore, the current samples do not include 'psychopaths' as described by Hare.

---

[4]It should be noted that some men in this sample have also committed sexual offences against younger victims.

Individuals who agreed to be interviewed were seen for approximately an hour and a quarter, during which they were asked to provide background information on their offence(s) as well as undertake a short intellectual assessment. Participants also completed two self-report personality inventories and a questionnaire about their upbringing. It should be noted here that these questionnaires were completed as part of a battery of tests that the individuals took away with them to complete. For varying reasons, not all individuals completed these questionnaires and therefore sample sizes are considerably smaller for these comparisons. Of the total sample of 170 men, 129 (76%) were Caucasian, 25 (15%) were African-Caribbean, 9 (5%) were Asian and 7 (4%) were from other ethnic groups. These figures are very similar to those reported for the prison population as a whole in England and Wales (Home Office, 2005). As in Grubin's study, rapists and sexual murderers differed significantly on ethnicity, with a greater proportion of rapists (32%) compared to sexual murderers (5%) being from a minority-ethnic background (χ^2 (1) = 11.55, $p<0.01$).

MEASURES

Shipley Institute of Living Scale (Shipley, 1940)

This intellectual assessment is primarily a measure of verbal intelligence, and has been found to be a useful screening instrument for mild degrees of intellectual impairment in individuals of normal original intelligence. The scale consists of a vocabulary test and an abstract thinking test. The extent to which an individual's abstract thinking falls short of his vocabulary score (which is a good measure of pre-morbid IQ) is an indicator of the level of impairment, if present. A WAIS-R (Wechsler Adult Intelligence Scale – Revised; Wechsler, 1981) conversion can be made from this assessment.

Memories of childhood (s-EMBU) (Perris et al., 1980)

This instrument is a self-report measure of an individual's perception of their parents' behaviour towards them as they were growing up. The questionnaire was developed in Sweden, with the title 'EMBU' being an acronym for 'Egna Minnen Beträffande Uppfostran', translated into English as 'One's memories of upbringing'. The questionnaire prompts the respondent to rate, on a four-point Likert scale ranging from 'No, never' to 'Yes, most of the time', the frequency with which they feel their mother and their father, in turn, displayed certain behaviours towards them. In the current study, a shortened version of the questionnaire, developed in 1999 by Arrindell and colleagues was used, consisting of 23 items as opposed to the original 81. This shortened version comprises three factors: rejection; emotional warmth; and overprotection. Recent studies (Arrindell et al., 1999) have demonstrated that this shortened version has good validity and reliability (internal consistency coefficients – Cronbach's alphas = 0.72), and that it can be regarded as a reliable equivalent to its 81-item predecessor.

Multiphasic Sex Inventory (MSI) (Nichols & Molinder, 1984)

This is a 300-item true/false self-report inventory specifically designed to be used with sex offenders. The MSI has 20 scales, six of which are validity scales assessing the respondent's attitudes at time of testing. The remaining 14 scales include a variety of sexual deviance measures, a sex knowledge and belief measure, a measure of sexual dysfunction and an assessment of motivation for treatment. Reliability data has only been reported for those scales (SSD and SO) where internal consistency analysis was possible. Items in all the other MSI scales are not equivalent in item difficulty. Therefore, such analysis was not appropriate. Test–retest reliability studies showed the MSI to be stable over time (scale coefficients ranged between 0.64 and 0.92, and total test–retest correlation was 0.89).

The Multidimensional Assessment of Sex and Aggression (MASA) (Knight, Prentky & Cerce, 1994)

The MASA is a self-report inventory that was specifically designed to assess the multiple dimensions required for MTC:R3 (Massachusetts Treatment Center Typology for Rapists, Version 3), the only empirically tested system of classification for rapists. The inventory consists of six booklets, the first three of which focus on life experiences, including work and social history, child and adolescent behaviours, including own childhood victimization (physical and sexual). In addition, individuals are asked about their lifetime use of pornography.

Millon Clinical Multiaxial Inventory-III (MCMI-III) (Millon, 1994)

This is a standardized 175-item self-report personality questionnaire that has been constructed in line with the Diagnostic and Statistical Manual of Mental Disorders or DSM-IV (American Psychiatric Association, 1994) model. It has been designed to distinguish the more enduring personality characteristics of individuals (axis II) from the acute clinical disorders they display, such as anxiety or depression (axis I). Base-rate (BR) scores are indicative of level of pathology, with BR scores of 75 and above suggesting a personality disorder trait, or presence of a scale's clinical syndrome, and BR scores of 85 or more providing strong support for the presence of the pathological symptom. The assessment procedure is sensitive to an individual's tendency to exaggerate or minimize their difficulties, whether this is by a conscious attempt to distort their answers or as a result of a personality style that inadvertently produces the same result. In addition, three validity questions are included. Endorsement of two or more of these items renders the profile invalid. Invalid profiles were not included in the analysis. Millon (1994) reported test–retest reliability coefficients for the various MCMI-III scales generally in the high 0.80s and low 0.90s over a short retest interval.

Antisocial Personality Questionnaire (APQ) (Blackburn & Fawcett, 1996)

This is a 125-item self-report inventory that measures eight primary traits (self-control, self-esteem, avoidance, paranoid suspicion, resentment, aggression, deviance and extraversion) and two higher-order dimensions (hostile impulsivity and social withdrawal) that are of relevance to antisocial populations. The questionnaire is based on the Special Hospitals Assessment of Personality and Socialisation (SHAPS; Blackburn, 1982) and was developed for assessing dangerous mentally disordered offenders. The questionnaire has been found to have satisfactory reliability (coefficient alpha ranges from 0.77 to 0.87).

RESULTS

Offender characteristics

Table 10.1 shows the differences found between the rapist and sexual murderer samples on individual offender characteristics. Other than IQ data (which were obtained in the pre-treatment interview), information was derived mainly from case files.

Table 10.1 shows that the sexual murderers had a higher estimated IQ (based on the Shipley Institute of Living Scale – SILS) compared to the rapists (t [df $= 153$] $= 3.73$, $p < 0.001$), although both groups' mean IQ was in the average range. The sexual murderer sample were significantly older than the rapist sample (t [df $= 96.2$] $= 2.74$, $p < 0.01$) at the time of interview, although comparatively younger at the time they actually committed their index offence (t [df $= 122.2$] $= 4.22$, $p < 0.001$). The two groups also differed in terms of their relationship status at the time of their index offence ($\chi^2 = 13.69$, $p < 0.01$), with significantly fewer sexual murderers being involved in any sort of relationship; the majority (38%) had no relationship at the time

Table 10.1 Differences in background characteristics

	Valid N^*	Rapists (N = 112)	Valid N^*	Sexual murderers (N = 58)	p^a
Mean age at assessment (sd)	112	34.9 (8.4)	58	39.3 (10.5)	< 0.01
Mean age at index offence (sd)	69	30.4 (9.5)	56	24.2 (7.1)	< 0.001
Mean IQ[b] (sd)	103	93.6 (13.7) (range 65–116)	52	102.2 (13.3) (range 69–119)	< 0.001
Shipley vocabulary raw score		28.5 (6.3)		32.5 (5.7)	< 0.001
Shipley abstract raw score		22.3 (9.7)		26.2 (9.3)	< 0.05
Previous violent offences[c]	94	55 (58%)	54	22 (41%)	< 0.05
Relationship status at time of offence:	89		52		
Married/one main partner		39 (44%)		18 (35%)	
Casual partners only		13 (15%)		6 (11%)	
Recently separated/ relationship breakdown		26 (29%)		8 (15%)	
No relationship at time of the offence		11 (12%)		20 (38)%	< 0.01

*Note that valid sample sizes vary considerably due to the research team's ability to obtain relevant information from case files, which, in turn, was effected by variations in information recording practices between prison establishments.
[a]Independent samples t tests and Pearson χ^2 were used as the statistical measures of significance where appropriate.
[b]WAIS-R equivalents derived from Shipley Institute of Living Scale (SILS). IQ information is only available on those individuals who agreed to be interviewed.
[c]Includes both actual convictions as well as offences admitted but not convicted for.

of their offence, compared to the rapists, the majority of whom (44%) were married, or had one main partner.

Forensic history

The two groups did not differ significantly in terms of age at which they committed their first ever sexual offence (includes index offence where applicable) (mean for rapists: 24.6 (s.d. 8.6); mean for sexual murderers: 22.6 (s.d. 7.3)). Neither were there any differences in terms of amount or type of self-reported juvenile sexual offending, as evidenced from the MASA scales. Forty-nine percent (N = 53) of the rapist sample and 34% (N = 19) of the sexual murderers had committed previous sexual offences, although this difference was not significant. In terms of previous offences in general, however, a greater proportion of the rapist sample had committed violent offences (includes those convicted for, as well as those admitted to but not necessarily convicted for) compared to the sexual murderers ($\chi^2 = 4.3$, $p < 0.05$). Specifically, the rapists scored higher on the 'Armed Robbery and Possession of a Weapon Behavior' scale of the MASA inventory ($z = 2.5$; $p < 0.05$).

Sexual history (interests/paraphilias)

A comparison of the two groups using self-report data from both the MSI and the MASA revealed no differences in terms of types of sexual interests (including paraphilias) or degree of interest in, or preoccupation with, sexual matters.

Own victimization

In line with Grubin's (1994) findings, sexual murderers and rapists did not differ in terms of self-reported childhood victimization. Findings from this study revealed that over half of the individuals in both samples had experienced sexual abuse at the hands of another (rapists: 52%; sexual murderers: 65%), with the average age at which the abuse started being 10 years old. In the majority of cases, the abuse involved a male perpetrator (64% and 61%, respectively) who, on the whole, tended to be a family friend or acquaintance (58%; 37%). However, of note is that in both offender groups, over a third of those who had reported having been sexually abused identified a female perpetrator acting alone (36% of rapists; 38% of sexual murderers). Here, the most frequently reported abusers were family friends or acquaintances, although two of the sexual murderers identified their biological mothers as having victimized them. Where specified, the most extreme act of abuse reported in the majority of both cases was of a penetrative nature (rapists: 37%; sexual murderers: 33%). The vast majority of participants, for whom information was available, reported having been physically abused in childhood (rapists: 82%; sexual murderers: 68%), the most frequent form of which was being hit with an object, for example, a belt or a stick.

General perceptions of upbringing

In terms of the offenders' general perceptions of their upbringing, an overall MANOVA showed no main effect of group, suggesting that, overall, the two offender groups did not differ in the degree to which they felt their parents had behaved in an overprotective, warm or rejecting manner towards them. Unfortunately, although individuals were required to make individual ratings on both their mother and father separately, due to the design of the questionnaire, this was not immediately obvious and the majority of the sample simply made a rating for their parents combined. Therefore, from the current study, it was not possible to determine whether the two groups differed in their relationships with their two parents.

Psychiatric history

Prior contact with psychiatric services was a feature of both groups (difference not significant), with almost half the rapist sample (48%) and over two thirds of the sexual murderers (68%) having had some sort of psychiatric assessment or intervention in the past (excluding pre-sentence evaluation). This ranged from being referred to a psychiatrist as a child, for example, because of conduct disorder problems, to periods of admission to a psychiatric institution in adulthood.

Personality assessment

In terms of personality, results comparing the two groups' MCMI-III scores showed that, overall, they differed in their response styles (F (3,97) = 2.82, $p < 0.05$), in that the rapists appeared to be more self-revealing (higher scores on the Disclosure Scale) compared to the sexual murderers. However, on the main personality scales, no main effect of offender type was found, indicating that the samples of rapists and sexual murderers did not differ significantly overall on personality variables according to this measure. Analysis of BR cut-offs in terms of the proportion of each of the two groups scoring in the clinically significant ranges on each of the various scales revealed no differences between the groups.

Table 10.2 shows the proportion of each of the two groups with BR scores of 75 or above and 85 or above. It can be seen from Table 10.2 that the rapists and sexual murderers have similar elevated prevalence rates of avoidant and antisocial personality traits, anxiety and alcohol dependence. The two groups differed, however, in terms of mean scores on three of the subscales of the APQ. These differences are shown in Table 10.3.

Table 10.3 shows that the rapist sample had significantly higher mean scores on the paranoid suspicion, resentment and self-esteem subscales, the latter reflecting poorer self-esteem, feelings of dysphoria and helplessness, and worry (Blackburn & Fawcett, 1996). These findings might suggest that the rapists, as a group, are more likely to have a negative view of others and life in general, compared to the sexual murderers. In terms of how the two groups' scores relate to a normative sample (males only),

Table 10.2 Percentage of rapists and sexual murderers with BR scores over 74 and over 84 on the personality and clinical syndrome scales of the MCMI-III

MCMI-III scale	Rapists (%) (N = 58) BR score		Sexual murderers (%) (N = 44) BR score		
	75–84	> 84	75–84	> 84	p
Schizoid	10.3	3.4	6.8	0.0	n.s.
Avoidant	19	6.9	20.5	2.3	n.s.
Depressive	17.2	10.3	25	9.1	n.s.
Dependent	13.8	3.4	11.4	11.4	n.s.
Histrionic	3.4	1.7	4.5	0.0	n.s.
Narcissistic	6.9	3.4	2.3	0.0	n.s.
Antisocial	24.1	5.2	15.9	6.8	n.s.
Sadistic	3.4	3.4	4.5	0.0	n.s.
Compulsive	8.6	1.7	6.8	0.0	n.s.
Negativistic (passive-aggressive)	12.1	8.6	6.8	6.8	n.s.
Masochistic (self-defeating)	12.1	6.9	15.9	6.8	n.s.
Schizotypal	6.9	1.7	0.0	2.3	n.s.
Borderline	8.6	8.6	4.5	4.5	n.s.
Paranoid	1.7	8.6	0.0	4.5	n.s.
Anxiety	27.6	13.8	36.4	18.2	n.s.
Somatoform	0.0	0.0	0.0	2.3	n.s.
Bipolar: manic	3.4	0.0	0.0	2.3	n.s.
Dysthymia	12.1	3.4	18.2	0.0	n.s.
Alcohol dependence	25.9	6.9	15.9	9.1	n.s.
Drug dependence	15.5	6.9	13.6	2.3	n.s.
Post-traumatic stress disorder	3.4	0.0	9.1	2.3	n.s.
Thought disorder	1.7	0.0	0.0	2.3	n.s.
Major depression	1.7	5.2	2.3	2.3	n.s.
Delusional disorder	0.0	1.7	0.0	2.3	n.s.

t-scores were obtained and the proportion of scores falling one standard deviation (SD) or more above the mean were calculated. Results showed that 44% of the rapist sample, compared to only 17.9% of the sexual murderer sample, had scores of one SD or more above the mean on the

Table 10.3 Differences in mean scores on the antisocial personality questionnaire (APQ)

APQ subscale	Rapists (N = 58) Mean	sd	Sexual murderers (N = 44) Mean	sd	F	p
Paranoid suspicion	6.16	4.64	3.59	3.76	5.17	< 0.01
Resentment	8.99	4.64	6.41	4.14	5.64	< 0.05
Self-esteem	7.61	5.09	5.03	4.19	6.42	< 0.05

paranoid suspicion scale ($p < 0.01$), 38.7% of rapists, compared to 20.5% of sexual murderers, scored more than one sd above the mean on resentment ($p = 0.05$), and 42.7% of rapists, compared to 17.9% of sexual murderers, fell into this category on the self-esteem subscale ($p < 0.01$). In addition, a greater proportion of the rapists scored beyond the normal range on the deviance subscale (rapists: 48%; sexual murderers: 17.9%, $p < 0.01$), a scale measuring general criminality and delinquency, as well as on the Factor 1 (impulsivity) scale (rapists: 37.3%; sexual murderers: 15.4%, $p < 0.05$), a scale which, according to Blackburn and Fawcett (1996) is a general factor of awareness and expression of hostile, rebellious and aggressive impulses, with higher scores reflecting impulsivity, antagonism and noncompliance.

Victim and offence characteristics

Table 10.4 shows how the two offender groups differed in terms of victim characteristics, relationship with victim and offence context.

The findings in the current study relating to victim age are similar to those found by Grubin (1994). Table 10.4 shows that the two samples differed significantly in terms of victim age (data relating to victim age includes all sexual convictions for an individual), where the average age of

Table 10.4 Differences in victim and offence characteristics

Victim characteristics	Rapists (N = 112)		Sexual murderers (N = 58)		p
	Valid N*		Valid N*		
Mean age of youngest victim (sd)[a]	107	25 (15.4) (Range: 3–88 yrs)	57	34.2 (23.1) (Range: 7–86)	< 0.05
Offended against adults only (>16 yrs old)[a]	112	99 (88.4%)	58	48 (82.8%)	n.s.
Offended against children only (<16 yrs old)[a]	112	0[b]	58	9 (15.5%)	n.a.
Offended against adults and children[a]	112	13 (11.6%)	58	1 (1.7%)	< 0.05
Offended against older adult (>65yrs old)[a]	108	6 (5.6%)	57	9 (15.8%)	< 0.05

*Note that valid sample sizes vary considerably due to the research team's ability to obtain relevant information from case files, which, in turn, was affected by variations in information recording practices between prison establishments.
[a]Includes all prior sexual convictions. Therefore, offences such as indecent assault and gross indecency may also be included here.
[b]Note: only men who had an offence of rape or attempted rape against an adult were included in the study.

the youngest victim was higher for the sexual murderers compared to the rapists (t [df $= 83.3$] $= 2.53$, $p < 0.05$). In addition, a greater proportion (16%) of sexual murderers compared to rapists (6%) were found to have offended against 'older adults' (defined here as being over the age of 65) ($\chi^2 = 4.73$, $p < 0.05$). However, this finding must be interpreted with caution, given that it is only as a result of the victim dying that the perpetrator becomes a 'sexual murderer' as opposed to a 'rapist'. As elderly victims are perhaps less likely to survive a violent attack, those who offend against this victim group are more likely to find themselves convicted of sexual murder.

For both offender groups, in approximately half of the cases (rapists: 56%; sexual murderers: 50%), the victims were strangers, i.e., unknown to the perpetrator until that day. Thirty-one percent of the rapists and 21% of the sexual murderers had attacked complete strangers, where no prior conversation or interaction had taken place. An example of this is where a victim is selected and followed, then attacked from behind. Prostitutes accounted for 8% of the rape victims and only 2% of the murder victims. Alcohol or nonprescribed-drug use featured in the majority of cases, with 75% of the rapists and 77% of the sexual murderers having consumed alcohol and/or taken illicit substances, such as cannabis, prior to the index offence. In terms of self-reported lifetime substance misuse, analysis of the MASA data revealed no differences between the two groups. Of note was that a significant minority of offenders (12% of rapists and 7% of sexual murderers) committed their index offence with a co-defendant (difference not significant).

DISCUSSION

As in previous studies, fewer differences than similarities were found between men who had killed in a sexual context compared to men who had sexually attacked but not killed a woman. However, the current study did show that sexual murderers were less likely than rapists to have been in a relationship prior to their offence, perhaps supporting previous findings that sexual murderers are more socially isolated. The victims of the sexual murderers also tended to be older, although, as previously mentioned, this is somewhat of a tautology, as rapists only become sexual murderers if the victim dies, and elderly victims are perhaps more likely to die as a result of their injuries, if severe. Therefore, rather than concluding that sexual murderers are more likely drawn to older victims, it might be said that, among sexually aggressive men, there are some who attack older victims and sometimes, those victims die. Having said this, clearly, there is a subcategory of offenders who kill intentionally, such as the sadistic murderer described in detail by Brittain (1970), but this description is by no means true of all 'sexual murderers' and may well also characterize a proportion of 'rapists' whose victims do not die because the offender is disturbed in the commission of the offence, or else the victim survives despite extensive injuries.

A comparison of the two offender groups in terms of personality characteristics as measured by the MCMI-III and the APQ revealed few differences. The rapists were more disclosing about their problems and scored higher on scales measuring historical deviance (nonsexual), paranoid suspicion and resentment. In addition, they reported lower self-esteem. Blackburn and Fawcett (1996) found a negative correlation between the self-esteem subscale of the APQ and length of detainment, showing that individuals detained for longer tended to have higher self-esteem, were more trusting and more sociable and friendly. These findings would concur with those of the current study, where the sexual murderers may well have spent a lot longer incarcerated than the rapists, given the nature of their crime, and consequently acclimatized to prison life, although, unfortunately, length of detainment prior to interview was not measured. The findings that the rapists were more disclosing, yet more paranoid and resentful are hard to interpret, but again, may reflect differences in their current situation as opposed to pre-existing traits, in that they may still harbour feelings of bitterness and resentment in relation to their conviction, perhaps towards their victim, who they may feel provoked them, or was 'asking for it'. Arguably, due to the unequivocal nature of their offence, the sexual murderers can have fewer grievances in relation to their conviction. Alternatively, the real difference may only lie in the degree to which they are prepared to acknowledge such feelings, rather than the feelings themselves. It is of note that the difference in the two groups' scores on the paranoid subscale of the MCMI-III was not significant once adjustments had been made for response style. In sum, these findings support those of Proulx et al. (2002), who found that rapists and sexual murderers have extremely similar personality styles and similar prevalences of personality disorders.

CONCLUSION

In summary, the current research compared the characteristics of incarcerated rapists and sexual murderers in terms of personal background, personality, offence and victim characteristics. A caveat to the findings is that they do not necessarily relate to psychopathic individuals, as these were not included in the study and therefore caution should be exercised in generalizing the findings to all rapists and sexual murderers in prison. In addition, not all individuals approached by the research team were prepared to complete psychometric tests and therefore comparisons on these measures are not without bias. However, from the subsamples studied, there is little evidence to support the hypothesis that rapists and sexual murderers differ from each other, either in terms of their life experiences, personality or offence characteristics. In fact, it might be concluded that, to a large extent, sexual murderers are rapists who ended up killing their victims, either through extreme anger, as a way of covering their tracks, or because the victim was elderly. Having said this, clearly there is a subcategory of individuals who have been primarily motivated to kill, either because the killing itself is arousing or because they are motivated to engage in postmortem sexual activity. However, excluding this category, few differences can be seen when comparing rapists and sexual murderers, as a whole, on static background characteristics or personality features. The question as to how, or if, the two groups differ in terms of dynamic or changeable factors, such as attitudes and beliefs, remains, and should be the focus of future research, as it is these which are primarily targeted in treatment, and which may, if differences are found, lead to differences in treatment provision between the two offender groups.

Chapter 11

IDENTIFICATION OF MOTIVATIONS FOR SEXUAL MURDER

Dawn Fisher and Anthony R. Beech

INTRODUCTION

Very little has been written on the belief systems of sexual murderers. Given that the underlying motive for an individual committing a particular offence is best formulated by accessing the offender's beliefs and attitudes about themselves, the world in general and their offending behaviour (Ward & Keenan, 1999), it is important to find ways of assessing these beliefs. This can then help to understand the function of the behaviour for each individual, which is necessary for identifying level of future risk and treatment for this type of sexual offender. In this chapter we will describe a study where we investigated the underlying cognitions of a group of sexual murderers in the UK and how their cognitions related to their offending. From this work we were able to find further evidence of a classification system of sexual murderers and rapists (sexual aggressors of women), which we believe may be useful in the treatment of these groups. Before we describe this study we want to first give a very brief overview of some of the classification systems, which have had an input into our thinking about the motivations for sexual murder and the work that has shaped our thinking over the last few years.

Sexual Murderers: A Comparative Analysis and New Perspectives Edited by Jean Proulx Éric Beauregard, Maurice Cusson and Alexandre Nicole
© 2007 John Wiley & Sons, Ltd.

CLASSIFICATION OF SEXUAL MURDERERS

It is widely acknowledged that sexual murders are committed for different reasons and that different 'types' of sexual murderers have different motivations for offending. In understanding the different types and motivations of those who commit such acts it is important to look at the characteristics of the different groups to determine whether they are indeed distinct groups or whether it may simply be due to circumstantial reasons that they have committed one type of crime rather than another. Elsewhere in this book there is a more thorough review of classification systems of sexual murderers, but for our purposes we would note that classification systems in the forensic area, can be said to broadly classify (from Blackburn, 1993): (1) *pragmatically* by examining the offence demographics in order to generate useful categories of offender; (2) by *identifying attributes* of central concern to a particular theory and distinguishing types of offenders based on this; (3) by *clinical descriptions*, which represent the prototypical features of particular types of offenders; and (4) by using *statistical techniques* to generate psychometric profiles that determine group membership. It is worth noting here that these different approaches have tended to be used by different agencies/professionals depending upon their needs. For those involved in crime investigation, often the pragmatic approach is used. For those involved in treatment, clinical description is the preferred method. For academics furthering theory, identifying attributes is the preferred method, and for those involved in risk assessment, statistical techniques are often preferred. We think this framework is also useful in grouping the different approaches to the classification of sexual murder, which we will outline below.

Pragmatic classification

The FBI has developed the probably best-known pragmatic classification, and types murders into *organized* and *disorganized* (Ressler, Burgess, Douglas et al., 1986). *Organized* murders are planned, conscious and methodical acts in which the victim is typically not previously known, whereas *disorganized* murders are spontaneous, where often the victim is known to the perpetrator. Individuals are generally typed as organized/ disorganized by the clues left at the crime scene (FBI Law Enforcement Bulletin, 1985). An organized killer in this system is described as 'socially competent', 'average to above-average intelligence', 'to have high birth-order status' and 'be more likely to use alcohol with the crime'. The disorganized killer, on the other hand, is identified as displaying the opposite characteristics in this system. In terms of crime-scene differences, the organized killer demands a submissive victim, while a disorganized killer exhibits sudden violence to the victim to gain submission; the organized killer hides the body, while the disorganized killer leaves the body in view. Douglas et al. (1992) developed two further categories of murder: *mixed* and *sadistic*. The mixed category contains elements of both the organized and disorganized categories, while an offender who gains satisfaction from causing suffering and pain, through torture, commits a sadistic killing.

Pragmatic analysis of the crime scene can be said to be useful, as it has suggested various motivations for different types of sexual murder, i.e. sadistic, instrumental and anger. Many authors have suggested that sexual murders are motivated by *sadistic impulses* (e.g. Dietz, Hazelwood & Warren, 1990; Prentky, Knight et al., 1989; Warren, Hazelwood & Dietz, 1996), where the act of killing is the primary sexual motive. Here the fusion of sexual assault and killing (Myers et al., 1999) is often characterized by an overt (penile penetration), or symbolic sexual assault (such as insertion of a foreign object into one of the victim's orifices). Others have suggested (i.e. Hazelwood & Douglas, 1980) that for some sexual murderers, killing may play an *instrumental* role in either the commission of a sexual assault, by keeping the victim quiet during the sexual attack to avoid detection, or by avoiding subsequent identification by the victim. Revitch (1980) also notes that some sexual murders may be motivated by *anger*, where there is an angry outburst, or in response to rejection of a proposed or actual sexual advance such that the victim is killed.

Theory-led classification

An example of the theory-led approach is Keppel and Walter's (1999) system of classification of rape murderers, based on work by Hazelwood and Burgess (1987) on a typology of rapists. Keppel and Walter suggest that this approach is more likely to address the behaviours, motivational continua and effects of experiential learning by the perpetrators of sexual murder. Therefore this is more a theory of serial sexual killers. Keppel and Walter suggested four categories of sexual murderer:

1. *Power-assertive rape/murder*. Here the rape is planned, but the murder is an unplanned response of increasing aggression to ensure control of the victim. Therefore, the killing is about exerting control and overcoming resistance. The victim is usually a stranger who has been found by chance—in the home, if the perpetrator is a burglar—or on the street. The killer gains a feeling of power and control through the rape and killing of his victim. According to Keppel and Walter the killer usually leaves an organized crime scene in order to cover up and protect his identity.
2. *Power-reassurance rape/murder*. This type of crime is typified by a planned rape and the unplanned 'overkill' of the victim. The crime is motivated by an idealized fantasy of sexual seduction, which the murderer attempts to act out with his victim. When the victim does not respond in the way

he imagines, panic or a feeling of failure drives his murder/assault through which he gains a sense of control. The perpetrator feels a need for 'emotional catharsis and victim control' (Keppel & Walter, 1999, p. 424). The perpetrator is described as acting out his sexual fantasies with his victim after death. This may extend to keeping souvenirs or news-paper clippings to extend the relationship. The perpetrator is likely to leave a mixed crime scene.

3. *Anger-retaliatory rape/murder*. This type of crime is typified by a planned rape, with the murder resulting from a violent attack, to retaliate against or get revenge on women. Hence the murder is due to a sense of grievance by the perpetrator towards the victim, who he feels has power and control over him and who has been critical of him. The victim may also act as a surrogate for the woman he feels angry towards. The rape/assault is often incomplete, as the murderer is unable to have an erection. The perpetrator is likely to leave a disorganized crime scene.

4. *Anger-excitation rape/murder*. Here the rape and the murder are both planned, with the aim of inflicting fear and pain on the victim for the gratification of the perpetrator. The sadistic satisfaction is gained from the process of killing and not in the death. The assault on the victim is likely to be lengthy and ritualistic in character.

The above example of a theory-led classification again highlights the fact that there are differing motivations for sexual murder, here identified as power, anger and sadistic pleasure. However, the weakness of the theory-led approach is the strength of the theory that the classification system is based on and the fact that it is actually based on little empirical evidence, and, as with the pragmatic approach, imputes motives from crime-scene analysis rather than any clinical insights.

Clinical description

The third approach to classification is by clinical description. An example of this approach is reported by Clarke and Carter (2000), who identified four types of sexual murderers through work with this group in a specialized treatment centre in Brixton Prison in London in the late 1990s:

1. *Sexually motivated*. In this group, characterized by a primary sexual motivation to kill, there are sophisticated and detailed masturbatory fantasies of killing, where the victim is usually unknown and has been specifically targeted, and the method of killing is sexually stimulating to the offender. These could best be described as sadistic murderers in previous classification schemes.

2. *Sexually triggered/aggressive control*. This type of sexual murderer is characterized by Clarke and Carter as having a primary motivation to

sexually offend, where the killing is intentional, e.g. to keep the victim quiet during the offence or to avoid subsequent detection by removing the main witness, i.e. the victim, of their sexually assaultative behaviour.

3. *Sexually triggered/aggressive dyscontrol.* This type of sexual murderer has no prior intention to kill or sexually offend. The offender explains the killing as having resulted from something the victim said or did in a sexual context, triggering a substantial sense of grievance held for some time against an intimate party. Extreme violence or humiliation against the victim takes place in the offence, suggesting loss of control and perspective. Sexual intercourse may or may not take place, but violence against the victim has sexual characteristics, e.g. mutilation of the genital area.

4. *Sexually triggered-neuropsychological dysfunction.* Clarke and Carter describe this type of sexual murderer, where there is an unclear motivation to kill or for that matter sexually offend. They suggest that such an offender would behave aggressively in a sexual context, and that such a perpetrator had led a life where sexual encounters have led to feelings of aggression or that aggressive encounters have led to sexual arousal. It should be noted that this group was generated from one offender with clear neuropsychological deficits, and therefore may not say much about a particular group of sexual offenders.

The clinical types identified by Clarke and Carter could be said to have close correspondence to the motivational types suggested by pragmatic classification, namely sadistic, instrumental and anger/grievance-driven. Clarke and Carter have also made some attempt to suggest how those offering treatment should be aware of the differing treatment needs of these different types of offenders. However, this is only briefly mentioned in Clarke and Carter's published work and really only touches upon the sexual component of the sexual murder, and says little about how to deal with the sadistic impulses of Group 1 and the anger and grievance aspects of Group 3 offenders.

Statistical description

The final approach to classification of offenders, according to Blackburn (1993) is the statistical approach. As far as we are aware there has been no other approach, apart from our own, that has attempted to derive a statistical classification system of sexual murderers. Hence the rest of the chapter will illustrate how we have generated a statistical description of sexual murderers based on their belief systems and what this may say about treatment. Here we investigated the presence and type of the 'implicit theories' held by the offenders (Beech, Fisher & Ward, 2005).

It has been argued by Ward (2000) that sexual offenders' cognitive distortions emerge from underlying causal theories rather than stem from unrelated, independent beliefs. In effect, these underlying beliefs generate the offence-supportive attitudes/cognitive distortions that are measured at the surface level (Ward et al., 1997). Ward (2000) further suggests that these beliefs are in effect 'implicit theories' (ITs) that the offender has about the world. These theories are similar to scientific theories in that they are used to explain, predict and interpret interpersonal phenomena. Polaschek and Ward (2002) suggested the following five ITs for describing rapist motivations: women are unknowable; women as sexual objects; dangerous world; male sex drive is uncontrollable; and entitlement. We (Beech, Ward & Fisher, 2006) have found evidence for the presence of these five ITs in rapists. Our hypothesis regarding sexual murderers was that the same ITs would be present in this group, suggesting that in a number of ways sexual murderers are not too dissimilar to rapists in terms of their motivations to offend.

METHODS

Subjects

The study involved examining transcripts of interviews of 28 sexual murderers. They were all serving a life sentence for murder. The murder was judged to have a definite sexual element and all the subjects had been offered treatment for sexual offending in the UK prison system (for an outline of the treatment provided see Beech, Oliver, Fisher & Beckett, 2006). At the time of the interviews the entire sample had completed the treatment programme. Of the total sample, 24 had committed their offences against adult women, three against young girls, and one against a nine-year-old boy. Thirteen men (46%) had committed offences against a stranger; two (7%) against an ex-wife/ex-partner; three (11%) against a family member; nine (32%) against a friend/acquaintance; and one against a prostitute. Their average age when they had committed the offence for which they were currently incarcerated was 23.82 (SD 7.29). Twenty-four men in the sample were white; four were African-Caribbean. Eight of the subjects (29%) had previous convictions for sexual offences, nine (32%) had previous convictions for violent offences, and 18 (64%) had previous convictions for nonsexual/nonviolent offences. Just under a third (nine) were in a relationship at the time of the offence, four (14%) were in a casual relationship, and four had been in a relationship that had broken up at the time of the offence. In 11 cases (39%) there was no evidence that they were in a relationship. Eleven men reported that they had received some form of psychiatric treatment prior to the commission of the murder (three for depression, four for personality disorder and four unspecified).

Procedure

All men participated in a semi-structured interview following completion of a sex offender treatment programme to address the sexual aspects of their offending. As part of this, in interview, they were asked to give an account of how they saw their offending and what had led to their offence. Care was taken to use open-ended questioning and avoid leading or closed questions. Typically, questions in the first part of the interview would be about: who they had offended against, whether they knew the victim prior to the offence and what had led to the offence. Prompt questions were asked about the offender's motivation. Other areas covered in the interview were: their feelings at the time of the offence towards their victim (if he or she was known to them), and others in their lives; distal and proximal antecedents of their offending, including fantasies around sex and violence; sexual behaviours they had committed in the offence/s, and the modus operandi of the killing. Where appropriate, questions were also asked about their previous offences. Other prompt questions were asked of the offender on the basis of their answers to these questions.

All interviews were tape-recorded, transcribed, and coded for the presence of ITs by two independent raters. Both of these raters looked at the context of the whole offence chain before identifying whether an IT was present or not. There were some borderline cases which required that a third rater make the decision as to whether an IT, identified by one of the raters, was present or not. Present. Any additional offence-supportive beliefs that did not fit into one of the five categories reported by Polaschek and Ward were put into a miscellaneous category. Once the coding was completed, this category was examined to see if there were any other ITs of significance. The inter-rater reliability of whether an IT was present was high across the two raters (Spearman's rho $= 0.77$, $p < 0.001$).

RESULTS

The results of the study showed that the same five ITs found in rapists were also present in the sexual murderer sample. It was clear that there were no appreciable differences in the kinds of ITs exhibited by rapists and individuals who had committed a sexual murder. It therefore seems that both types of offender hold the same range of underlying beliefs and attitudes. It may be that the differences between them are less than may be assumed and that situational circumstances may be more an explanation as to why one individual ends up killing his victim when others do not. We will now examine each of the five ITs in terms of their prevalence in the sample.

1. Dangerous world

This IT relates to how the offender sees the world as a dangerous place and believes that other people are likely to behave in an abusive and rejecting manner in order to promote their own interests. Therefore, it is necessary to fight back and achieve dominance and control over other people. This involves punishing individuals who appear to inflict harm on the offender. If women are perceived as threats, they may become victims of sexual abuse. The beliefs and desires of other people, particularly those signifying malevolent intentions, are a focus of this IT.

This IT was the most common in the sample; it was present in 22 (79%) of the cases and typically was related to extreme episodes of violence and anger. The form this IT took in the sexual murderers' descriptions of their offending behaviour was that of generalized malevolence. The individual concerned viewed other people as being unreliable and having treated them abusively and unjustly. This view resulted in entrenched feelings of resentment and anger and the use of interpersonal strategies of retaliation. Thus many of the sexual murderers decided to retaliate against the individuals who they believed had wronged them, or else simply selected someone else that they could vent their frustrations against as a form of displacement of their anger. A typical example is the situation where an individual had become angry with a specific individual such as their sexual partner and then gone out in an angry mood state and offended against another female, almost as a substitute.

Examples

Responses to the question 'What do you think the motivation for your offence was?' 'I committed the offence because I was not thinking of anybody but myself, I was taking my anger, bitterness, my hatred and my frustration out'.

Another offender said that, 'The pain I was feeling I wanted to transfer it onto someone else and all that...because it's stuff that's happened in the past and also stuff that was going on around at the time. It meant quite a lot too, everything just boiling up, boiling it all up, then it all came out at the same time. I was abused as a child by my foster father...I think it was kind of like, the humiliation part was from then, the abuse was, it was all inside of me and I just wanted it out, I wanted it out'.

While another said, 'We went to a night-club, started to have sex and she refused to have sex with me and because of all the anger and the emotions of the previous events. A break-up previous to that, an assault charge previous to that all got on top of me that night and I took all my frustrations and anger out on X.' In terms of what he did to the victim this offender said 'OK now you've been hurt as much as I've been hurt, you won't mess me, or anybody else, about again'.

2. Male sex drive is uncontrollable

Individuals who hold this IT believe that men's sexual energy is difficult to control and that women have a key role in its loss of control. Many offenders attribute the causes of their offending to external factors (i.e. external to the self and personal responsibility). These factors can be located in the victim or in other features of the environment (e.g. availability of alcohol). According to this IT, it follows that a woman denying reasonable sexual access is one cause of loss of control for men.

This was the second most common IT, being present in 20 men (71%) of the sample. There were three strands to this IT. First, the participants would often report feeling powerless in their lives and unable to control their actions, including their sexual behaviour. Second, the aggressive emotions that resulted in the murder were often described as external to the person; they simply overwhelmed him. Third, individuals described feeling over-whelmed by their sexual fantasies and the associated sexual urges. The sexual element in their offending was viewed as particularly compelling and compulsive in nature. It was as if the sexual fantasies took on a life of their own and it was inevitable that sooner or later the individual would rape and/or murder a woman. In some instances, the fantasies contained explicitly sadistic components that revolved around the infliction of pain and suffering (and death) on the victim.

Examples

One offender, when asked about what he had been fantasizing about prior to the sexual murder reported: 'All sorts. Rapes, murders. . .all kinds of fantasies. Anything that made me feel good as, I would fantasize about. The majority of them were about; I suppose rape, yeah, because sex became involved then. . . It was mostly about having somebody within my power so I could, because I felt power-less, at the time'.

Another offender said: 'I lost it. I lost my temper and I lost it all together. I tried to dominate physically, by using physical force and then she went for me, that's where it was. . .I've got to get the upper hand here and that's where I lost it and the physical violence started'.

Another offender, to explain the escalation of his behaviour to the point where he had targeted someone to rape and subsequently murder, said that. . .'things have built up for a long time. . .which allowed me in a way to chose a deviant set of behaviours as a sexual outlet, peeping and exposing and stuff like that. If I liked someone I'd expose myself to them. . .On the night I killed X if that had been someone else I would have chosen that person [to rape]. I recognized her so I assumed that she'd recognize me and I panicked'.

3. Entitlement

This IT is based on the core idea that some people are superior to and more important than others. Because of their superior status, such individuals have the right to assert their needs above others, and to expect that this will be acknowledged and agreed to by those who are judged to be less important. The source of legitimacy for this sense of entitlement might be based on gender, class or some other factor. For example, men might be viewed as more powerful and important than women, and therefore have the right to have their sexual needs met when they want and with whom they want. In this IT the desires and beliefs of the offender are paramount and those of the victim ignored or viewed as only of secondary importance.

This IT was found in 12 men (43%) of the sample. There was a sense in this IT that offenders were entitled to take sex if they wanted it because they were males, more physically powerful or simply deserved it because the woman concerned had sexually aroused them or was in an existing (or had been) relationship with them.

Examples

One offender reported that he was being 'strung along' by a prostitute, saying: 'I got angry because she was stringing me along, playing games, if you know what I mean she wanted more money...I thought well I'm going to have sex with her whatever... I thought she's a prostitute and she's holding out for more money.'

While another offender said that he ... got round there [the victim's house] and I was talking to her and during the course of the evening, it was pretty late, say about half an hour into the conversation. I was telling her about my problems...and I made a pass at her. Which was, I kissed her for a couple of seconds. She pushed me away so because of not being able to handle the rejection, I took my frustrations and anger out on her which I regret and after that I killed her which was, how should I say, very over the top, but I'm used to getting everything my own way y'know?'.

4. Women as sex objects

Men holding this IT view women as existing in a constant state of sexual reception, and individuals who hold this IT believe that women have been created to meet the sexual needs of men. In this IT, women's most significant needs and desires centre around the sexual domain. Therefore it is anticipated that women will constantly desire sex, even if it is coerced or violent, and that they are primarily sexual entities. Individuals with this IT also believe that women should always be receptive and available to meet men's sexual needs when they arise. One implication of this theory is that there is often a discrepancy between what women say and what they actually want. This inconsistency arises because their sexual needs may be unknown to them. This aspect is different from the 'Women are unknowable/Women are dangerous' IT in that it is not that women deliberately deceive men; it is that they simply don't know that they are fundamentally 'sex objects', i.e. they are fundamentally unaware of the unconscious messages their bodies are emitting.

This IT was only present in nine (32%) of the cases. In this IT, the participants reported viewing women as sexual objects or existing merely as recipients of males' sexual attention. They were regarded as conduits of male sexual interest and not viewed as autonomous beings with preferences and interests of their own. This IT functioned to set up expectancy in the offender where he expected sex; if it was not forthcoming, he would respond by becoming aggressive.

Examples

One offender described his life prior to the offence as, 'I took on so much y'know proving myself to be top dog at work, living a life of a lie, with having two girlfriends, lying to them, seeing women as sex objects, having bets with work colleagues over how many you could bed, things like that'.

Another offender who was asked whether the focus on reducing deviant sexual thoughts in therapy had been useful to him said, 'I had a tendency to sexualize, I still have a tendency to sexualize women, is that a trait of a sex offender or is that just me being . . .a Neanderthal type man? A bit of both I suppose. I think what I learnt is not so much a problem per se, initially it's where you go, that's the problem, that's where the problem starts to arise. Personally if I saw a women with a great arse, I personally do not consider that to be a problem. If I pursue it and it starts leading into thoughts of offending, or I start to properly sexualize this women, then there would be a problem.'

5. Women are unknowable/Women are dangerous

This IT was relatively rare, as it was only found in five cases. With this IT, women were viewed as deliberately misleading men and causing them to feel inadequate and rejected. The participants expressed frustration and confusion and tended to behave in a sexually aggressive way to teach the women a lesson. Thus the key idea seems to be that women are believed to be responsible for failed relationships and intentionally set out to make life difficult for some men.

Examples

About actions committed on his murder victim, the offender said that, 'So what I had to do then. . .was to humiliate her enough to satisfy my need, if you like, to say O.K now you've been hurt as much as I've been hurt, you won't mess me or anybody else about again, and I said to myself she wasn't dead. . .'.

Of an assault on a previous girlfriend two weeks earlier the offender said that, . . .she went into a verbal assault on me which I couldn't handle so I said to myself the only way I can get you back for hurting me is to rape you. So [I] dragged her up stairs'.

About his motivation another offender said, 'I used to think it was a case of just rape and it being a sex thing but it wasn't, it was much deeper than that, and I realize I was carrying a lot of bad attitude about women, and the way I've not dealt with rejection at all, it was my fault, I was the one carrying all the crap if you were, because I never coped with it and dealt with it and it all came out on my victim that day'.

Miscellaneous

There were very few cognitions that could not be coded into the five ITs and those, on closer inspection, were found to be closely related to one of these primary categories. A number of the participants stated that they committed the offence because they were expressing displaced anger toward a parent or caregiver because of the abuse they had inflicted on them as children. This is really an example of the 'Dangerous world' IT. Other men described feeling sexually attracted to women or to the prospect of violent sex. On reflection, it was felt that these were instances of 'Women are sexual beings', 'Uncontrollability', or 'Dangerous world' ITs.

Categorization of sexual murderers by implicit theories

Having found the same ITs in a group of sexual murderers as in rapists we then went on to look at the pattern of occurrence of the ITs. 'Dangerous world' was present in 79% of cases and 'Male sex drive is uncontrollable' in 71%. By a process of sorting the most common ITs, it was found that there appeared to be three main groups in these data. When these groups were compared on a number of offence demographics (see Table 11.1), clear differences were found between the groups. These are described below.

From Table 11.1 it can be seen that *Group 1* can best be described as a 'sadistic' group, in that they report that they were motivated by a prior intention to kill, and by violent and sadistic thoughts and fantasies. Some men in this group also reported specific thoughts around control and domination. The ITs present for this group were 'Dangerous world', 'Male sex drive is uncontrollable', and, in half of the group, 'Entitlement' (where the offender holds that his desires and beliefs are paramount). The victims were significantly more likely to be targeted strangers than in the other two groups combined. A high level of sexualized violence was committed in these men's offences and the level of sexual mutilation was high (significantly more likely to have occurred than in the other two groups combined), as was sexual interference after death. Mutilation and interference included acts such as: exposure of, and bites to, the breast; partial severance of the breast; and vaginal mutilation. This behaviour can be considered ritualistic in nature. In at least one case the offender committed necrophilic acts on the victim's body. Strangulation was often used as a method of killing in the group, which was rare in the other two groups. Strangulation can be considered as a method of killing where the perpetrator has complete control over the life of the victim at all times until she/he has died. Members of this group were found to be the most dangerous repeat sexual offenders, in that half were rated as having a high or very high risk of sexual reconviction, as measured by the actuarial risk predictor, Risk Matrix 2000 (Thornton et al., 2003).

Group 2 is best described as being 'violently motivated'. The members of this group were characterized by being driven by grievance towards women. Most men in this group reported that their motivation to offend was primarily driven by anger and resentment towards women. The

Table 11.1 Offence characteristics of men, grouped by the presence/absence of 'Dangerous world'/'Male sex drive is uncontrollable' implicit theories

	Group 1 (N = 14) (Dangerous world + Male sex drive uncontrollable)	Group 2 (N = 8) (Dangerous world)	Group 3 (N = 6) (male sex drive is uncontrollable)
Reported motivation	To carry out fantasies	Grievance	Avoid detection
Reported thoughts/ fantasies prior to murder	3 (21%) intent to murder 3 (21%) rape/murder 3 (21%) sadistic 2 (14%) control/ domination 3 (21%) none reported	7 (87%) resentment/ anger towards women 1 (13%) sexual fantasies	5 (83%) sexual fantasies 1 (17%) intent to murder
Method of killing	6 (43%) strangulation 5 (36%) stabbed 1 (7%) stabbed/set on fire 1 (7%) beaten 1 (7%) beaten/killed by train	5 (63%) beaten 1 (12%) drowned 1 (12%) stabbed 1 (12%) suffocated	3 (50%) stabbed 2 (33%) beaten 1 (17%) strangulation
Targeted stranger	9 (65%)*	2 (25%)	1 (17%)
Known victim	2 (28%)	4 (50%)	2 (33%)
Age of victim (SD)	36.79 (6.24) range 9–86	38.25 (10.33) range 14–85	29.17(6.12) range 18–56
Sexual mutilation	9 (65%)*	1 (13%)	1 (17%)
Sexual interference after death	5 (36%)	3 (37%)	1 (17%)
History of violence against women	10 (71%)*	2 (25%)	1 (17%)
Risk of sexual reconviction[1]			
High/ Very High	7(50%)*	2(25%)	0(0%)
Medium	5(36%)	4(50%)	3(50%)
Low	2(14%)	2(25%)	3(50%)
Previous sexual convictions	5(36%)	1(13%)	2(33%)
Previous violent convictions	6(43%)	1(13%)	2(33%)
Other convictions	7(50%)	7(88%)	4(67%)

*Significant differences between Group 1 and Groups 2 and 3 combined
[1]As measured by Risk Matrix 2000 (Thornton et al., 2003)

'Dangerous world' IT appeared to be the primary underlying IT in terms of how men viewed the world, with thoughts about punishment and control primary motivators. The sexual murder itself was characterized by a high level of expressive violence, with multiple attacks on the victim, using different weapons (knives, blunt instruments and hands) and evidence of 'overkill' (gouging the victims eyes out, attempted scalping, numerous stabbings or repeated blows such that body parts were partially severed). For example, one victim had received over 140 different wounds to her body. Sexual mutilation of the victim's body was low in this group, although a third of the group had sexually interfered with the body after death. This behaviour took the form of further humiliating acts on the victim such as inserting knives or other objects into the vagina. This group was the most likely to have known their victim prior to the offence.

Group 3 is best described as being 'sexually motivated'. They were characterized by the murder being generally carried out in order to keep the victim quiet during the offence, or in order to avoid detection by making sure that the victim was not around to subsequently identify the perpetrator. Some men in this group admitted that they were prepared to murder their victim before they had committed their sexual offence. The primary IT found in this group was 'Male sex drive is uncontrollable'; hence there was generally little evidence of a history of overt hostility towards women or overkill in this group, as seen in Group 2. There was also little evidence of ritualized elements in the murder itself, in that there was a low level of sexual mutilation and sexual interference after death. 'The 'Male sex drive is uncontrollable' IT acts as a motivator to commit a sexual offence whatever the cost to the victim. Thus, these offenders were determined to have sex regardless of what they had to do to obtain it.

DISCUSSION

The three groupings reported above seem to relate to motivations that have been described in the profiling literature concerning sexual murder which have been detailed earlier. Group 1 appears to contain what might be considered the prototypical, usually serial, sexual murderer, where the killing is the *primary* sexual motive. Group 2 appears similar to those described by Revitch (1980), which is *motivated* by an angry outburst or in response to rejection of a proposed or actual sexual advance. Group 3 is similar to the type described by Hazelwood and Douglas (1980) where the murder plays an *instrumental* role to avoid detection or to keep the victim quiet.

These groups, identified purely on the basis of identified ITs, also seem to relate to clinical descriptions of sexual murderers involved in treatment, reported by Clarke and Carter (2000). Although there are a number of differences in the offence demographics of the men identified in this study, there are a number of commonalities that warrant mentioning. In Clarke and Carter's clinical descriptions, the *sexually motivated murderer* is similar to the profile of Group 1 men. The *sexually triggered/aggressive dyscontrol* sexual murderer, in the Clarke and Carter system, shows striking similarities with offenders contained in Group 2. The *sexually triggered/aggressive control* sexual murderer is similar to Group 3.

Implications for treatment

The findings of the study have implications for treatment as they suggest that sexual murderers are not qualitatively different from rapists in terms of the underlying cognitive schemas they have about the world. Therefore, it would appear that schema-focused treatment, such as that employed by the UK Prison Service in England and Wales, would be just as beneficial with this type of sexual offender as it has been with other high-risk sexual offenders as reported by Thornton and Shingler (2001). The particular type of IT present in each individual should guide specific treatment needs.

Group 1, i.e. those who have both 'Dangerous world' and 'Male sex drive is uncontrollable' ITs running at the same time, are very dangerous offenders. They need a high level of treatment intervention in order to reduce the possibility of committing further serious sadistic sexual crimes. There clearly needs to be behavioural work to modify deviant sexual arousal to their violent/sadistic fantasies. However, the identified synergism of the two specific strands of how the offender views the world should be addressed and disentangled in targeted schema-focused therapy. The sadistic arousal to their offending calls into question the advisability of doing any victim empathy work with these individuals.

For *Group 2*, where the 'Dangerous world' IT is operating without 'Male sex drive is uncontrollable', problems appear to underpin grievance and hostile thoughts about women rather than any deviant thoughts/fantasies that are specifically sexual in origin. Here, the data would suggest that offence-focused work may be better targeted towards anger and hostility problems, as well as schema-focused work around these men's longstanding grievance schemas about women.

For *Group 3*, where the 'Male sex drive is uncontrollable' IT is operating, there is a willingness to undertake sexual assaults to satisfy sexual urges and a general failure to control such deviant sexual thoughts and behaviours. These men might be considered as individuals driven by urges to commit sexual offences. Therefore, cognitive-behavioural techniques typically employed with sexual offenders (Beech & Fisher, 2002; Marshall, Anderson & Fernandez, 1999) may be useful with this group. Here, any offence/schema-focused work should be clearly related to getting the offender to control his actions so that he does not regard any sexual or offence-related thoughts as being unstoppable and translating to a sexual assault. Self-regulation and impulsivity problems need to be addressed with these individuals.

CONCLUSION

This chapter has briefly examined some of the approaches to the classification of sexual murderers, noting there would appear to be four main approaches that are employed, depending upon what the particular professional aims to get out of classification, broadly speaking: offender identification, theory advancement, treatment and risk assessment advances. We would note that the findings in our research around the identification of implicit theories in sexual offenders indicate that it is possible to identify an offender's underlying motivations (without his necessarily explicitly acknowledging these). This observation suggests that the identification of ITs prior to the commencement of treatment could indicate treatment paths for offenders who are less than honest and open about their reasons for offending, and hence has very real treatment implications. Understanding an offender's motivation could also have very real implications on the advancement of risk assessment with this group of sexual offenders. Therefore, using an open questioning style that allows the individual to give a 'free narrative' would seem to be a promising approach to assessment with this group. In conclusion, the preliminary study of sexual murderers' ITs, originally reported by Beech et al. (2005) gives us some intriguing insights into the values and beliefs underlying their devastatingly destructive behavior. It also provides a rather simple map of the significant interpersonal and personal concerns of this group of extremely violent individuals and has the potential to inform both aetiological theories and clinical practice. We feel that it is important to look for similarities as well as differences between clinical populations, and the results of our study indicate that rapists and sexual murders would appear to think in a similar way, and that the differences in the outcome of their offending may have more to do with situational factors.

PART III
PRACTICAL ISSUES

Chapter 12

THE ROLE OF PROFILING IN THE
INVESTIGATION OF SEXUAL HOMICIDE

Éric Beauregard

Criminal profiling can be defined as the identification of a suspect's principal personality and behavioural characteristics on the basis of the characteristics of his crimes (Cook & Hinman, 1999; Davies, 1992, 1994; Douglas et al., 1986; Egger, 1999). The goal of criminal profiling is to provide answers to the following questions (Egger, 1999; Rossmo, 2000):

1. What happened at the crime scene?
2. Why did the events in question occur?
3. What type of individuals could have committed these acts?

Criminal profiling has four axiomatic principles. First, the crime scene reflects the criminal's personality (Holmes & Holmes, 1996). In other words, the manner in which the victim was killed, as well as evidence collected at the crime scene, reveal information about the criminal's personality. Second, a criminal's modus operandi remains similar from crime to crime. Third, the crime signature remains constant from crime to crime. The crime signature is the unique way in which the crime is committed, e.g. the technique used to kill, specific words spoken by a sexual aggressor to his victim. The crime signature is, in other words, a set of behaviours that are specific to individuals but not essential to the commission of the crime (Douglas et al., 1992; Holmes & Holmes, 1996; Keppel, 2000; Keppel &

Sexual Murderers: A Comparative Analysis and New Perspectives Edited by Jean Proulx Éric Beauregard, Maurice Cusson and Alexandre Nicole

Birnes, 1997). Fourth, the criminal's personality does not change. Although individuals are capable of modifying some aspects of their personality, the basic elements remain unchanged. Criminals' personalities develop over many years, and cannot radically change rapidly. Because the personality stays the same, the crimes committed exhibit similarities (Holmes & Holmes, 1996).

Studies of criminal profiling have identified a number of uses for this investigative tool. First, the profile can provide a psychological and social profile of the suspect. It should therefore predict personality and demographic characteristics (e.g. age, sex, race, employment status, civil status, religion, education), thereby helping to identify the type of person having committed the crime. A profile may also prove useful during interrogation. Since different people react differently to police interrogation, a valid profile may help investigators select the most effective interrogation techniques and attitudes (Ainsworth, 2001; Holmes & Holmes, 1996; St-Yves, 2002). Other uses that have been suggested for criminal profiling include limiting the number of potential suspects, suggesting proactive investigative strategies, and preventing other violent crimes (Cook & Hinman, 1999).

Not all crimes lend themselves to profiling. Profiling is most effective in crimes suggesting an offender with a psychopathology and who did not know the victim previously (Holmes & Holmes, 1996). More specifically, it is most useful for sexual assault, satanic or ritualized crimes, paedophilia and sexual murders involving evisceration or pre- or postmortem mutilation (McCann, 1992). Serial crimes of a nonsexual nature, such as arson, may also lend themselves to profiling. Crimes in which there is staging of the crime scene or a signature yield better results than 'normal' violent crimes. Finally, crimes in which the offender verbalizes provide more information on which to base the profile (Cook & Hinman, 1999).

According to Ainsworth (2001), there are three reasons that profiling is most successful with the crimes enumerated above, all of which involve the assault of a stranger of either sex. First, these crimes are the most resistant to traditional investigative techniques, particularly as there tend to be many suspects. Second, the evidence at the crime scenes sheds light on the criminal's personality and motivation. Third, these crimes are often associated with intense media pressure and anxiety in the general public; consequently, police use all investigative tools available, regardless of financial or temporal constraints.

CRIMINAL PROFILING: INDUCTIVE OR DEDUCTIVE?

Although there have been few evaluative studies of criminal profiling, an ideological debate has already arisen among researchers and profilers over the relative merits of inductive and deductive criminal profiling (McGrath, 2000; Turvey, 1998, 2001).

Inductive criminal profiling uses experimentation, inductive generalization (extrapolation of premises from a smaller to a larger group of individuals) and statistical analysis to generate a profile of the individuals responsible for specific crimes. According to McGrath (2000), this method may be compromised by biased sampling or by the probabilistic nature of its results. Another disadvantage of this method is that it provides no insight into the more intelligent and talented criminals, i.e. criminals who manage to elude the police, as the databases it relies on comprise only apprehended criminals. According to Turvey (1998, 2001), the inductive method is most common among FBI teams, profilers working for police agencies, criminologists, forensic psychologists and forensic psychiatrists.

The deductive method has been defined as:

> . . . a process of interpreting forensic evidence, including such inputs as crime scene photographs, autopsy reports, autopsy photographs, and a thorough study of individual offender victimology, to accurately reconstruct specific offender crime scene behavior patterns, and from those specific, individual patterns of behavior, deduce offender characteristics, demographics, emotions, and motivations (Turvey, 1998, p. 5).

This method allows investigators to deduce the criminal's emotions during the crime, behaviours and personality characteristics on the basis of forensic evidence, crime scene characteristics and victim characteristics.

The advantages of the deductive method are its ability to characterize the motivation of even the most sordid criminals, follow the evolution of criminal behaviour, and identify the modus operandi and crime signature. Furthermore, by so doing, it can reveal relationships with other unsolved crimes (Turvey, 1998; McGrath, 2000). The technique is not without its drawbacks, however, chief of which is its reliance on the validity of the basic premise: as in all deductive techniques, if the basic premise is false, the conclusions will also, inevitably, be false.

THE EVOLUTION OF CRIMINAL PROFILING

Psychological profiling

Although criminal profiling seems relatively recent, the first profile dates back to the investigation of Jack the Ripper in 1888. At that time, Dr Thomas Bond, a surgeon and an expert in forensic medicine, conducted an autopsy of Mary Kelly, the last victim of Jack the Ripper, in an attempt to identify some characteristics of the criminal (Rossmo, 2000). More recently, in the 1950s and 1960s, James A. Brussel, a psychiatrist, was asked to construct a personality profile of the criminal responsible for bomb attacks (the Mad Bomber) and murders by strangulation (the Boston Strangler) (Geberth, 1996; Pinizzotto, 1984). Later, Brussel and several other mental health professionals were asked to help police apprehend serial murderers, including David Berkowitz, the 'Son of Sam' murderer. Nevertheless, the systematic recourse to mental health professionals in the investigation of violent crimes was sporadic until 1978, when the FBI established a criminal profiling programme in its Behavioral Science Unit, now known as the Investigative Support Unit, within its Critical Incident Response Group (CIRG) at its academy in Quantico, Virginia (Ainsworth, 2001; Petee & Jarvis, 2000).

Brussel's approach, which entails interpreting abnormal behaviours and applying psychiatric expertise to real-world police investigations, has proven itself to be an effective method (Geberth, 1996). However, rather than following a rigorous methodology, this approach relies on the experience and knowledge of specific mental health professionals. The construction of a profile requires the identification of the psychopathology specific to the crime in question, but different professionals may well arrive at divergent diagnoses. This idiosyncratic approach hinders the establishment of comparative evaluations of the validity of its approach (Wilson, Lincoln & Kocsis, 1997). Furthermore, behavioural specialists with experience in police investigation and related fields (for example, criminalistics) are rare (Dietz, 1985; Hazelwood et al., 1995). Despite these limitations, psychological profiling continues to grow in popularity in many countries, particularly because of its apparent effectiveness.

Crime-scene profiling

Despite the limited number of mental health professionals capable of helping the police, the FBI's criminal profiling team has conducted research in order to better understand criminal personalities and motivations. The best-known FBI study entailed interviews with serial sexual murderers about their techniques for avoiding capture (Burgess et al., 1986; Ressler, Burgess & Douglas, 1988; Ressler, Burgess, Douglas et al., 1986; Ressler, Burgess, Hartman et al., 1986). The main types of information collected concerned the modus operandi, the crime scene and the personality of the murderers. On the basis of this information, the FBI's team developed a typology comprising two primary types: 'organized' and 'disorganized' murderers (see Chapter 8).

Although the FBI is renowned for having established and made available a research-based profiling technique (Davis, 1999), some authors have criticized their technique. First, most of the FBI's published studies do not describe the methodology used to construct their typology of murderers (Beauregard, 1999; Beauregard & Proulx, 2002). Second, their approach has no theoretical basis, and tends to reduce human behaviour to a limited number of observable features related to the characteristics of the unknown criminal (Wilson et al., 19997). Lastly, Ainsworth (2001) points out that even though the FBI have produced some empirical results related to criminal profiling, their real-world use of this technique has been characterized by subjective interpretations resulting from leaps of intuition. Despite these criticisms, it is important to bear in mind that the FBI was the first to collect data and propose a model of criminal profiling.

In Holland, criminal profiling has been inspired by the best elements of the FBI approach (Ainsworth, 2001; Jackson, van den Eshof & de Kleuver, 1997). The two main principles of the Dutch approach are that criminal profiling is a combination of investigative experience and behavioural sciences expertise, and that profiles are not ends in themselves but rather tools to guide investigations (Ainsworth, 2001; Jackson et al., 1997). The main difference between the Dutch and FBI approaches is that Dutch researchers have made an effort to validate the tool and determine its reliability. Criminal profiling units should therefore not only be involved in criminal investigations but also be scientifically active (Jackson & Bekerian, 1997).

In 1997, the Netherlands Institute for the Study of Criminality and Law Enforcement (NISCALE) undertook four evaluative studies of profiling. The first study examined the reasoning applied by police investigators and profilers to crime-scene evidence (Jackson et al., 1997). The second compared profilers and nonprofilers, using an expert/novice approach. The third study analysed the criminal records of convicted sexual aggressors, in order to determine whether criminal record can be deduced from crime-scene characteristics. The fourth study consisted of a survey of investigators' satisfaction with the profiling technique. It thus appears that the Dutch approach to criminal profiling has successfully taken into account criticisms of this technique, and improved its validity.

Statistical profiling

Statistical profiling is based on multivariate statistical analysis of characteristics of offenders and offending processes. For some years now, researchers interested in criminal profiling have attempted to increase its scientific value by using predictive statistical models. Knight et al. (1998) brought their experience in typological studies to bear on criminal profiling, and studied the contribution of crime-scene variables to the identification of sexual-offender types. Their results indicate that it is possible to predict the antisocial and expressive violence types in the MTC-R-3 typology (Knight & Prentky, 1990; Knight et al., 1998). Warren et al. (1999) were able to distinguish, in a sample of 108 serial sexual aggressors responsible for 565 sexual assaults, between those who used increasing amounts of force in their crimes ('increasers') and those who used a constant amount of force ('non-increasers'). Increasers are characterized by being Caucasian, and by a first rape that involves lengthy assault and verbal humiliation of the victim.

Following his success in establishing the profile that led to the arrest of John Duffy, the serial rapist known as 'The Railway Rapist', David Canter began studying the investigation of violent crimes. Relying on key concepts in criminology, social psychology and forensic psychiatry, he gathered empirical data with which to produce profiles for violent criminals. His conceptual model is composed of five major axes: interpersonal consistency; spatiotemporal features; offender characteristics; criminal history; and criminalistics (Canter, 1995; 2000; Wilson & Soothill, 1996).

Canter and Heritage (1990) developed an empirical multivariate model of the behaviour of sexual offenders based on five components: attempted intimacy with the victim; sexual behaviours; overt violence and aggression; impersonal interactions; and criminal behaviours and intent. The model is based on Smallest Sample Analysis (SSA) (or Smallest Space Analysis) of data from 66 assaults committed by 27 sexual criminals. This analytical method, related to Facet Theory, is based on the correlations between variables, and identifies variables most likely to co-occur. The analysis yields a graphical measure of similarity on a two-dimensional map (Greenberg, 1979) in which variables close to the centre are more frequent and more specific to the crime in question, and variables far from the centre are less frequent. Variables that map close to each other tend to co-occur. This method allows identification, through the use of cutting lines, of the crime's dimensions.

Salfati (Salfati, 2000a, 2000b; Salfati & Canter, 1999) developed a typology of murder based on Facet Theory and SSA. Her results indicated the existence of two types of murders: instrumental (cognitive and opportunistic) and expressive (impulsive). Instrumental murder is characterized by the manual infliction of wounds (especially in the neck region), the hiding of the face of the victim, and the presence of sexual elements (e.g. the victim is often sexually assaulted and left partially naked) (Salfati & Canter, 1999). In these cases, the murderer takes care not to leave evidence, and moves the corpse. Expressive murder is characterized by the infliction of multiple wounds (i.e. with no anatomical localization) with a weapon found at the crime scene or brought by the murderer.

Although both SSA and Facet Theory appear to yield valuable results, they also have their limits. First, the number and location of dimensions on the map are based on subjective decisions by researchers and are thus open to question (Ainsworth, 2001). Second, some variables or facets may be central to more than one dimension, indicating the possible existence of a mixed type. Finally, SSA arranges variables in a multidimensional space but interprets them in a two-dimensional space (Rossmo, 2000).

Taxometric procedures (cluster analysis, multidimensional scaling, etc.) appear to provide good results, particularly in the case of sexual murder. The results obtained by Beauregard and Proulx (described in Chapter 8) have many similarities with those of Salfati (Salfati, 2000a, 2000b; Salfati & Canter, 1999) and those of the FBI (Douglas et al., 1986, 1992; Ressler et al., 1988). It is interesting to note that these similarities were obtained with totally different samples and methodologies. However, the use of typologies in criminal profiling is frequently criticized because the rigid nature of the types often does not accommodate nonprototypical criminals.

Davies (Davies, 1997; Davies, Wittebrood & Jackson 1996) has proposed a model that predicts the criminal-record history of sexual offenders on the basis of the characteristics of their offending process. Using logistic regression, the authors demonstrated that the best models were those that predicted previous convictions for breaking and entering, violent assault and sexual assault by inexperienced rapists.

Aitken (Aitken, Connolly et al., 1996; Aitken & Gammerman, 1989; Aitken, Gammerman et al., 1996) used both logistic regression and a Bayesian Belief Network model to predict the characteristics of sexual murderers of children. The sample for these analyses was composed of cases in the CATCHEM database (a database of all cases of sexual murder and child kidnapping in Great Britain since 1960). At the end of 1997, the database contained 3310 cases, and a more detailed subset comprised 417 offenders responsible for 470 victims. Statistical profiles were generated from solved cases in the database (Rossmo, 2000). With the PRESS system, the relationship between the variables included in the profile is represented visually. The graph of the Bayesian network is composed of nodes and arcs. Each node represents a specific characteristic and each arc connects two characteristics. The direction of the arc represents the direction of the causal relationship or the influence of one characteristic on the other (Figure 12.1).

In Figure 12.1, A and B are the parent and child nodes, respectively. In the example, A corresponds to 'aggressor lives with a partner' and B corresponds to 'victim is male'. Using a database, two conditional probabilities can be determined: Pr (B | A) and Pr (B | A'): the probability that B (victim is male) is true if A (aggressor lives with a partner) is true, and the probability that B (the victim is male) is true if A is false (A': the aggressor does not live with a partner). The existence of such a bi-nodal network implies that the choice of victim may be influenced by the marital status of the aggressor (Aitken, Connolly et al., 1996). From a criminal profiling perspective, it is the inverse of this proposition that is of interest: if we know the sex of the victim, what is the probability that the aggressor lives with a partner?

Aitken et al. (Aitken, Connolly et al., 1996; Aitken, Gammerman et al., 1996) developed a belief network for murderers of children, composed of

Figure 12.1   Graphical representation of a Bayesian Belief Network

the following seven nodes: (1) victim age; (2) victim sex; (3) last site at which victim was sighted; (4) method used to kill victim; (5) marital status of aggressor; (6) relationship between aggressor and victim; (7) criminal record. The network was developed in order to predict the aggressor characteristics (nodes 5,6,7) on the basis of victim and crime-scene characteristics (nodes 1,2,3,4). To illustrate this, the authors calculated the probabilities associated with aggressor characteristics for a female victim aged 0–7 found strangled outside her house. If the victim lay strangled in her house, the probability that she knew her aggressor was 0.57. However, when she was found outside her house, the probability fell to 0.11 (Aitken, Connolly et al., 1996).

Aitken et al. (Aitken, Connolly et al., 1996; Aitken, Gammerman et al., 1996) claim that this method, by combining objective (statistical analysis) and subjective (investigative expertise) approaches, significantly advances criminal profiling. The experience of the investigator is fully exploited in the determination of networks, while statistical analysis is necessary for the calculation of probabilities. Furthermore, the primary advantages of Bayesian Belief Networks are their great flexibility and the clarity of the intervariable relationships that are automatically represented graphically. This method also allows new networks to be rapidly created, tested and modified as new information becomes available. However, a method such as this, which incorporates a degree of subjectivity, may yield variable results, depending on the expertise of researchers and investigators.

Fuzzy logic, often used in electronics, engineering and mathematics, is another mathematical method that has been applied to criminal profiling. In fuzzy logic, Boolean logic (in which variables may have only two, extreme, values, e.g. yes/no) is adapted to accommodate concepts that entail a spectrum of responses (Verma, 2001). For example, witnesses' descriptions of suspects are often subjective: tall, dark skin, young, long hair, etc. Such fuzzy descriptions are difficult to include in traditional statistical analyses.

Zadeh (1965) developed a new form of logic system that he called fuzzy logic, in which he stipulated that an element can be a member of a given set in a uncertain manner. Unlike the classical mathematical set theory in which an element can be only in two situations, a member of the set or not its member, fuzzy logic generalizes the possibilities and introduces the concept of shades of membership patterns.

Fuzzy logic assigns a degree of membership which may range from 0 (absence of feature) to 1 (presence of feature) rather than being limited to either extreme. For example, a witness of an armed robbery may state that the suspect was tall – but the precise meaning of 'tall' may be very different in different witnesses. Fuzzy logic allows police to use a scale to determine individual threshold for 'tallness'. This strategy improves the precision of profiles by taking into account the extent to which a feature is present rather than forcing investigators into yes/no decisions that may vitiate the collection of precious information or even wrongly exclude a suspect. Although fuzzy logic appears promising, further research is required before it can be considered an effective police tool.

It is interesting to note that most of the recent studies on criminal profiling have relied on multivariate statistical methods. The authors of these studies have thus responded to the criticisms that this investigative tool is unscientific. While statistical methods such as logistic regression, Bayesian Belief Networks, fuzzy logic and taxometric procedures methods appear to produce coherent and valid results, it must be recalled that the application of these techniques to criminal profiling is in its infancy, and that further work is necessary before they can be used directly in real investigations.

EVALUATIVE STUDIES OF CRIMINAL PROFILING

Few studies have attempted to measure the effectiveness of criminal profiling. An unpublished study by Douglas dating back to 1981 examined the value of profiling to police forces in 192 cases between 1978 and 1981 (Copson, 1995). Criminal profiling helped reduce the scope of investigation in 77% of cases in which the criminal was eventually identified, and resulted in the arrest of the criminal in 15 cases. The investigators estimated that criminal profiling saved 594 person-days of investigation. Furthermore, all the investigators having used profiling services wanted it to remain available. It should be noted, however, that the methodology of the study was not described.

Another study was conducted in 1992 by Paul Britton, head of the forensic psychology unit of the Trent region in England. According to Copson, this study revealed that the profiles produced were imprecise and did not lead to arrests. However, Britton concluded that profiling could be useful under certain conditions (Copson, 1995).

Goldblatt studied the effectiveness of the psychological profiling unit founded at the University of Surrey (now at the University of Liverpool). The unit had been established by David Canter, and Goldblatt's study was in fact primarily based on information provided by Canter himself. Of the 57 profiles produced by the unit, 12 resulted in charges being laid. The analysis of these 12 cases indicated that of the 114 elements suggested by the profiles, 72% were accurate, 19% were incorrect and 9% could not be evaluated without further information (Copson, 1995).

In 1993, a survey was conducted by NISCALE on satisfaction with criminal profiling. The survey studied only 20 cases and of these, only six could truly be considered typical examples of criminal profiling. The study came to two primary conclusions. First, the investigators interviewed stated that they were satisfied with the profiling technique. Secondly, a majority of investigators admitted having learned much during their discussions with the profiling specialist, and stated that new ideas had been triggered that could be applied to future investigations (Jackson, Van Koppen & Herbrink, 1993).

Copson (1995) analysed 184 investigations in which criminal profiling had been used in Britain. The two most frequent types of crimes were homicide (61.4%) and sexual assault (21.7%). The results indicate that criminal profiling was not only used to obtain a predictive profile but also to better understand criminals' offending behaviours. The criminal profile was useful for solving only 14.1% of cases, and opened new avenues of investigation in only 16.3%. Nevertheless, 82.6% of the investigators considered that profiling concretely advanced the investigation. Profiling was viewed as more useful in advancing understanding of the crime and the offender (60.9%) than in identifying suspects (only 2.7%).

Two other studies have used an expert/novice approach to the evaluation of criminal profiling. Pinizzotto and Finkel (1990; see also Pinizzotto, 1984) analysed intergroup differences among profilers, investigators, psychologists and students. In cases of sexual assault, profilers produced reports that were more detailed and whose validity was higher than those produced by the other groups; no intergroup differences were observed for murder (Pinizzotto & Finkel, 1990). The researchers obtained equivocal results with regard to the ability of the various groups to predict the characteristics of a suspect.

Kocsis et al. (2000) conducted a similar study, comparing groups of profilers, police officers, psychologists, students and psychics. Profilers were slightly better than the others at identifying the criminal's cognitive processes, physical characteristics, lifestyle characteristics, social history and offending behaviours. Psychologists, on the other hand, were better at determining personality characteristics. To determine whether the profilers performed better than the other groups, profilers were compared to a composite group comprising all the other groups. Profilers obtained a significantly higher number of correct predictions than the nonprofiler group. (For an extensive evaluation of profiling, see Kocsis, 2006.)

In brief, these studies demonstrate that criminal profiling is an investigative tool that is appreciated by police officers, not only for its ability to predict the characteristics of the offender but also because of the new ideas that emerge during the profiling process and the light it sheds on offending behaviour. However, the evaluative studies presented above only studied certain types of criminal profiling, and none of them attempted to quantify the profiles generated in order to evaluate their real predictive value.

GEOCRIMINOLOGY AND GEOGRAPHICAL PROFILING OF SEXUAL MURDERERS

Geocriminology, or environmental criminology, is the study of the relationships between places, using statistical methods and computerized tools.

Geocriminology is founded on three theories: routine activities theory; rational choice theory; and the crime pattern theory. The routine activities theory holds that illegal acts occur when there is a spatiotemporal convergence – in the context of everyday activities, i.e. work or leisure – of a motivated offender, a victim or potential target, and the absence of a capable guardian (Felson, 1998). The rational choice theory explains crimes in terms of decision-making processes, especially cost-benefit analyses (Cornish & Clarke, 1986). According to Felson, the rational choice theory better accounts for the content of decisions, while the routine activities theory better accounts for ecological features that provide criminal opportunities about which decisions are made. Finally, the crime pattern theory posits that crimes rarely occur at random locations, and that there is a rational basis for the geography of crime (Brantingham & Brantingham, 1991). Thus, crimes are committed in spaces through which an offender moves and in which potential victims are identified. An offender constructs a mental map of his city on the basis of the knowledge he acquires as he moves between his workplace, leisure spaces and residence. Criminals do not differ from noncriminals in this respect: everyone's daily activities form the basis of their mental map of their environment. What is different is that in criminals, this process also leads to the identification of criminal opportunities. More specifically, according to the crime pattern theory, crimes are more likely wherever there is an intersection of an awareness of space and the presence of potential victims or targets (Brantingham & Brantingham, 1991).

Certain fundamental principles are essential to the understanding of the geographical mobility of individuals in general and of sexual murderers in particular. The principle of least effort (Zipf, 1950) holds that an individual faced with alternative courses of action will choose the one requiring the least effort. Although this principle is of great value in explaining the movements of individuals, other factors also intervene. For example, the distance an individual travels depends on several factors:

1. The means of transport: distances seem longer when travelled on foot than by car, and people without cars have a shorter radius of activity than people with cars.
2. The attractiveness of the destination and the pathways taken to get there. Route selection depends on many factors, including convenience, number of stops and attractiveness of the landscape.
3. Knowledge of roads and highways.
4. The number and types of obstacles (e.g. rivers, highways, borders).
5. The existence of alternative routes. The existence of multiple routes increases a criminal's flight possibilities.
6. The real distance (Holmes & Holmes, 1996).

The distance-decay function refers to the inverse relationship between frequency and distance: the farther a destination is, the less frequently it is visited, principally because of the financial and time costs associated with long travel. Concretely, this means that people choose locations close to home for their most common activities.

The relationship between the mobility of sexual offenders and modus operandi

The distance travelled by sexual offenders to commit their crimes has been studied by a number of authors. Lebeau (1987) found that the distance travelled by sexual aggressors of adult women depended on the approach used to contact the victim. Thus, serial and nonserial sexual aggressors who travelled the shortest distance contacted their victims by breaking into their homes, while those who travelled the greatest distance depended on obtaining the confidence of the victim. Warren et al. (1998) studied the relationship between distance travelled to commit a crime, demographic variables, crime-scene variables and criminal record in a sample of 108 serial sexual aggressors responsible for 565 sexual assaults. Almost 50% of the sexual aggressors had committed at least one sexual assault within 0.5 miles of their home, which entailed significant exposure to apprehension. Aggressors who were older and white travelled greater distances than did those who were younger and members of a visible minority. This may reflect young aggressors' greater impulsivity and older aggressors' greater access to vehicles (Warren et al., 1998). A positive and significant association was found between the distance travelled, on the one hand, and ritualized behaviours and the use of physical restraints on the other. Thus, sexual aggressors who committed their crimes in a ritualized manner and who used physical restraints travelled longer distances. These ritualized behaviours and the use of physical restraints may be caused by specific sexual fantasies that motivate the sexual assault, and the selection of a specific type of victim. Finally, sexual aggressors with extensive criminal records, who broke into their victims' homes, and who robbed their victims, tended to travel longer distances. According to the authors, this result reflects these aggressors' greater motivation and greater experience in the commission of nonsexual crimes.

The geographical mobility of sexual murderers has also been studied. Aitken, Connolly et al. (1996) reported that in their sample of paedophilic sexual murderers, 91.6% travelled less than 5 miles to commit their crime. Safarik, Jarvis and Nussbaum (2002) reported that in their sample of sexual murderers of elderly women, 56% lived within six blocks of their victims' homes, and 30% lived on the same block. Canter and Hodge (1997) observed that 25% of serial sexual murderers travelled less than 5 kilometres to commit their crimes, while 50% of sexual murders were committed within a distance of 15 kilometres. Finally, Shaw (1998) reported that the mean distance travelled by sexual murderers in his sample was 2.4 miles, and that 85% of the sexual murderers travelled less than 9.5 kilometres to commit their crime. Furthermore, 25% of the murders were committed in the murderers' homes.

The application of geocriminological principles to police investigations

In some investigations of violent crimes, geocriminological principles have been applied to the identification of the area of residence of criminals. For example, in the case of the Yorkshire Ripper, a special unit composed of four police officers and a forensic scientist was formed after five fruitless years of investigation. The investigators were divided on the probable area of residence of the criminal. Some, including the chief inspector, believed he lived in the region of Sunderland, while others believed him to be found in the region of West Yorkshire, where the majority of the murders had been committed (Kind, 1987). To test these hypotheses, the special unit subjected their spatiotemporal data to two navigation metric tests. The first test consisted of determining the spatial mean of the Yorkshire Ripper's 17 murders. The result pointed toward Bradford, an area located in West Yorkshire. The second test consisted of establishing links between the temporal and geographical patterns of the Yorkshire Ripper's crimes. Assuming the killer had no geographical preference and returned home as quickly as possible after each murder, his attacks would tend to be later at night, when he was near his home, in order to minimize the risk of apprehension. Murders occurring later in the day thus can be assumed to be nearer the murderer's home. A correlation analysis of the time of the murder and the length of daylight (estimated from the month) was performed, and the results suggested a seasonal effect on the time of day at which the murders occurred. These results indicated that the Yorkshire Ripper resided near Bradford and Leeds (Kind, 1987).

The results of the two navigation metrics thus indicated that the Yorkshire Ripper indeed came from the Bradford region, near West Yorkshire. The special unit accordingly concentrated its efforts on this region, and in January 1981, Peter William Sutcliffe, a trucker living in Heaton, a suburb of Bradford, was arrested by two patrol officers in the Sheffield region and confessed to being the Yorkshire Ripper. Although the arrest was not the direct result of the special unit's work, the unit had been correct in its analysis, and investigators could have identified the murderer earlier if the unit's work had been taken into account.

Canter and Larkin (1993) evaluated two hypotheses concerning the spatial behaviour of serial sexual aggressors, using a sample composed of 45 English serial sexual aggressors responsible for 251 sexual assaults (mean: 5.6 sexual assaults). The 'marauder hypothesis' suggests that aggressors use their home or a site of significant activity as a base from which to commit sexual assaults. This implies that there is an overlap between the territory in which crimes are committed and the territory in which the criminal carries out his routine activities. As a corollary, the greater the distance between the crime scenes the greater the distance travelled by the aggressor from his home. This is consistent with the position of Brantingham and Brantingham (1993), who considered the home to be the central point of criminal opportunity. The 'commuter hypothesis' suggests that aggressors travel from their homes to another territory to commit their crimes. This does not imply that the territory to which they travel is unfamiliar, merely that it is a considerable distance from their non-offending territory. There is thus no overlap between the territory in which the crimes are committed and the territory of residence. Using circle and range tests, Canter and Larkin could confirm only the marauder hypothesis, i.e. almost all the sexual aggressors had committed their assaults near their homes.

Canter and Gregory (1994) reanalysed their original data in order to verify the hypothesis that aggressors with more resources (money, geographical knowledge, time) travelled greater distances to commit their crimes. They analysed the distances travelled in terms of dichotomous variables such as race, age, day of the week (weekend/weekday) and type of location. The results revealed that aggressors who were older and white, who committed their crime during the week, tended to travel greater distances.

Kocsis and Irwin (1997) reported that 82% of serial arsonists, 70% of serial sexual aggressors and 49% of burglars in Australia lived close enough to the scenes of their crimes to be considered marauders. Similarly, 56% of a sample of American serial sexual aggressors (Warren et al., 1998) and 72% of a sample of Japanese serial arsonists (Tamura & Suzuki, 1997) were considered marauders.

Alston (1994, 2001) pointed out several limitations of Canter and Larkin's marauder hypothesis (1993). First, differences in the organization of European (older) and North American (newer) cities may well result in differences in the microspatial behaviours of sexual aggressors in these locales. Second, circle and range tests may fail to effectively narrow the scope of the search in cases involving long distances, as the resultant circles may encompass entire cities. Third, the commission of a single sexual assault near his home is enough to classify a serial sexual aggressor as a marauder, regardless of the number of assaults committed far from home. Fourth, Canter and Larkin did not consider anchor points other than the home in their analysis. For example, how should the test be modified to accommodate an aggressor who commits his assaults from his workplace? Finally, Canter and Larkin's tests do not take into account the fact that some types of victims are found in specific territories. For example, aggressors who target prostitutes tend to search for victims in specific sectors of the city, e.g. red-light zones.

In light of these criticisms, Alston (1994) proposed the use of the Kolmogorov–Smirnov test in geocriminological studies, and tested its utility in a sample composed of 30 serial sexual assaults (at least two assaults per aggressor) known to the Vancouver RCMP's E unit. The study evaluated aggressors' awareness of space on the basis of their routine pathways (main roads close to their homes), and clearly revealed that victim selection is dependent on offender activity nodes. In fact, 97% of assaults occurred within 3.5 kilometres, and 94% within 2.5 kilometres, of the offender awareness space. Furthermore, in 56% of cases, the mean distance between the site of the assault and a principal activity node of the aggressor was less than 2.5 kilometres.

In Russia, the police used geocriminology in their search for the worst serial sexual murder in the country's history. The murderer in question was responsible for the death and mutilation of many women and children in the Rostov Woods over a 12-year period. Investigators believed that on the train to his work, the murderer selected his victims and manipulated them in order to bring them to the woods, where he attacked them. The study of aerial surveillance maps proved ineffective in establishing the point of origin of the murderer. Uniformed police officers were therefore posted at every train station on the outskirts of the woods with the exception of the three highest-risk stations, at which undercover officers were posted. This operation (Operation Forest Strip), involving 360 police officers, led to the arrest of Andrei Chikatilo in November 1990, and to his eventual execution for 53 sexual murders (Rossmo, 2000).

Rigel: a geographical profiling program

A geographical profiling system called Rigel was developed by Kim Rossmo, a former Vancouver police officer, during his doctorate in criminology at Simon Fraser University. The program relies on the crime pattern theory developed by Brantingham and Brantingham (1984, 1991, 1993) but applies it in the opposite direction than was originally intended: rather than predicting crime locations from suspects' home or workplace, it predicts the home or workplace from known crime locations.

Rigel uses the Criminal Geographic Targeting (CGT) algorithm to generate a three-dimensional probability distribution, termed a 'jeopardy surface', from the spatial data related to a series of crime locations. This surface is then superimposed on a map of the crime location, creating a 'geoprofile' that quantifies the probability of finding the aggressor at any given location (Rossmo, 1993a, 1993b, 1994, 1995a, 1995b, 1996, 1997, 1998, 2000). Thus, the geoprofile suggests optimal search strategies rather than identifying specific locations.

The geographical profile includes both objective and subjective components. The objective component comprises analyses of the spatial relationships between crime locations (using geographical techniques and quantitative measures), and of streets and highways, psychological and physical borders, the type of area (industrial, commercial, residential), and the sociodemographics of the neighbourhood, the type of offender, predation behaviours, and victims' daily activities and movements. The subjective component comprises the reconstruction and interpretation of the offender's mental map. For example, sexual murderers who select prostitutes as victims seek victims in neighbourhoods where prostitution occurs (e.g. dense urban zones) rather than in cosseted neighbourhoods.

The use of geographical profiling is, however, subject to a number of conditions. First, there must be multiple – ideally, at least five – crime-related locations to analyse. These may be either multiple single-location crimes or multiple locations related to even a single crime. Crime-related locations may include locations at which credit cards were used, telephone calls made, vehicles borrowed or abandoned, objects or clues found, victims met, criminal acts committed, and bodies abandoned. However, as the model's predictive power is a function of the number of locations, the more locations, the better. A further prerequisite is that the crime be serious enough to justify the time and effort needed to construct the profile (Rossmo, 2000).

Although geographical profiling has been primarily used in cases of serial sexual murder and serial sexual assault, the technique is also useful in cases of bombing, armed robbery, kidnapping, missing person cases and serial arson.

Geographical profiling is an appropriate complement to traditional investigative tools when: (1) there is a series of crimes; (2) traditional investigative techniques have not proven useful; (3) there is evidence of relationship between the crimes in the series; (4) a psychological profile exists. The geographical profile is constructed on the basis of existing reports (investigation reports, autopsy reports and, if available, psychological profiles) and analysis of the crime scene and crime-related locations. In addition, the profiler should consult the investigators, analyse the neighbourhoods' criminal statistics and demographics, and analyse the streets, zoning and main arteries.

Value of geographical profiling in the investigation of violent crimes

Even though the nominal goal of geographical profiling is the prediction of the probable area in which a criminal lives, the technique has also proven useful in the prioritization of the many suspects investigations of serial crimes often generate. For example, in 1998, a series of 11 sexual assaults over a period of 35 days in the region surrounding Mississauga, Ontario, was attributed to a single criminal. The investigation generated a list of 300 suspects, but geographical profiling prioritized these suspects on the basis of a probable residence zone of 0.03 square miles. The local police force collected a DNA sample from the suspect identified as the most probable, and subsequently charged him (Rossmo, 2000). Similarly, from 1984 to 1995, a serial sexual aggressor was responsible for 14 sexual assaults in Lafayette, Louisiana. In 1998, with the criminal still at large, the police force requested psychological and geographical profiles. The profiles resulted in the identification of a hitherto unsuspected search territory and of the crucial clue out of the 2000 available. Fingerprints and a DNA sample were taken from a suspect on the basis of his living within 0.5 square miles of the territory identified by geographical profiling. When presented with the results, which were incriminating, the suspect confessed, and was subsequently convicted (Rossmo, 2000).

Geographical profiling may also prove useful in establishing surveillance or patrol strategies, allowing police resources to target regions in which suspects are most likely to be found and in which they are most likely to strike again. For example, in 1996, the RCMP detachment in Burnaby, British Columbia, investigating a case of serial arson involving 24 fires had psychological and geographical profiles of the criminal produced. The geographical profile allowed the search territory to be reduced to 0.02 square miles (0.6%). One of the suspects matched both the geographical and psychological profiles, which led the investigators to intensify their surveillance, adopt offender-specific interrogation strategies and ultimately lay charges (Rossmo, 2000).

Another way in which geographical profiling can help identify suspects is through its use in conjunction with governmental and commercial databases. In one case of serial sexual assaults, the psychological profile indicated that the suspect was a frequent consumer of pornography. A CD-ROM directory of stores was consulted to identify all the stores selling or renting pornographic films in the territory targeted by the geographical profile. Armed with the knowledge that most people frequent stores located near their homes, the investigators then showed a police sketch of the suspect to the employees of the stores, and asked about regular clients (Rossmo, 2000).

Geographical profiling may also provide information that improves the success of police interrogations. For example, in the case of missing persons or of persons assumed to be dead but whose body has not been found, geographical profiling may indicate the most likely locations of the missing body. Incorporation of maps or photographs of these locations into polygraph interrogations may improve the likelihood of locating the body, as polygraphs allow investigators to observe physical reactions, rather than oral responses, to photographs, objects and maps.

Geographical profiling may yield valuable results when used jointly with police information systems (e.g. Canada's SALVAC, the United States' VICAP) or registers of criminals, and helps investigators find clues, orient meetings with witnesses during the establishment of search frameworks, and train task forces.

Rossmo developed the CGT hit score, a quantitative measure of the performance of a geographical profile. It is calculated by dividing the territory investigated following the geoprofile up to the offender's arrest by the total territory over which the crimes in question were committed. Thus, if a serial sexual aggressor committed his assaults in a territory of 12 square kilometres and his home is found within an area of 0.6 square kilometres, the CGT hit score for the geographic profile is 5% (0.6/12) (Rossmo, 2001).

Between 1991 and 2001, several polices forces, including the Vancouver Police Force, the RCMP, the Ontario Provincial Police and the National Crime Faculty, submitted a total of 1426 crimes involving 1726 locations to geographical profiling. Overall, the mean CGT hit score was 4.7% (median: 3.0, standard deviation: 4.4), with murders obtaining a mean score of 5.1%, sexual assaults 4.7%, arsons 2.2% and armed robberies 7.1% (Rossmo, 2001).

CONCLUSION

Criminal profiling has undergone rapid evolution since James A. Brussel's work in the 1950s, and the last two decades have seen the emergence of new approaches. Unfortunately, these advances and innovations have tended to be drowned out by debates over the scientific validity of the technique. Recently, however, researchers have developed predictive models based on statistical methods that are increasingly good descriptors of criminal behaviour. Regardless of whether they are based on regression, Bayesian networks, fuzzy logic or classification methods, the models have produced interesting and quite encouraging results. However, these scientific innovations have been ignored by the many practitioners who cling to the semi-mystical nature often ascribed to the technique. In this connection, it is instructive to recall Grubin's observation (cited by Rossmo, 2000) that prudence should be exercised when the profiler becomes more popular than the profile.

However, as a result of academic researchers' criticisms of criminal profiling, the technique now appears to be more open to interdisciplinarity and teamwork. The era of the solitary profiler is, in general, long gone. We believe that partnerships between researchers and investigators can only improve the quality of criminal profiling. Thanks to statistical methods, the method of choice of social scientists, researchers have already developed predictive models (Aitken, Connolly et al., 1996; Aitken, Gammerman et al., 1996). But for profiling to be as effective as possible, approaches must be developed that fully exploit the joint expertise of scientists and investigators, and converge towards the apprehension of criminals.

Applied research in criminal profiling must be encouraged. Technological advances have made possible the development of new and extremely useful profiling tools, e.g. geographical profiling (Rossmo, 2000), but the information on specific criminal behaviours on which these tools are based must be updated on an ongoing basis. Furthermore, because some types of crimes, such as sexual murder, are relatively infrequent, it is particularly important for researchers to collaborate and share their data on these types of crime. Collaboration of this type would allow more complete profiles to be produced, and social and demographic differences to be controlled for.

Similarly, it is now clear that profilers must maintain records of all their profiles, so that cumulative analyses may be performed. To date, evaluative studies have indicated that investigators appreciated the contribution of profiling, particularly its clarification of criminal behaviour and identification of new avenues of investigation. Nevertheless, it is equally important to assess the ability of profiling to predict the characteristics of the author of a crime. Surveys on this question indicate that there is still much to be done.

In addition, researchers must continue to study several types of criminals in order to better understand them and produce more valid classifications. It should be borne in mind, however, that criminal profiling is concerned with why a criminal committed his crime *in the way he did*, not why he committed the crime *at all*. This requires understanding the significance of modus operandis and signatures, as well as motivations. In addition, future research should attempt to determine the individual characteristics with the greatest influence on the modus operandi. In criminal profiling, it is important to know which factors determine the characteristics of the crime scene, so as to be able to reconstruct the crime and make predictions about the suspect.

The development of a theory of criminal profiling requires that all the scientific knowledge that we do possess about some types of criminals (sexual murderers, sexual aggressors, etc.) be exploited to its fullest. For example, studies of sexual criminals' offending processes (Proulx et al., 1999; Proulx, Perreault & Ouimet, 1999; Ward, Louden et al., 1995) may also shed light on pre-crime phase processes and help establish a theoretical framework for the profiling of these criminals.

It is important to bear in mind that despite the obvious infatuation in recent years for criminal profiling – both among police agencies and in popular culture – this technique does not solve crimes. Confessions, the cooperation of witnesses and the collection of clues continue to be essential to solving crimes (Rossmo, 2000). Nothing can ever replace traditional investigative work. In fact, profiling cannot be dissociated from investigation: the more complete the investigation, the more accurate the profile.

Chapter 13

PSYCHOTHERAPEUTIC AND PSYCHODYNAMIC ISSUES WITH SEXUAL MURDERERS

Monique Tardif, Benoît Dassylva and Alexandre Nicole

The leitmotif of this chapter, like that of the other chapters of this book, is that the more disturbed an individual's developmental trajectory the more serious crimes he will be prone to commit. Nonetheless, the treatment of sexual murderers remains a cloudy, if not frankly confusing, issue. To undertake treatment of such offenders implies that the therapeutic techniques and underlying clinical concepts have undergone consistent and repeated testing. However, both clinical experience and treatment-related knowledge are limited when it comes to sexual murderers, due to the heterogeneous nature of these offenders and the rarity of their crimes. Accordingly, rather than setting out a detailed basis for treatment, this chapter will pursue more modest goals: the description of particularly helpful conceptual elements, and the presentation of clinical guidelines and techniques likely to be used in an exploratory therapeutic process.

THE EFFECTIVENESS OF TREATMENT

The last 50 years have seen a remarkable evolution in the techniques used to assess and treat sexual offenders (Marshall et al., 2006). Thus, early

Sexual Murderers: A Comparative Analysis and New Perspectives Edited by Jean Proulx Éric Beauregard, Maurice Cusson and Alexandre Nicole
© 2007 John Wiley & Sons, Ltd.

therapeutic approaches attempted to modify sexual offenders' sexual preferences through the use of conditioning techniques (Laws & Marshall, 2003). Subsequently, as affects and cognitive processes were taken into account, the target of therapy extended to social skills deficits, difficulties in managing affect, empathy deficits and cognitive distortions (Abel, Mittleman & Becker, 1985; Kirsch & Becker, 2006; Marshall & Laws, 2003). In the 1980s, it was noted that sexual aggression and addiction to psychoactive substances had several features in common. The principles of relapse prevention developed in work with substance abusers were therefore adapted and integrated into treatment programmes for sexual offenders (Marlatt, 1982; Marlatt & Gordon 1985; Pithers et al., 1983; Prentky & Burgess, 2000). The principle of this approach is that offenders can learn self-control and avoid relapses, through identification of the sequence of affective, cognitive and behavioural precursors of sexual aggression. Offenders must also learn coping skills to deal with these precursors. Although sexual aggression is now considered multifactorial, several authors believe that behaviour modification is the most appropriate therapeutic objective, and that the focus of treatment should therefore be on the factors directly responsible for the emergence and maintenance of sexual aggression (Hanson et al., 2002; Kirsch & Becker, 2006; Prentky & Burgess, 2000).

The efficacy of sexual offender treatment programmes continues to preoccupy clinicians and researchers (Alexander, 1999; Furby, Weinrott & Blackshaw, 1989; Gallagher et al., 1999; Hall, 1995; Hanson et al., 2002; Marques et al., 2005). The results of meta-analyses indicate that treatment programmes yield variable or modest results. Some authors have expressed concern about the absence of standard treatments and the value of assessing effectiveness solely in terms of relapses, rather than including, for example, relative changes in risk factors (Gallagher et al., 1999; Hanson et al., 2002; Hanson, 2000; Kirsch & Becker, 2006; Marques et al., 2005). In addition, the need for further research has been pointed out (Marshall et al., 2006). Marshall and Serran (2000) deplored the fact that no study has assessed the effectiveness of the various components of treatment programmes, which precludes identification of the active *elements* of observed changes.

Treatment must be tailored to the type of sexual offender. Furthermore, as different types of sexual offenders respond to treatment differently, particular attention must be paid to treatment planning (Hanson et al., 2002; Marshall et al., 1991; Marshall and Barbaree, 1990b). Only one study has investigated the effectiveness of programmes intended to prevent sexual murderers from relapsing (Clarke & Carter, 2000); the programme was observed to have positive effects but to be less effective than relapse prevention programmes for other types of sexual offenders. In the same vein, Kirsch and Becker (2006) state that it is inappropriate to apply current treatment programmes to all types of offenders.

The next section will clarify several concepts, especially those related to the sadistic nature of sexual murderers, in order to avoid the frequently arbitrary extrapolation of knowledge acquired from other types of offenders to sexual murderers.

DEFINITIONS OF SADISM AND OF SEXUAL MURDERERS

Lexical difficulties related to the definition of sexual murder is prejudicial not only to research on this type of crime but also to theorization and clinical work. For Douglas et al. (1992), the defining characteristic of sexual murder is that 'sexual homicide involves a sexual element (activity) as a basis for the sequence of acts leading to death' (p. 123). According to this definition, the sexual element is the primary motivational factor, while the sequence of events may demonstrate the coexistence of sexual and violent elements, or the preponderance of violent elements. Accordingly, while an individual may be classified as 'sexual murderer' because an outburst of anger during sexual assault pushes him to kill, another may be so classified because he systematically executes a sexual scenario involving murder. The imprecision of the key concepts of sexual murder hinders the establishment of reliable diagnostic criteria and the development of interventions adapted to the severity and intensity of these extreme criminal behaviours.

From a psychodynamic perspective, sexual murderers' problems are said to stem from a childhood (pre-oedipal) fixation characterized by sexual and aggressive instincts, i.e. sadistic urges. Fixation may generate sexual problems when the libido is so strongly attached to a mode of satisfaction of one of the developmental stages (oral, anal, phallic) that it shapes the character of the individual. The consequence of fixation may be manifest in the individual's sexual expression or may be latent (see, for fixation, Doron & Parot, 1991, pp. 303–4; Laplanche & Pontalis, 1967, pp. 160–4). The importance accorded to fixation by Freud (1905) has led to the mistaken notion that sadism in adults is merely a pathological exacerbation of a normal developmental phase of childhood libido. However, sexual sadism in adults is a sexual perversion in which satisfaction is derived from suffering and humiliation inflicted on others (Laplanche & Pontalis, 1967). In children, the expression of sexual drive does not require the finality of satisfaction, or even the presence of another person. Furthermore, among adults, the structuring of sadistic sexual fantasies and drives in sexual problems require other psychological processes to be in place (Bonnet, 2002).

Since our conception does not view 'ordinary' and 'criminal' sadism as two poles of a common continuum of severity, some differentiating factors are necessary. The availability of a partner may lead an 'ordinary' sadist to form a sadomasochistic relationship. Here, the expressions of sadistic and masochistic paraphilias are symmetric and complementary: this is a consensual relationship that allows the sadist to impose violence on his or her partner. This consensual relational game allows one party to evacuate their suffering and obtain pleasure, and the other party to endure this suffering in order to master it and transform it into pleasure. As long as this sadomasochistic game remains within the subjectively acceptable boundaries of the partners, each obtains satisfaction.

In contrast, sadism drives some individuals to seek a victim, not a sexual partner. In this case, the scenario of a symbolic acting out of inflicted suffering no longer suffices. Only a victim's real suffering (i.e. suffering that is not transformed into pleasure) is an acceptable finality. However, some individuals require a real victim to completely realize their fantasies or drives, and go beyond some personal boundaries of violence. Thus, most sadistic sexual aggressors do not commit sexual murder, although they may fantasize about it. In contrast, sadistic murderers have core sexual fantasies in which the finality of killing is central. These sexual murderers seek a great dehumanization of their victims and exhibit intense desire for omnipotence in several areas of their lives, especially their modus operandi. This point will be discussed in greater detail in the section on the role of the victim. Angry sexual murders, on the other hand, tend to be less sadistic and react more defensively to threats to their psychological integrity. Threats to integrity are feelings of being threatened because of the non-satisfaction of a psychological need or an intense emotional reaction to an external threat. For angry sexual murderers, the most common external threats are related to their individual freedom, their life, or their virility. The great diversity of threats is explained by the fact that losses of integrity are contingent on individual vulnerabilities, which are highly subjective.

THERAPEUTIC FRAMEWORK

The usual framework for therapy for sexual murderers is long-term incarceration that offers sufficient time for assessment and psychotherapeutic work. However, even before the initial assessment, clinical staff must anticipate the issues associated with the arrival of the sexual murderer. Measures designed to ensure safe environments for the staff, co-detainees and the murderer must be planned and must take into account the specific characteristics of the offender. For example, sexual murderers of children, who may be the object of violence from co-detainees, do not require the same management measures as do sexual murderers whose victims were adult females. Concrete measures such as the establishment of a security score, specific security measures for female staff and discussion of counter-transference must be implemented.

Initial evaluation

The pre-treatment assessment begins after sentence is pronounced and all the diagnostic evaluations (psychiatric, psychological, psychophysiological) have been completed. Therefore, there are no short-term objectives related to social reinsertion at this stage. Imprisonment often provokes a feeling of relief in offenders, who attempt to comprehend what has happened to them and obtain support. According to Zagury (2002), the function of containing of prison allows some compulsive sexual murderers to live calmly day to day and maintain adequate relationships. Once outside this framework, however, they become disorganized and commit many crimes in a quest for a feeling of omnipotence. The absence of manifest psychopathological symptoms attendant on confinement may thus strongly bias the assessment of risk presented by these murderers, particularly if their criminal history is partially unrecorded or unknown. Other sexual murderers lead incarcerated lives that are as exemplary as their previous lives in the community had been; in these cases, problematic behaviours in prison are not a concern, which renders the evaluation of change much more difficult.

As soon as pre-treatment assessment begins, the crime must be explored with the offender, in order to clearly identify its repercussions on the offender himself and on others (victims, those close to the murderer, co-detainees, correctional personnel). This initial assessment determines the offender's ability to manage his immediate situation and to talk about his crime, and the possibility of offering him support. In fact, authentic self-questioning appears unlikely initially. Simply bringing up the murderer's crime and history may present several problems. Basically, these are related to doubt about the sexual nature of the crime (due to conceptual and empirical diagnostic weaknesses), the absence of charges for sexual crimes, the often imprecise official version of the crime, and the poor reliability of the murderer's version of the crime. The information obtained from self-administered questionnaires and inventories and from phallometric assessments also may be biased. Following sentencing, offenders are less likely to hide or deform information. Nevertheless, the information they do provide must still be scrutinized carefully. It is therefore recommended that information be collected from multiple sources (professionals, spouses, members of his entourage and correctional or clinical staff). This first step provides a benchmark for further assessments of the murderer's openness and authenticity. Other clinical instruments that may be used include the Aggressive Sexual Behaviour Inventory (Mosher, 1988; Mosher & Anderson, 1986), the Coercive Sexual Fantasies Questionnaire (Greendlinger & Byrne, 1987), the Sex Fantasy Questionnaire (SFQ) (O'Donohue, Letourneau & Dowling (1997), the Sexual Arousability Inventory (Chambless & Lifshits, 1984) and the Multidimensional Assessment of Sex and Aggression (MASA) (Knight, Prentky & Cerce, 1994).

THE ANALYSIS OF THE CRIME SCENARIO

The entry point of choice for the treatment of sexual murderers remains the analysis of the modus operandi. The murderer's active, concrete role in the crime is more readily explored than is his inner world, which is less readily consciously accessible. Similarly, the contextual aspects of the crime (type of victim, location, acts, etc.) are related to elements of the offender's specific psychological process (Bonnet, 2002).

It appears that the types of sexual murderers can be distinguished from each other on the basis of their premeditation and murder scenario. Thus, some murderers whose crimes reflect anger and rage only exhibited indicators of violence reflecting control, power and domination. However, there are other criteria of sadism, namely humiliation of the victim, torture of the victim, interest in sexual sadism (self-reported or phallometric evidence) and sexual mutilation (Marshall, Kennedy, Yates & Serran, 2002). In our opinion, at least one of these other criteria is necessary for a diagnosis of sexual sadism. Marshall and his colleagues also recognize additional criteria of sexual sadism: kidnapping and confinement of the victim, taking the victim to a predetermined place, postmortem mutilation, sodomization of the victim, keeping souvenirs of the victim and recording of the crime. The value of Marshall et al.'s analytical checklist is its ability to distinguish between sadism and the expression of gross violence (which appears to be associated with a relationship of mastery) (Dorey, 1994). In this latter type of relationship, there is a drive for the control, domination and appropriation of another person. Although the victim may suffer intensely, inflicting suffering is not the goal, and suffering may even be ignored by the offender, who is indifferent to it (see Doron & Parot, 1991, p. 253). This important differentiation allows for a more coherent theorizing of the issues underlying sexual murder.

The concepts that facilitate the analysis of the crime acts and scenario are prevalence of negativity, matrix of repetition and process of fascination. The 'prevalence of negativity' (Winnicott, 1971, 1986) is the principle that negativity exerts a stronger influence than positivity on individuals' construction of their personal conception of concrete reality, and on their fantasies of imaginative reality. Thus, the analysis of the crime should be two-fold, focusing on both concrete reality (e.g. expressions of omnipotence during crime) and the corresponding absent reality (e.g. complete submission to his mother). For example, an angry sexual murderer expresses anger and domination during his crime, but the source of his frustration is absent; furthermore he does not express feelings of powerlessness. The concept of the repetitive matrix of sexual murders (Zagury, 2002) holds that a serial killer's first crime shapes his subsequent murders, as it simultaneously troubles and subjugates him. Far from triggering introspection, this impact of the first murder appears to incubate, eventually surfacing in a new, modified scenario. In the same vein, according to Ressler (1993), serial killers attempt to have their crimes exemplify their sadistic sexual fantasies as closely as possible from one murder to another. These considerations underscore the necessity of performing longitudinal analyses of offending pathways and sexual fantasies in order to better understand the underlying process of such crimes. The concept of the process of fascination (Dorey,

1994) holds that content considered destructive may, by its association with content considered striking and contrasting, become aesthetic, even erotic, because it engenders a fascination with destruction and death. For example, a sexual murderer may carefully arrange the decor of his murder scene so as to produce a theatrical effect (location, accessories, ritual, etc.) that induces fascination (*Dictionnaire de Psychanalyse*, 2001, p. 775–6). He attempts to lend meaning, sometimes enigmatic, to the murder scene, contrasting it with reality and the abject machinations of his crime. It is nevertheless important to mark as separate the bizarre fantasy content that reflects an underlying psychotic pathology. In these situations, the modus operandi usually appears less controlled, more disorganized, more chaotic.

In the planning and execution of their crime scenarios, sadistic sexual murderers are inclined to use contrasts to produce, consciously or not, a process of fascination. They consider themselves superior to other sexual murderers because they consider their crimes to be associated with more or less symbolized and enigmatic meaning. The targets of their effects of fascination are the media, the public and experts. The precautions they take in order to avoid apprehension only amplify reactions of horror and fascination, which give them a feeling of omnipotence.

Typically, therapists seeing these offenders in treatment feel intruded upon and violated with regard to their personal boundaries – in short, a victim–aggressor relationship is initiated. Another typical phenomenon is the establishment of a process of fascination which neutralizes the therapist's function. In these situations, therapists must re-establish their freedom of action by moderating the content addressed in therapy in order to limit its effect. Some sexual murderers are so invested in their position of omnipotent aggressor that they remain completely opposed to the idea of exploring their inner world. Although some adopt a more conciliatory position in treatment with regard to noncriminal content, their refusal to discuss their crimes often appears to simply be a systematic avoidance strategy.

Analysis of the function of the victim

Some sexual murderers insist on explaining their crimes on the basis of their uncontrollable urges towards their victims. However, their criminal actions towards their victims is only a subset of the complex relational issues underlying such crimes (Rousillon, 2002). In revenge scenarios, the victim remains a human being, as can be seen by such formulaic utterances as 'You're the one suffering, not me'. In this context, pleasure does not come from the victim's suffering but rather from a reversal of powerlessness into domination. Thus, in some murderers, the desire to dominate the victim is part of a need for self-affirmation to counter persistent feelings of powerlessness, passivity and dependence. In this context, the victim is a threat to his personal integrity and self-esteem, and must therefore be mastered to the point of becoming a true object of 'mastery' (Jeammet, 2002). Some sexual murderers of this type were only expecting to commit sexual assault, in an attempt to satisfy their urge for vengeance, with the murder occurring only as a result of uncontrollable situational factors. The violence inflicted on the victim in these cases is intended to negate her personal integrity and right to self-determination. According to Dorey (1981), the characteristics of the instinct for mastery are capture, appropriation and domination. These relational dimensions are usually present in the assaults by angry sexual murderers. Sexual murderers who commit this type of violence do not intend to inflict pain on the victim – they are in fact oblivious to it. Strictly speaking, this type of crime is not sadistic in intent, but is an assault determined by an impulsive act of self-preservation. The victim thus serves as a surrogate for other women who the murderer wishes to spare, since women remain, after all is said and done, a recognized source of satisfaction. The angry sexual murderer, generally nonserial, knows his victim in some 60% of cases. The quest for affirmation and self-preservation reflects a more defensive reaction that hides the offender's suffering. The victim must be mastered and become the receptacle of the offender's anger, as befits her status of victim. The crime thus has an interactive dimension, as evidenced by the reactions of the victims who resist and the aggressor's verbalized anger in response to this resistance.

Among other sexual murderers, aggression represents an offensive act that elicits no distress from the offender. Due to splitting, suffering is completely detached from the murderer's consciousness and not accessible. In this context, it is the affect of suffering that is completely split from other affects (omnipotence, for example). The victim is usually previously unknown to the murderer, and merely plays an ancillary role in the murderer's scenario. She is reduced to the status of a nonhuman object. The objective of the crime is to destroy the notion of being human and the normality of interpersonal and social relationships and corporeal representation. For example, the internal organs are made external, and objects are misused both for destructive purposes and to produce chaos and disorganization. The reactions of the victim are of no consequence to the offender   it is the magnitude of the destruction and the feelings of omnipotence that count. In these extreme cases, the damage to otherness and to the normality of life transcends the crime scene and targets the rest of the world, sowing terror, drawing media attention and challenging the law and experts. The quest for omnipotence is pitiless, insatiable even, and seeks a triumph recognized by others. In these types of crimes, victims are caught in a true system of destruction and torture.

CLINICAL ISSUES

Having reviewed definitional and theoretical issues related to sexual murderers, we will now outline some empirical and clinical issues, and establish some principles underlying therapeutic intervention.

Early relational problems and guilt

The family environment of sexual offenders is usually thought to be violent and unpredictable, which produces a predisposition to sexual coercion and relational difficulties (Malamuth et al., 1993; Marshall, 1984). As we have seen (Chapter 2), sexual murderers come from family environments that are more disturbed than those of other types of offenders. However, several authors believe that it is important to also take into account the role of developmental factors in the emergence and maintenance of coercive sexual aggression (Arrigo & Purcell, 2001; Burgess et al., 1986; Hickey, 2001; Malamuth et al., 1993; Marshall & Barbaree, 1993; Ressler et al., 1988). It therefore appears relevant to explain the primitive nature of the relational pathology of sexual murderers in terms of developmental factors.

In their study of sadomasochism among 111 children (boys and girls), Novick and Novick (1996) concluded, on the basis of clinical observation, that a child does not choose to develop permanent stable fantasies of omnipotence. A child's self-assertive and aggressive impulses are transformed into sadism when adults fail to satisfy their basic and relational needs. The feelings of rage and powerlessness thus provoked trigger a strong desire for destructive omnipotence, given the difficulty with which very young children feel guilt and concern for another. At this stage, a child is incapable of constructing a representation of another human (Winnicott, 1958). Since he is not yet differentiated, he is only attentive to reaching his goals, with little concern for the repercussions of his behaviour (Cupa, 2002). This allows him to express an intense dehumanized destructive impulse in his relationships with adults. In contrast, during the normal process of development, adults help children humanize their contacts and modulate their experience of omnipotence in ways that are more respectful of others. Novick and Novick (1996) noted in their adult patients that parental figures had contributed to this illusion of omnipotence and to a permanent distortion of reality, which reinforced the illusion of omnipotence and their distorted perceptions of themselves and of others. In the process, the regulation of self-esteem and impulse satisfaction became strongly linked to omnipotence and the capacity to control others. Furthermore, the tendency to seek fantasy-based solutions to conflicts and to difficulties adapting to reality becomes fixed during the latent period (between 6 and 12 years old), and becomes part of the character (Novick & Novick, 1996). In adolescence, individuals with sadomasochistic traits associate reality with displeasure and their fantasy world with pleasure (Novick & Novick, 1996). This in turn leads to the avoidance of the demands of reality and further strengthens reliance on the magic solution of omnipotence and the commission of destructive acts that deny reality.

The great value of the work by Novick and Novick (1994) is the identification of two systems of self-regulation and conflict resolution: an *open system*, oriented towards joy, competence, creativity and reality; and a *closed system*, oriented towards avoidance of reality, development of sado-masochism and illusions of omnipotence. Ideas of omnipotence must be validated by external factors if they are to become psychologically integrated. Such contributive factors concerning family environment include serious health problems, death or injury due to inadequate parenting. The illusion of omnipotence thus becomes a necessary belief, a subjective vision of reality that organizes the individual's thoughts and acts (Novick & Novick, 2000; Weiss, 1993, 1998). If the individual becomes convinced that their system of omnipotent illusion is reliable, the system will come to resemble an addiction, hindering openness to new experiences and the development of adequate forms of conflict resolution. It is in this way that a system of conflict resolution and pathological self-regulation of self-esteem becomes increasingly closed, repetitive and resistant to change.

Intervention goals, limitations and other considerations

We suggest that the theoretical model of Novick and Novick, as well as Dorey's model of relationships of mastery are good fits to the phenomenon of sexual murder. In the light of the theoretical aspects outlined above, clinical indicators may be proposed concerning sentence management and treatment goals. Current sexual offender treatment programmes have not been developed with sexual murderers in mind. It must therefore be recognized that their unquestioning application is likely to cause problems of several kinds. On the clinical level, sexual murderers, more than any other group of sexual offenders, present deeply anchored, very primitive psychological problems. It is therefore necessary to rethink, for example, the relevance of attempting to convince a sadistic sexual murder to enter a relapse prevention programme when (a) he feels himself to suffer from no problem, (b) he 'specializes' in well-planned crimes and (c) he is serving a 20-year sentence. Therapeutic interventions targeting the sexual nature of sexual murder should not be proposed at the beginning of sexual murderers' incarceration. It is, on the other hand, suggested to adopt a progressive approach that involves interventions that target the murderer's current life situation and take a more global approach to problems.

In this context, two guidelines stand out: address realistic intervention objectives and choose general, rather than specific, objectives. Some sexual murderers, disturbed by their crimes, request help understanding the reasons for their crimes and, in an attempt to give themselves hope, what the future reserves for them. Frank and direct discussions of the gravity of their crimes, the usual length of sentences for these crimes, society's and the legal system's scepticism about their reinsertion into society and limitations of treatment are necessary. Sincerity and frankness during the therapist's initial discussions will tend to counter sexual murderers' tendency to lie and trick to obtain what they want. Better management of incarceration and improvement of the murderer's quality of incarcerated life are realistic initial goals. Subsequently, general objectives related to developmental factors may be addressed. It should be recalled that the sexual murderer has a tendency to maintain a closed system of thoughts and actions (Novick & Novick, 1994). Self-absorbed, the sexual murderer attempts to avoid experiencing reality and acquiring new experiences, in favour of maintaining his feeling of omnipotence and relying on his fantasy world. At this stage, the recommended treatment objectives are therefore: encourage the murderer to participate in social and educational activities that foster openness to others; help the murderer to develop a realistic perception of himself and others; and find concrete and socially appropriate solutions to daily conflicts. Over the long term, achieving these general objectives will help the murderer escape his closed system, differentiate himself and solve problems without relying on his deviant sexual fantasies. At this point, we believe that these types of objectives may be achieved through nonspecific interventions such as psychoeducational and social activities, support therapy and learning of social skills. In this clinical context, the general objective of these interventions is to humanize the murderer's relational interactions. To this end, treatment staff's observations and interventions should be discussed in individual interviews or group discussion, in order to promote integration of learning and self-awareness. If these interventions yield long-term results, the clinician may attempt specific interventions targeting the murderer's sexual crime process, bearing in mind the dates of eligibility for parole or discharge.

The absence of major mental disorders among most sexual murderers may surprise therapists. In fact, murderers may appear organized, calm and detached from their crimes. Other murderers may intimidate therapists to the point that they feel symbolically victimized. Still others are capable of directing their attention to the therapist's narcissism and seducing them in an attempt to make them forget that they are the authors of violent crimes. The delivery of extremely violent content in a calm and innocent tone is disconcerting. In such cases, the therapist must suppose the existence in the murderer of a capacity for identification with others, neglected suffering and unconscious affects (Roussillon, 2002). If therapists find themselves becoming the receptacle for verbal, not physical, aggressive and sadistic content, they can avoid the victim role by using the content of interviews and their therapeutic relationship to identify the underlying problems and pursue self-awareness on the part of the murderer. The therapist also attempts to establish a relational mode in which they can progressively identify with the offender and ultimately the victim in order to use their subjective reactions as the basis for future therapeutic work. The danger in this type of therapeutic process is to be trapped in a single counter-transference reaction. To be the 'ally' of the offender, for example, may exacerbate murderer's splitting, and thus consolidate a split perception, of either the treatment staff or of himself.

Although daily observations by the treatment staff are valuable indicators of the murderer's state of mind, clinicians should be careful about extrapolating the murderer's progress in detention to a community-life context. Sexual murderers with good cognitive abilities are quite capable of showing successful integration of treatment. Others may exhibit the signs of consistent change while they are observed in closed detention or escorted outings. It is recommended that sexual murderers be observed systematically over the long term, with particular attention to the way *they* deal with their specific or challenging difficulties, which are indicators of therapeutic progress. Murderers whose crime was completely split from the other, relatively normal, spheres of their lives (occupational, social, marital) may not exhibit behavioural changes while incarcerated, rendering the assessment of the treatment impossible. Yet others, often of the angry type, have limited intellectual and cognitive abilities and are more opposed to therapy and less inclined to collaborate. Furthermore, the tendency of several murderers to dupe the therapist and keep their deviant imaginary sexual life active and secret is an important obstacle to the assessment of effects of therapy. These different clinical situations clearly show the necessity of determining specific indicators of therapeutic progress in detention.

The limitations outlined above regarding the assessment and treatment of this category of sexual offender are all the more problematic because of the limited number of cases (particularly in the case of sadistic murderers). For example, there is no data on recidivism or the impact of treatment. This being so, and in light of the grave consequences of recidivism in this context, the therapist bears a very high level of responsibility to society. For this reason, and because of a desire to avoid involvement in a murderer's eventual reinsertion in society, some therapists may refuse to treat sexual murderers. This burden of responsibility may be particularly acute when a therapist is obliged to evaluate the effects of their treatment. In this case, therapists may be faced with a conflict of loyalty that opposes the therapist–client relationship and the duty to protect society, and may find themselves in the paradoxical position of attempting to demonstrate that their treatment was ineffective – despite positive clinical indicators! It should be recognized that the therapist is the object of several types of internal and external pressure. Thus, their concern to avoid further victims and fulfil their duty to protect society influences their attitude to offering treatment and evaluating its effects. It should also be borne in mind that the media constitute an important source of pressure, due to their coverage of violent sexual crimes. With each new event, the media question the social reinsertion of sexual offenders, the abolition of the death penalty, the effectiveness of treatments and the competence of therapists. Furthermore, there is a real danger in extrapolating positive treatment results from other groups of sexual offenders to sexual murderers (Hollin, 1997). In our opinion, therapeutic trials performed with sexual murderers must be adapted to the subjects, realistic, progressive and congruent with the limitations of current knowledge.

CASE STUDIES

The presentation of two case studies is intended to illustrate the issues related to the treatment of angry and sadistic sexual murderers.

Frank: a sadistic murderer

At first glance, Frank appears to have led a banal life. Although married and employed, he had little social network and lived a quiet life. The appearance of a staid life is, however, deceiving, as for several years, starting some time after he married, Frank carried out behavioural try-outs related to his fantasies of controlling, confining, sexually assaulting, torturing and murdering women. Most of his free time appears to have been centred on preparatory activities for the crime: nourishing sadistic sexual fantasies and making contact with women in order to determine whether he could exert enough control to allow him to act out the subsequent steps of his scenario and partially satisfy his desire for omnipotence. His emotional register was marked by sexual arousal and feelings of power, without, however, underlying elements of suffering or malaise.

Frank's crime was scripted well beyond simple murder and was founded on deception, as his subterfuge consisted of offering a young woman a job in the field of fashion or high-end prostitution. His plan was to recruit a woman, trap her (capture), have consensual sexual contact with her (appropriation), humiliate her, torture her (domination), kill her and dismember her. It is possible to identify the three components of the relationship of mastery—namely capture, appropriation and domination—in this plan, but Frank did not stop there, as we shall see. It took Frank more than seven years of nourishing his deviant sexual fantasy to commit his murder. He made an appointment to observe a woman without her knowing and test if she would follow his requests concerning her clothing, namely to wear nylon stockings. It should be noted that the presence of the fetish element does not reflect true fetishism but is rather a sign of control that aroused him intensely. He pursued his scenario by beginning the job interview and asked whether she would agree to perform high-end prostitution. When she agreed, he asked her to demonstrate her skills and then killed her. After she was dead, he stabbed her in the heart seven times with a screwdriver, in an act of symbolic power. He kept the body of the victim one week before dismembering it and putting the parts in garbage bags (a denaturation of the victim to a nonhuman object, which adds to the horror), another way to symbolize his scorn for human life. He had a feeling of absolute power. After the crime, he talked to coworkers about the killer's profile, followed the story in the media and took great satisfaction in the failure of the police to apprehend him. All this demonstrates his rejection of the human, the law, society. The crime was completely split from his professional and marital life. Following this, he continued to take pleasure in collecting evidence of his triumph in the media and of the police's impotence. He felt proud of what he had done, and was satisfied. The analysis of the pre-crime, crime and post-crime phases revealed that Frank is a sadist and that self-regulation of his self-esteem was based on a feeling of omnipotence.

Short-term objectives

- Humanize his interpersonal relationships.
- Favour his participation in activities in order to develop his acceptance of the real world.
- Explore other aspects of his personality and his interests, in order to develop self-esteem less oriented towards omnipotence.

Long-term objectives (if previous objectives were effective)

- Discuss his crimes, to understand their meaning.
- Make him aware of his rejection of his real world and of the human, as well as of underlying aspects of his desire for omnipotence.

Therapeutic course

- Do not pursue objectives oriented towards release, as the likelihood of this is low.
- Do not undertake only cognitive behavioural modalities, as it is too easy for this offender to conform and manipulate.
- Do not confuse the murderer's capacity to conform to treatment with real therapeutic progress.
- Channel his desire for omnipotence into a more human and socially acceptable outlet, so as to increase his capacity for interaction with the real world (principal indicator of progress).

Paul: an angry murderer

Paul's life was a constant stream of frustration, stemming from conflict with women, low self-esteem and feelings of rejection. As a defence mechanism, he came to believe that women are merely objects of pleasure to be dominated and mastered. In his relationships with women, he sought to establish a relationship of mastery. Feelings of malaise and distress prior to the commission of his crimes are identifiable retrospectively, indicating a defensive role of the offending pathway. In such cases, the victim is not dehumanized, as she is perceived as an object of both frustration and, because of her capacity to provide pleasure, satisfaction. His first, unplanned, crime occurred when a prostitute with whom he was to have sex ridiculed him in front of a taxi driver, calling him an easy client. Once alone with the prostitute, he exploded in rage and strangled her to death. This was an impulsive act with no evidence of sadism, as he took no pleasure in the victim's suffering. It was only after he had killed the victim that he undressed her, had intercourse but did not ejaculate, and masturbated until ejaculation. He left the crime scene without drawing attention to himself and did not attempt to hide his crime. After the crime he felt relieved and free of all tension. The motivation of the crime appeared to have been vengeance for a narcissistic affront inflicted by a woman. Two weeks later, he made an appointment with a prostitute working out of her home, with whom he had already had sex on several occasions. He got to the appointment a little earlier than expected, and the prostitute asked him to wait because she was with another client. He was frustrated and angry at this situation, because he felt entitled to special treatment. He interpreted the prostitute's behaviour as a form of control in a situation in which he himself sought to dominate a woman. Following this loss of power, he strangled her in an outburst of rage, had sex with her postmortem and ran away from the crime scene. The two crimes lasted 30 minutes in all. Two months later, incapable of living with his crimes, he turned himself in to the police. Paul felt relieved initially, then guilty.

Short-term objectives

- Offer support therapy in order to help him cope with emotions related to his crime's consequences for himself and others, and express his feelings of malaise.
- Favour his participation in relational activities in order to develop his interaction with others less oriented towards domination–submission relationships.
- Explore other aspects of his personality and his interests, in order to develop self-esteem less oriented towards omnipotence and sexuality.

Long-term objectives (if previous objectives were effective)

- Discuss his crimes, to understand their meaning and make him aware of his feelings of impotence.
- Teach him to better manage situations in which he suffers narcissistic affronts, particularly from women.
- Foster his sense of self-esteem.
- Help him develop more egalitarian relationships with women.

Therapeutic course

- Undertake specific treatment designed to improve anger control; work on the development of social skills; reduce his cognitive distortions, especially his idea that women are always trying to dominate and humiliate men; develop relapse-prevention strategies.
- Be vigilant about the murderer's participation in his treatment.
- The primary indicators of changes are related to: more egalitarian interpersonal relationships (particularly with women); a form of sexuality less oriented towards domination; a less interpretive relationship with women; better tolerance of frustration; a more appropriate, less sexualized form of self-esteem.
- Avoid undue generalization of the therapeutic progress.

CONCLUSION

Given the current state of knowledge, the gravity of the issues and the limited clinical experience with subjects, treatment of sexual murderers is more open to debate than the treatment of any other category of sexual offender. Some conceptual elements related to the desire for relationships of mastery and extreme desire for omnipotence appear to help better understand and differentiate between angry and sadistic sexual murderers. The circumstances surrounding the onset of treatment of sexual murderers not only are key determinants of the establishment of realistic objectives but also impose limits on the therapeutic framework and process. The length of the sentence and the implementation of a secure intervention framework are crucial. A therapeutic process focusing on short-term objectives at the beginning of incarceration favours the exploration of post-crime repercussions and the humanization of the murderer. Subsequently, objectives related to issues underlying the commission of the crimes can be pursued with some sexual murderers. A therapist working with these subjects must remain particularly vigilant about subjective reactions that can interfere with therapeutic work. Although many caveats related to the treatment of sexual murderers have been discussed, it is nevertheless true that these subjects may benefit from therapeutic interventions, and that therapists may acquire new insights about sexual murderers over the course of the therapy.

CONCLUSION

Jean Proulx

In the introduction and in Chapter 1 of this book, we presented the sexual murderer as typically portrayed by scientific and literary authors. In this view, the sexual murderer is a psychopath with no empathy for his victims and no guilt over his crimes. In addition, he is a serial killer specializing in sexual crimes that originate in long-nurtured sadistic sexual fantasies predominated by the torture and the humiliation of his victims. This aberrant proclivity is rooted in an infancy characterized by sexual, physical and psychological victimization. Finally, in the popular mind, there is a belief that a huge number of sexual murderers are at large.

Unfortunately, this model of sexual murderers has limited empirical basis. Some studies have relied on a limited amount of data, taken from a limited number of subjects. Others have relied on samples that are biased by the overrepresentation of serial murderers. In yet others, no distinction is made between sexual murderers of women, of children, or of men, despite the possibility that these three types of sexual murderers differ with respect to development, psychological profile and offending process. In addition, several studies have relied on data of dubious validity (for example, biographies) rather than on semi-structured interviews, official records (police reports, victim statements) and standardized psychometric instruments. Finally, few comparative studies have been conducted, and those few have some limitations.

Sexual Murderers: A Comparative Analysis and New Perspectives   Edited by Jean Proulx and Éric Beauregard,
Maurice Cusson and Alexandre Nicole
© 2007 John Wiley & Sons, Ltd.

In order to avoid the pitfalls of previous studies, both the Montreal and Birmingham studies relied on large unbiased samples, as well as on comparison groups and standardized assessment procedures. In the Montreal study, 40 nonserial sexual murderers of women were compared to a group of 101 sexual aggressors of women. Each offender was evaluated with a set of standardized psychometric instruments (e.g. MCMI) and participated in a semi-structured interview. The results of these procedures were complemented by information from official records. In the Birmingham study, 58 sexual murderers were compared to 112 sexual aggressors. As in the Montreal study, offenders were evaluated using standardized psychometric instruments (e.g. MCMI, MSI, MASA) and participated in semi-structured interviews. Results from these two studies were convergent and differ in several ways from previously reported results.

In the Montreal study, the developmental, psychopathological and situational features of sexual murderers of women were compared to those of sexual aggressors of women. The prevalences of sexual and psychological victimization did not significantly differ in the two groups. However, sexual murderers were the victims of physical violence more often than were sexual aggressors of women. In addition, inappropriate behaviours in childhood (social isolation, daydreaming, reckless behaviours), deviant sexual fantasies and low self-esteem were more prevalent among sexual murderers than among sexual aggressors. Also, more than half of the subjects in both of these two groups of offenders reported having been exposed to psychological and physical violence. Finally, the majority of subjects possessed previous criminal records (murderers: 71.8%; sexual aggressors: 80.9%); violent crimes were more frequent among sexual murderers, property crimes among sexual aggressors. Neither group specialized in sexual crimes (only 22% of all the crimes committed by sexual murderers, and 17% of the crimes committed by sexual aggressors, were sexual in nature). Thus, these results indicate that the developmental and criminal backgrounds of sexual aggressors and sexual murderers do present certain differences, even if they are not diametrically opposed.

In terms of psychopathological factors – as measured by the MCMI personality disorder scales – sexual murderers were quite similar to sexual aggressors. In both groups, the most commonly observed personality disorders were schizoid, avoidant and dependent. Subjects with this profile are typically considered socially isolated, shy and having low self-esteem, which perfectly matches our results concerning the childhood and adolescence of sexual murderers. Accordingly, we find the classical view of the sexual murderer as psychopath highly debatable, in light of our finding that only 10% of our subjects had significant scores on the antisocial scale of the MCMI.

Several of the situational factors were good predictors of a sexual crime ending in murder. In fact, an attack by an assailant who was angry prior to the crime was more likely to end in a sexual murder. Sexual murder was also more likely if the assailant had consumed alcohol prior to the crime or was armed with a blunt object. On the other hand, sexual murder was much less likely if the victim and assailant were intimates or members of the same family. These results indicate that situational factors, independent of developmental and psychopathological factors, are crucial determinants of the escalation of sexual assault to sexual murder.

Nonserial sexual murderers in the Montreal study were compared to serial sexual murderers of the FBI study. In the latter sample, a larger number of subjects had a disturbed development which was characterized by social isolation, cruelty toward animals, self-mutilation and compulsive masturbation. Fortunately, however, serial sexual murderers represent only 2% of sexual murderers incarcerated in Canada and in United States. Again, the classical model, in which serial sexual murderers are seen as archetypical, is not confirmed by empirical data.

Apart from the comparative analysis, the Montreal study included typological analyses. These analyses reveal three types of sexual murderers: the sadistic murder, the angry murderer and the murderer who kills to eliminate witnesses. The sadistic sexual murderer is a good fit to the classical model of sexual murderers, since he is overwhelmed by deviant sexual fantasies, and his murders are well planned. In addition, sadistic sexual murders included elements of psychological and physical violence. In contrast, the angry sexual murderers had no deviant sexual fantasies prior to their crimes. However, the murders committed by angry sexual murderers are characterized by alcohol intoxication and anger, two disinhibitory factors. This type of murder is not planned and involves a high level of expressive violence. Finally, the primary motivation of sexual murderers who kill to eliminate witnesses is sexual gratification. This typology clearly demonstrates that only some sexual murderers are sadistic.

In the Birmingham study, as in the Montreal study, a sample of sexual murderers was compared to a sample of sexual aggressors, and typological analyses were carried out. The majority of the subjects had previous criminal records. The prevalence of sexual victimization in the two groups of sexual criminals did not significantly differ. With regard to psychopathological characteristics, as measured by MCMI scales, sexual murderers were quite similar to sexual aggressors, with only 10% of both groups exhibiting antisocial personality characteristics. Finally, the typological analyses revealed three types of sexual murderers: sadistic, violently motivated and sexually motivated.

The results of the Birmingham study are very similar to those obtained in the Montreal study. Apart from their results, these two studies share the following characteristics: (1) a large unbiased sample of sexual murderers; (2) a comparison group; (3) standardized psychometric instruments and (4) semi-structured interviews of each offender. Since these two studies were carried out independently in Canada and in England, their convergent data may be considered a solid basis for a model of sexual murderers.

Although the Montreal and Birmingham studies produced similar results, further studies are necessary before the classical model of sexual murderers can be dismissed. Since sexual murder is a rare phenomenon, an international study is necessary to obtain a large unbiased sample in a relatively short period. Such a study would use the same protocol in several countries and include standardized measures of developmental, psychopathological and criminological factors. Ideally, a prospective longitudinal study, based on a birth cohort, should be carried out, but this strategy is unrealistic, given the low prevalence of sexual murder. Consequently, a retrospective approach is suggested. The limitations of this type of research strategy may be improved by using multiple sources of information (family, school and police). In addition, neuropsychological and endocrinological factors must be investigated with newly developed laboratory methods. For example, functional MRI and phallometry could be carried out during the presentation of violent and erotic stimuli, in order to assess sexual murderers' information processing in sexual and violent contexts.

Scientific investigation of sexual murderers is necessary from both theoretical and practical points of view. Although the development of an adequate model of sexual murderers is a scientific goal in itself, it also has practical benefits, as it provides police officers, as well as forensic psychologists and criminologists involved in the treatment of sexual murderers, with a solid basis for dealing with these offenders. In addition, profilers rely on the results of empirical studies to maximize the accuracy of the portraits of specific sexual murderers they are called upon to produce, and clinicians involved in the treatment of sexual murderers rely on the results of empirical studies to identify the most relevant therapeutic goals for specific offenders. While decisions to release sexual murderers to the community must partially be grounded in the assessment of their therapeutic progress following prolonged incarceration, a delicate question remains: Should any sexual murderer be released to the community, given the catastrophic consequences of recidivism? However, this question takes us far from the realm of science, and drives into the domains of ethics and politics.

REFERENCES

Abel, G. G., Blanchard, E. B., Becker, J. V. & Djenderedjian, A. (1978). Differentiating sexual aggressives with penile measures. *Criminal Justice and Behavior*, *5*, 315–32.

Abel, G. G., Gore, D. K., Holland, C. L., Camp, N., Becker, J. V. & Rathner, B. A. (1989). The measurement of the cognitive distortions of child molesters. *Annals of Sex Research*, *2*, 135–53.

Abel, G. G., Mittelman, M. S., & Becker, J. V. (1985). Sex offenders: results of assessment and recommendations for treatment. In M. H. Ben-Aron, S. J. Hucker & C. D. Webster (Eds), *Clinical Criminology: The Assessment and Treatment of Criminal Behavior* (pp. 207–20). Toronto: M & M Graphics.

Ainsworth, P. B. (2001). *Offender Profiling and Crime Analysis*. New York: Willan.

Aitken, C. G. G., Connolly, T., Gammerman, A., Zhang, G., Bailey, D., Gordon, R. & Oldfield, R. (1996). Statistical modelling in specific case analysis. *Science and Justice*, *36*, 245–55.

Aitken, C. G. G. & Gammerman, A. (1989). Probabilistic reasoning in evidential assessment. *Journal of the Forensic Science Society*, *29*, 303–16.

Aitken, C. G. G., Gammerman, A., Zhang, G., Connolly, T., Bailey, D., Gordon, R. & Oldfield, R. (1996). Bayesian belief networks with an application in specific case analysis. In A. Gammerman (Ed.), *Computational Learning and Probabilistic Reasoning* (pp. 169–84). Chichester: John Wiley & Sons, Ltd.

Alder, C. (1984). The convicted rapist: a sexual or a violent offender? *Criminal Justice and Behavior*, *11*, 157–77.

Alexander, M. A. (1999). Sexual offender treatment efficacy revisited. *Sexual Abuse: Journal of Research and Treatment*, *11*, 101–16.

Alston, J. D. (1994). The serial rapist's spatial pattern of target selection. Unpublished master's thesis, Simon Fraser University, Burnaby, BC.

Alston, J. D. (2001). The serial rapist's spatial pattern of victim selection. In G. M. Godwin (Ed.), *Criminal Psychology and Forensic Technology: A Collaborative Approach to Effective Profiling* (pp. 231–49). Boca Raton, FL: CRC Press.

American Psychiatric Association (1980). *Diagnostic and Statistical Manual of Mental Disorders (DSM-III)*. Washington, DC: American Psychiatric Association.

American Psychiatric Association (1987). *Diagnostic and Statistical Manual of Mental Disorders (DSM-III-R)*. Washington, DC: American Psychiatric Association.

American Psychiatric Association (1994). *Diagnostic and Statistical Manual of Mental Disorders (DSM-IV)*. Washington, DC: American Psychiatric Association.

American Psychiatric Association (2000). *Diagnostic and Statistical Manual of Mental Disorders: Fourth Edition*: Text Revision. Washington, DC: American Psychiatric Association.

Amir, A. (1971). *Patterns in Forcible Rape*. Chicago: University of Chicago Press.

Arrigo, B. A. & Purcell, C. E. (2001). Explaining paraphilias and lust murder: toward an integrated model. *International Journal of Offender Therapy and Comparative Criminology*, 45, 6–31.

Arrindell, W. A., Sanavio, E., Aguilar, G., Sica, C., Hatzichristou, C., Eisemann, M., Recinos, L. A., Gaszner, P., Peter, M., Tomatis, C., Kállai, J. & Van der Ende, J. (1999). The development of a short form of the EMBU: its appraisal with students in Greece, Guatemala, Hungary and Italy. *Personality and Individual Differences*, 27, 613–28.

Aubut, J. (1993). *Les Agresseurs Sexuels: Théorie, Evaluation et Traitement*. Paris: Maloine.

Bandura, A. (1977). *Social Learning Theory*. Englewood Cliffs, NJ: Prentice Hall.

Barbaree, H. E., Seto, M. C., Serin, R. C., Amos, N. L. & Preston, D. L. (1994). Comparisons between sexual and non-sexual rapists subtypes: sexual arousal to rape, offense precursors and offense characteristics. *Criminal Justice and Behavior*, 21, 95–114.

Bard, L., Carter, D. Cerce, D., Knight, R., Rosenberg, R. & Schneider, B. (1987). A descriptive study of rapists and child molesters: developmental, clinical and criminal characteristics. *Behavioral Science and the Law*, 5, 203–20.

Barlow, D. H. & Abel, G. G. (1976). Sexual deviation. In W. E. Craighead, A. E. Kazdin & N. J. Maloney (Eds), *Behavior Modification: Principles, Issues and Applications* (pp. 341–60). Boston: Houghton & Mifflin.

Bartol, C. R. (1999). *Criminal Behavior: A Psychosocial Approach* (5th edition). Upper Saddle River: Prentice Hall.

Baxter, D. J., Marshall, W. L., Barbaree, H. E., Davidson, P. R. & Malcolm, P. B. (1984). Deviant sexual behavior: differentiating sex offenders by criminal and personal history, psychometric measures, and sexual response. *Criminal Justice and Behavior*, 11, 477–501.

Beauregard, E. (1999). *Typologie de scénarios délictuels de meurtriers sexuels*. Mémoire inédit, Université de Montréal.

Beauregard, E., Lussier, P. & Proulx, J. (2004). An exploration of developmental factors related to deviant sexual preferences among adult rapists. *Sexual Abuse: Journal of Research and Treatment*, 16, 151–61.

Beauregard, E. & Proulx, J. (2002). Profiles in the offending process of non-serial sexual murderers. *International Journal of Offender Therapy and Comparative Criminology*, 46, 386–99.

Beauregard E. & Proulx, J. (in press). A classification of sexual homicide against men. *International Journal of Offender Therapy and Comparative Criminology*.

Beauregard, E., Stone M. R., Proulx J., & Michaud, P. (in press). Sexual murderers of children: developmental, pre-crime, crime and post-crime factors. *International Journal of Offender Therapy and Comparative Criminology*.

Beck, A. T. & Freeman, A. (1990). *Cognitive Therapy of Personality Disorders*. New York: Guilford Press.

Beech, A. (2003). Sexual murderers. Unpublished manuscript.

Beech, A. & Fisher, D. (2002). The rehabilitation of child sex offenders. *Australian Psychologist*, 37, 206–14.

Beech, A., Fisher, D. & Ward, T. (2005). Sexual murders' implicit theories. *Journal of Interpersonal Violence*, 20, 1366–89.

Beech, A., Oliver, C., Fisher, D. & Beckett, R. C. (2006). *STEP 4: The Sex Offender Treatment Programme in Prison: Addressing the Needs of Rapists and Sexual Murderers.* Birmingham: University of Birmingham. Available electronically from www.hmprisonservice.gov.uk/assets/documents/100013DBStep_4_SOTP_report_2005.pdf.

Beech, A., Robertson, D. & Clarke, J. (2001). *Towards a sexual murder typology.* 20th Annual Conference of the Association for the Treatment of Sexual Abusers, San Antonio, Texas.

Beech, A., Ward, T. & Fisher, D. (2006). The identification of sexual and violent motivations in men who assault women: implications for treatment. *Journal of Interpersonal Violence*, 21, 635–53.

Bénézech, M. (1995). De quelques perspectives médico-psychologiques sur les homicides sexuels. Présentation de trois observations. *Annales Médico-psychologiques*, 153, 501–11.

Bénézech, M. (1997). L'homicide sexuel: diagnostic et classement criminologiques. *Journal de Médecine Légale et de Droit Médical*, 40, 289–94.

Bernard, G. & Proulx, J. (2002). Caractéristiques du passage à l'acte de criminels violents états-limites et narcissiques. *Revue Canadienne de Criminologie, January*, 51–75.

Blackburn, R. (1982). *The Special Hospitals Assessment of Personality and Socialisation.* Unpublished manuscript, Park Lane Hospital, Liverpool, UK.

Blackburn, R. (1993). *The Psychology of Criminal Conduct: Theory, Research and Practice.* Chichester: John Wiley & Sons, Ltd.

Blackburn, R. & Fawcett, D. (1996). *Manual for the Antisocial Personality Questionnaire (APQ).* Unpublished manuscript, University of Liverpool, UK.

Block, R. & Skogan, W. G. (1985). *The Dynamics of Violence between Strangers – Victim Resistance and Outcomes in Rape, Robbery and Assault.* Formerly the Center for Urban Northwestern University Institute for Policy Research, USA.

Block, R. & Skogan, W. G. (1986). Resistance and nonfatal outcomes in stranger-to-stranger predatory crime. *Violence and Victims*, 1, 241–53.

Blumstein, A., Cohen, J., Roth, J. A. & Visher, C. A. (1986). *Criminal Careers and Career Criminals* (vol. 1). Washington, DC: National Academy Press.

Blumstein, A., Cohen, J. & Farrington, D. P. (1988). Criminal career research: its value for criminology. *Criminology*, 26, 1–35.

Bond, I. K. & Evans, D. R. (1967). Avoidance therapy: its use in two cases of underwear fetishism. *Canadian Medical Association Journal*, 96, 1160–2.

Bonnet, G. (2002). Quand le sadisme devient une perversion. *Revue Française de Psychanalyse*, 66, 1043–53.

Boutin, S. (1999). *La carrière criminelle des agresseurs sexuels.* Rapport de stage inédit, Université de Montréal.

Brantingham, P. J. & Brantingham, P. L. (1984). *Patterns in Crime.* New York: Macmillan.

Brantingham, P. J. & Brantingham, P. L. (1991). *Environmental Criminology.* Prospect Heights, IL: Waveland Press.

Brantingham, P. L. & Brantingham, P. J. (1993). Environment, routine and situation: toward a pattern theory of crime. In R. V. Clarke & M. Felson (Eds), *Routine Activity and Rational Choice, Advances in Criminological Theory* (Vol. 5). New Brunswick: Transaction.

Brittain, R. P. (1970). The sadistic murderer. *Medicine, Science and the Law*, 10, 198–207.

Brown, J. S. (1991). The psychopathology of serial homicide: a review of the possibilities. *American Journal of Forensic Psychiatry, 12*, 13–21.

Brussel, J. A. (1968). *Casebook of a Crime Psychiatrist.* New York: Bernard Geis Associates.

Bumby, K. M. & Hanson, D. J. (1997). Intimacy deficits, fear of intimacy, and loneliness among sexual offenders. *Criminal Justice and Behavior, 24*, 315–31.

Burgess, A. W., Hartman, C. R., Ressler, R. K., Douglas, J. E. & McCormack, A. (1986). Sexual homicide: a motivational model. *Journal of Interpersonal Violence, 1*, 251–72.

Burgess, A. W., Prentky, R. A., Burgess, A. G., Douglas, J. E. & Ressler, R. K. (1994). Serial murder. In M. Hersen, R. T. Ammerman & L. A. Sisson (Eds), *Handbook of Aggressive and Destructive Behavior in Psychiatric Patients* (pp. 509–30). New York: Plenum.

Canter, D. V. (1995). Psychology of offender profiling. In R. Bull & D. Carson (Eds), *Handbook of Psychology in Legal Contexts.* Chichester: John Wiley and Sons, Ltd.

Canter, D. V. & Gregory, A. (1994). Identifying the residential location of rapists. *Journal of Forensic Science Society, 34*, 169–75.

Canter, D. V. & Heritage, R. (1990). A multivariate model of sexual offence behaviour: developments in offender profiling. *Journal of Forensic Psychiatry, 1*, 185–212.

Canter, D. V. & Hodge, S. (1997). *Predatory patterns of serial murder.* Unpublished manuscript, University of Liverpool, Institute of Investigative Psychology and Forensic Behavioural Science.

Canter, D. V. & Larkin, P. (1993). The environmental range of serial rapists. *Journal of Environmental Psychology, 13*, 63–71.

Chambless, D. & Lifshitz, J. L. (1984). Self-reported sexual anxiety and arousal: the expanded sexual arousability inventory. *Journal of Sex Research, 20*, 241–54.

Chéné, S. (2000). Le processus d'aggravation du viol au meurtre sexuel: intentions de l'agresseur et données situationnelles. Unpublished master's thesis, Université de Montréal.

Chessick, R. D. (1997). Archaic sadism. *Journal of the American Academy of Psychoanalysis, 24*, 605–18.

Clarke, J. & Carter, A. (1999). *Sexual murderers: their assessment and treatment.* 18th Annual Research and Treatment Conference, ATSA, Lake Buena Vista, Florida.

Clarke, J. & Carter, A. (2000). Relapse prevention with sexual murderers. In D. R. Laws, S. M. Hudson & T. Ward (Eds), *Remaking Relapse Prevention with Sex Offenders: A Sourcebook* (pp. 389–401). Thousand Oaks, CA: Sage.

Cohen, A. (1966). *Deviance and Control.* Englewood Cliffs, NJ: Prentice Hall (French translation, 1971).

Cohen, L. E. & Felson, M. (1979). Social change and crime rate trends: a routine activity approach. *American Sociological Review, 44*, 588–608.

Cook, P. E. & Hinman, D. L. (1999). Criminal profiling: science and art. *Journal of Contemporary Criminal Justice, 15*, 230–41.

Copson, G. (1995). *Coals to Newcastle? A Study of Offender Profiling: Part 1* (Special Interest Series: Paper 7). London: Police Research Group, Home Office Police Department.

Cornish, D. & Clarke, R. (1986). Rational choice approaches to crime. In D. B. Cornish & R. V. Clarke (Eds), *The Reasoning Criminal: Rational Choice Perspectives on Offending* (pp. 1–6) New York: Springer-Verlag.

Cuppa, D. (2002). La pulsion de cruauté. *Revue Française de Psychanalyse, 66*, 1073–89.

Cusson, F. (1996). La réitération de l'homicide au Québec de 1956 à 1995. Master's thesis, Université de Montréal.

Cusson, F. (1999). Les meurtriers qui tuent de nouveau. In J. Proulx, M. Cusson & M. Ouimet (Eds), *Les Violences Criminelles* (pp. 131–53). Québec: Presses de l'Université Laval.

Cusson, M. (1998a). La violence conflictuelle. In M. Cusson (Ed.), *Criminologie Actuelle* (pp. 22–35). Paris: Presses Universitaires de France.

Cusson, M. (1998b). Le rationnel et l'irrationnel. In M. Cusson (Ed.), *La Criminologie* (pp. 67–76). Paris: Hachette.

Cusson, M. (1998c). *Criminologie Actuelle*. Paris: Presses Universitaires de France.

Cusson, M., Beaulieu, N. & Cusson, F. (2003). Les homicides. In M. LeBlanc, M. Ouimet & D. Szabo (Eds), *Traité de Criminologie Empirique* (3rd edition, pp. 281–331). Montréal: Presses de l'Université de Montréal.

Cusson, M. & Cordeau, G. (1994). Le crime du point de vue de l'analyse stratégique. In D. Szabo & M. Leblanc (Eds), *Traité de Criminologie Empirique* (pp. 91–112). Montréal: Les Presses de l'Université de Montréal.

Davies, A. (1992). Rapist's behaviour: a three-aspect model as a basis for analysis and the identification of serial crime. *Forensic Science International, 55*, 173–94.

Davies, A. (1994). Offender profiling. *Medicine, Science and the Law, 34*, 185–6.

Davies, A. (1997). Specific profile analysis: a data-based approach to offender profiling. In J. L. Jackson & D. A. Bekerian (Eds), *Offender Profiling: Theory, Research and Practice* (pp. 191–209). Chichester: John Wiley and Sons, Ltd.

Davies, A., Wittebrood, K. & Jackson, J. L. (1996). Predicting the criminal antecedents of a stranger rapist from his offence behaviour. *Science and Justice, 37*, 161–70.

Davis, J.A. (1999). Criminal personality profiling and crime scene assessment: A contemporary investigative tool to assist law enforcement public safety. *Journal of Contemporary Criminal Justice, 15*, 291–301.

Dictionnaire de la Psychanalyse (2nd edition) (2001). Paris: Encyclopedia Universalis & Albin Michel.

Dietz, P. E. (1985). Sex offender profiling by the FBI: a preliminary conceptual model. In M. H. Ben-Aron, S. J. Hucker & C. D. Webster (Eds), *Clinical Criminology: The Assessment and Treatment of Criminal Behaviour* (pp. 207–19). Toronto: M & M Graphics.

Dietz, P. E. (1986). Mass, serial and sensational homicides. *Bulletin of the New York Academy of Medicine, 62*, 477–91.

Dietz, P. E., Harry, B. & Hazelwood, R. R. (1986). Detective magazines: pornography for the sexual sadists? *Journal of Forensic Sciences, 31*, 197–211.

Dietz, P. E., Hazelwood, R. R. & Warren, J. W. (1990). The sexually sadistic criminal and his offences. *Bulletin of the American Academy of Psychiatry and the Law, 18*, 163–78.

Dorey, R. (1994). La peau éclatée, entre l'hommage et la dette. In R. Kaës et al. (Eds), *Hommage à Didier Anzieu. Les Voies de la Psyché*. Paris: Dunod.

Doron, R. & Parot, F. (1991). *Dictionnaire de la Psychologie*. Paris: PUF.

Douglas, J. E. & Burgess, A. E. (1986). Criminal profiling: a viable investigative tool against violent crime. *FBI Law Enforcement Bulletin*, 9–13.

Douglas, J. E., Burgess, A. W., Burgess, A. G. & Ressler, R. K. (1997). *Crime Classification Manual*. New York: Lexington.

Douglas, J. E., Burgess, A. W., Burgess, A. G., & Ressler, R. K. (1992). *Crime Classification Manual: A Standard System for Investigating and Classifying Violent Crimes*. New York: Lexington.

Douglas, J. E., Ressler, R. K., Burgess, A. W. & Hartman, C. R. (1986). Criminal profiling from crime scene analysis. *Behavioral Sciences and the Law, 4*, 401–21.

Earls, C. M. & Proulx, J. (1986). The differentiation of francophone rapists and nonrapists using penile circumferential measures. *Criminal Justice and Behavior, 13*, 419–29.

Egger, S. A. (1999). Psychological profiling: past, present, and future. *Journal of Contemporary Criminal Justice, 15*, 242–61.

Fedora, O., Reddon, J. R., Morrison, J. W., Fedora, S. K., Pascoe, H. & Yendall, L. (1992). Sadism and other paraphilias in normal controls and aggressive and nonaggressive sex offenders. *Archives of Sexual Behavior, 21*, 1–15.

Feister, S. J. & Gay, M. (1991). Sadistic personality disorder: a review of data and recommendations for DSM-IV. *Journal of Personality Disorders, 5,* 376–85.

Felson, M. (1998). *Crime and Everyday Life* (2nd edition). Thousand Oaks, CA: Pine Forge.

Felson, R. B. & Krohn, M. (1990). Motives for rape. *Journal of Research in Crime and Delinquency, 27,* 222–42.

Felson, R. B. & Messner, S. F. (1996). To kill or not to kill? Lethal outcomes in injurious attacks. *Criminology, 34,* 519–45.

Felson, R. B. & Steadman, H. J. (1983). Situational factors in disputes leading to criminal violence. *Criminology, 21,* 59–74.

Fox, J. A. & Levin, J. (1999). Serial murder: popular myths and empirical realities. In M. D. Smith & M. A. Zahn (Eds), *Homicide: A Sourcebook of Social Research* (pp. 165–75). Thousand Oaks, CA: Sage.

Freud, S. (1905/1953). *Three Essays on the Theory of Sexuality* (standard edition, 7). London: Hogarth Press.

Fromm, E. (1973). *The Anatomy of Human Destructiveness*. New York: Holt, Rinehart & Winston.

Furby, L., Weinrott, M. R. & Blackshaw, L. (1989). Sex offender recidivism: a review. *Psychological Bulletin, 105,* 3–30.

Gacono, C. B. & Meloy, J. R. (1994). *The Rorschach Assessment of Aggressive and Psychopathic Personalities*. Hillsdale, NJ: Lawrence Erlbaum.

Gacono, C. B., Meloy, J. R. & Bridges, M. R. (2000). A Rorschach comparison of psychopaths, sexual homicide perpetrators, and nonviolent pedophiles: Where angels fear to tread. *Journal of Clinical Psychology, 56,* 757–77.

Gallagher, C. A., Wilson, D. B., Hirschfield, P., Coggeshall, M. B. & MacKenzie, D. L. (1999). A quantitative review of the effects of sex offender treatment on sexual reoffending. *Corrections Management Quarterly, 3,* 19–29.

Gassin, R. (1998). *Précis de Criminologie* (4th edition). Paris: Dalloz.

Geberth, V. J. (1995). Psychopathic sexual sadists: the psychology and psychodynamics of serial killers. *Law and Order, 43,* 82–6.

Geberth, V. J. (1996). *Practical Homicide Investigation: Tactics, Procedures, and Forensic Techniques* (3rd edition). Boca Raton, FL: CRC Press.

Geberth, V. J. & Turco, R. N. (1997). Antisocial personality disorder, sexual sadism, malignant narcissism, and serial murder. *Journal of Forensic Sciences, 42,* 49–60.

Godwin, G. M. (2000). *Hunting Serial Predator: A Multivariate Classification Approach to Profiling Violent Behavior*. Boca Raton, FL: CRC Press.

Gratzer, T. & Bradford, J. (1995). Offender and offense characteristics of sexual sadists: a comparative study. *Journal of Forensic Sciences, 40,* 450–5.

Greenberg, D. F. (1979). *Mathematical Criminology*. New Brunswick, NJ: Rutgers University Press.

Greendlinger, W. & Byrne, D. (1987). Coercive sexual fantasies of college men as predictors of self-reported likelihood to rape and overt sexual aggression. *Journal of Sex Research, 23,* 1–11.

Groth, A. N. & Birnbaum, H. J. (1979). *Men Who Rape: The Psychology of the Offender*. New York: Plenum.

Groth, A. N., Burgess, A. W. & Holmstrom, L. L. (1977). Rape: power, anger and sexuality. *American Journal of Psychiatry, 134,* 1239–43.

Grubin, D. (1994). Sexual murder. *British Journal of Psychiatry, 165,* 624–9.

Haas, H. (2001). *Agressions et Victimisations: une Enquête sur les Délinquants Violents Non Détectés*. Aarau: Sauerländer, wissenschaftliche Reihe Band 15.

Hall, G. C. N. (1995). Sexual offender recidivism revisited: a meta-analysis of recent treatment studies. *Journal of Consulting and Clinnical Psychology, 63,* 802–9.

Hall, G. C. N. & Hirschman, R. (1991). Towards a theory of sexual aggression: a quadripartite model. *Journal of Consulting and Clinical Psychology, 59,* 662–9.

Hanson, R. K. (2000). Treatment outcome and evaluation problems (and solutions). In D. R. Laws, S. M. Hudson & T. Ward (Eds), *Remaking Relapse Prevention with Sex Offenders: A Sourcebook* (pp. 485–99). Thousand Oaks, CA: Sage.

Hanson, R. K. & Bussière, M. T. (1998). Predicting relapse: a meta-analysis of sexual offender recidivism studies. *Journal of Consulting and Clinical Psychology, 66,* 348–62.

Hanson, R. K., Gordon, A., Harris, A. J. R., Marques, J. K., Murphy, W., Quinsey, V. L. & Seto, C. S. (2002). First report of the Collaborative Outcome Project on the effectiveness of psychological treatment for sex offenders. *Sexual Abuse: Journal of Research and Treatment, 14,* 169–94.

Hare, R. D. (1985). Comparison of procedures for the assessment of psychopathy. *Journal of Consulting and Clinical Psychology, 53,* 7–16.

Hare, R. D. (1991). *The Hare Psychopathy Checklist – Revised.* Toronto: Multi-Health Systems.

Hare, R. D. (1996). Psychopathy: a clinical construct whose time has come. *Criminal Justice and Behavior, 23,* 25–54.

Hazelwood, R. & Burgess, A. N. (1987). *Practical Aspects of Rape Investigation: A Multidisciplinary Approach.* New York: Elsevier North-Holland.

Hazelwood, R., Dietz, P. E. & Warren, J. I. (1992). The criminal sexual sadist. *FBI Law Enforcement Bulletin, 61,* 12–20.

Hazelwood, R. & Douglas, J. (1980). The lust murderer. *FBI Law Enforcement Journal, 49,* 1–8.

Hazelwood, R. & Warren, J. (1989). The serial rapist: his characteristics and victims. *FBI Law Enforcement Bulletin,* 10–17.

Hazelwood, R. & Warren, J. (1995). The relevance of fantasy in serial sexual crime investigation. In R. Hazelwood & A. W. Burgess (Eds), *Practical Aspects of Rape Investigation* (pp. 127–38). New York: CRC Press.

Heritage, R. (1992). Facets of sexual assault: first steps in investigative classifications. Unpublished master's thesis, University of Surrey.

Hickey, E. W. (1997). *Serial Murderers and Their Victims* (2nd edition). Belmont, CA: Wadsworth.

Hickey, E. W. (2002). *Serial Murderers and Their Victims* (3rd edition). Belmont, CA: Wadsworth.

Hollin, C. R. (1997). Sexual sadism: assessment and treatment. In R. Laws, W. T. O'Donohue (Eds), *Sexual Deviance: Theory, Assessment and Treatment* (pp. 210–24). New York: Guilford Press.

Holmes, R. M. & Holmes S. T. (1996). *Profiling Violent Crime: An Investigative Tool.* Thousand Oaks, CA: Sage.

Holt, S., Meloy, J. R. & Strack, S. (1999). Sadism and psychopathy in violent and sexually violent offenders. *Journal of American Academy of Psychiatry and the Law, 27,* 23–32.

Homant, R. J. & Kennedy, D. B. (1998). Psychological aspects of crime scene profiling: validity research. *Criminal Justice and Behavior, 25,* 306–19.

Home Office (2005). *Population in Custody Quarterly Brief. April to June 2005, England and Wales.* www.homeoffice.gov.uk/rds/pdfs05/prisq205.pdf.

Hucker, S. J. (1997). Sexual sadism: psychopathology and theory. In D. R. Laws & W. O'Donohue (Eds), *Sexual Deviance: Theory, Assessment and Treatment* (pp. 194–209). New York: Guilford.

Hucker, S. J., Langevin, R., Dickey, R., Handy, L., Chambers, J. & Wright, P. (1988). Cerebral damage and dysfunction in sexually aggressive men. *Annals of Sex Research, 1,* 33–47.

Jackson, J. L. & Bekerian, D. A. (1997). *Offender Profiling: Theory, Research and Practice.* Chichester: John Wiley and Sons, Ltd.

Jackson, J. L., van den Eshof, P. & de Kleuver, E. E. (1997). A research approach to offender profiling. In J. L. Jackson & D. A. Bekerian (Eds), *Offender Profiling: Theory, Research and Practice* (pp. 107–32). Chichester: John Wiley and Sons, Ltd.

Jackson, J. L., Van Koppen, P. J. & Herbrink, C. M. (1993). *Does the service meet the needs? An evaluation of consumer satisfaction with specific profile analysis and investigative advice offered by the scientific research advisory unit of the National Criminal Intelligence Division (CRI).* The Netherlands, NISCALE Report NSCR 93-05.

Jeammet, N. (2002). Un sadisme ordinaire. *Revue Francaise de Psychanalyse. 66*, 1117–32.

Jenkins, P. (1988). Serial murder in England 1940–1985. *Journal of Criminal Justice, 16*, 1–15.

Johnson, B. R. & Becker, J. V. (1997). Natural born killers? The development of the sexually sadistic serial killer. *American Academy of Psychiatry and the Law, 25*, 335–48.

Kaufman, K. L., Orts, K, Holmberg, J., McCrady, F., Daleiden, E. L. & Hilliker, D. (1996). *Contrasting Adult and Adolescent Sexual Offenders' Modus Operandi: A Developmental Process.* 15th Annual Meeting of the Association for the Treatment of Sexual Abusers, Chicago, Illinois.

Keppel, R. D. & Birnes, W.J. (1997). *Signature killers.* New York: Pocket Books.

Keppel, R. D. (2000). Investigation of the serial offender: Linking cases through modus operandit and signature. In L. B. Schresinger (Ed.) *Serial Offenders: Current Thoughts, Recent Findings* (pp.121–133). Boca Raton: CRC Press.

Keppel, R. D. & Walter, R. (1999). Profiling killers: a revised classification model for understanding sexual murder. *International Journal of Offender Therapy and Comparative Criminology, 43*, 417–37.

Kernberg, O. F. (1975). *Borderline Conditions and Pathological Narcissism.* New York: Jason Aronson.

Kind, S. S. (1987). Navigational ideas and the Yorkshire Ripper investigation. *Journal of Navigation, 40*, 385–93.

Kirsch, L. G. & Becker, J. V. (2006). Sexual offending: theory of problem, theory of change, and implications for treatment effectiveness. *Aggression and Violent Behavior, 11*, 208–24.

Klein, M. (1948). *Contributions to Psychoanalysis, 1921–1945.* London: Hogarth.

Knight, R. A. & Prentky, R. A. (1990). Classifying sexual offenders: the development and corroboration of taxonomic models. In W. L. Marshall, D. L. Law & H. E. Barbaree (Eds), *Handbook of Sexual Assault: Issues, Theories and Treatment of the Offender* (pp. 23–52). New York: Plenum.

Knight, R. A., Prentky, R. A. & Cerce, D. D. (1994). The development, reliability, and validity of an inventory for the multidimensional assessment of sex and aggression. *Criminal Justice and Behavior, 21*, 72–84.

Knight, R. A., Warren, J. L., Reboussin, R. & Soley, B. J. (1998). Predicting rapist type from crime scene variables. *Criminal Justice and Behavior, 25*, 30–46.

Kocsis, R. (1999). Criminal profiling of crime scene behaviors in Australian sexual murders. *Australian Police Journal, 53*, 113–16.

Kocsis, R. (2006). *Criminal Profiling. Principles and Practice.* Totowa, NJ: Humana Press.

Kocsis, R. & Irwin, H. J. (1997). An analysis of spatial patterns in serial rape, arson, and burglary: the utility of the circle theory of environmental range for psychological profiling. *Psychiatry, Psychology and Law, 4*, 195–206.

Kocsis, R., Irwin, H. J., Hayes, A. F. & Nunn, R. (2000). Expertise in psychological profiling: a comparative assessment. *Journal of Interpersonal Violence, 15*, 311–31.

Krafft-Ebing, R. (1886). *Psychopathia Sexualis* (F.S. Klaf-traduction, 1965). New York: Arcade.

Kruttschnitt, C. (1989). A sociological, offender-based study of rape. *Sociological Quarterly, 30*, 305–29.

Landry, M., Nadeau, L. & Racine, S. (1996). *Prévalence des troubles de la personnalité dans la population toxicomane du Québec*. Unpublished report, Recherche et intervention sur les substances psychoactives.

Langevin, R. (1991). The sex killer. In A. W. Burgess (Ed.), *Rape and Sexual Assault: A Research Handbook* (vol. 3., pp. 257–73). New York: Garland.

Langevin, R. (2003). A study of the psychosexual characteristics of sex killers: can we identify them before it is too late? *International Journal of Offender Therapy and Comparative Criminology, 47*, 366–82.

Langevin, R., Bain, J., Ben-Aron, M. K., Coulthard, R., Day, D., Handy, L., Heasman, G., Hucker, S. J., Purins, J. E., Roper, V., Russon, A. E., Webster, C. D. & Wortzman, G. (1985). Sexual aggression: constructing a predictive equation. In R. Langevin (Ed.), *Erotic Preference, Gender Identity and Aggression in Men: New Research Studies* (pp. 39–76). Hillsdale, NJ: Lawrence Erlbaum.

Langevin, R., Ben-Aron, M. H., Wright, P., Marchese, V. & Handy, L. (1988). The sex killer. *Annals of Sex Research, 1*, 263–301.

Laplanche, J. & Pontalis, J. B. (1967). *Vocabulaire de la Psychanalyse*. Paris: PUF.

Laws, D. R. & Marshall, W. L. (2003). A brief history of behavioural and cognitive behavioural approaches to sexual offenders: Part 1. Early developments. *Sexual Abuse: Journal of Research and Treatment, 15*, 75–92.

Lebeau, J. L. (1987). The journey to rape: geographic distance and the rapist's method of approaching the victim. *Journal of Police Science and Administration, 15*, 129–36.

LeBlanc, M. (1986). La carrière criminelle: définition et prédiction. *Criminologie, 19*, 79–97.

Lee, J. K. P., Pattison, P., Jackson, H. J. & Ward, T. (2001). The general, common, and specific features of psychopathology for different types of paraphilias. *Criminal Justice and Behavior, 28*, 227–56.

Levin, J. & Fox, J. A. (1985). *Mass Murder: America's Growing Menace*. New York: Plenum Press.

Leyton, E. (1986). *Hunting Humans: The Rise of the Modern Multiple Murderer*. Toronto: McClelland & Stewart.

Liebert, J. A. (1985). Contributions of psychiatric consultation in the investigation of serial murder. *International Journal of Offender Therapy and Comparative Criminology, 29*, 187–200.

Loeber, R. & LeBlanc, M. (1990). Toward a developmental criminology. *Crime and Justice: A Review of Research, 12*, 375–473.

MacCulloch, M. J., Snowden, P. R., Wood, P. J. W. & Mills, H. E. (1983). Sadistic fantasy, sadistic behaviour and offending. *British Journal of Psychiatry, 143*, 20–9.

Malamuth, N. M. (1986). Predictions of naturalistic sexual aggression. *Journal of Personality and Social Psychology, 50*, 953–62.

Malamuth, N. M., Heavy, C. L. & Linz, D. (1993). Predicting men's antisocial behavior against women: the interaction model of sexual aggression. In G. N. C. Hall, R. Hischman, J. R. Graham & M. S. Zaragoza (Eds), *Sexual Aggression: Issues in Etiology, Assessment, and Treatment* (pp. 63–97). Washington: Taylor & Francis.

Marlatt, G. A. (1982). Relapse prevention: a self-control program for the treatment of addictive behaviours. In R. B. Stuart (Ed.), *Adherence, Compliance and Generalization in Behavioural Medicine* (pp. 329–78). New York: Guilford Press.

Marlatt, G. A. & Gordon, J. R. (1985). *Relapse Prevention*. New York: Guilford Press.

Marmor, J. & Gorney, R. (1999). Instinctual sadism: a recurrent myth about human nature. *Journal of the American Academy of Psychoanalysis, 27*, 1–6.

Marques, J. K., Wiederanders, M., Day, D. M., Nelson, C. & Van Ommeren, A. (2005). Effects of a relapse prevention program on sexual recidivism: final results from

California's Sex Offender Treatment and Evaluation Project (SOTEP). *Sexual Abuse: Journal of Research and Treatment, 17*, 79–107.

Marshall, W. L. (1984). *Rape as a Socio-Cultural Phenomenon.* The J.P.S. Robertson Lecture, Trent University, Peterborough, Ontario.

Marshall, W. L. (1989a). Intimacy, loneliness and sexual offenders. *Behaviour Research and Therapy, 27*, 491–503.

Marshall, W. L. (1989b). Pornography and sex offenders. In D. Zillman & J. Bryant (Eds), *Pornography: Recent Research, Interpretations, and Policy Considerations* (pp. 185–214). Hillsdale, NJ: Lawrence Erlbaum.

Marshall W. L., Anderson D. & Fernandez, Y. (1999). *Cognitive Behavioural Treatment of Sexual Offenders.* New York: John Wiley & Sons, Inc.

Marshall, W. L. & Barbaree, H. E. (1988). An outpatient treatment program for child molesters. In R. Prentky & V. L. Quinsey (Eds), *Human Sexual Aggression: Current Perspectives. Annals of the New York Academy of Science* (vol. 528, pp. 205–14). New York: New York Academy of Sciences.

Marshall, W. L. & Barbaree, H. E. (1990a). An integrated theory of the etiology of sexual offending. In W. L. Marshall, D. R. Laws & H. E. Barbaree (Eds), *Handbook of Sexual Assault: Issues, Theories, and Treatment of the Offender* (pp. 257–75). New York: Plenum Press.

Marshall, W. L. & Barbaree, H. E. (1990b). Outcome of comprehensive cognitive-behavioral treatment programs. In W. L. Marshall, D. R. Laws & H. E. Barbaree (Eds), *Handbook of Sexual Assault: Issues, Theories, and Treatment of the Offender.* New York: Plenum Press.

Marshall, W. L., Earls, C. M., Segal, Z. & Darke, J. L. (1983). A behavioral program for the assessment and treatment of sexual aggressors. In K. D. Craig & R. J. MacMahon (Eds), *Advances in Clinical Behavior Therapy* (pp. 148–74). New York: Brunner Mazel.

Marshall, W. L., Fernandez, Y. M., Marshall, L. E., & Serran, G. A. (2006). *Sexual offender treatment: controversial issues.* Chichester: John Wiley & Sons.

Marshall, W. L., Hudson, S. M. & Hodkinson, S. (1993). The importance of attachment bonds in the development of juvenile sex offending. In H. E. Barbaree, W. L. Marshall & S. Hudson (Eds), *The Juvenile Sex Offender* (pp. 164–81). New York: Guilford Press.

Marshall, W. L. & Kennedy, P. (2003). Sexual sadism in sexual offenders: an elusive diagnosis. *Aggression and Violent Behavior: A Review Journal, 8*, 1–22.

Marshall, W. L., Kennedy, P. & Yates, P. (2002). Issues concerning the reliability and validity of the diagnosis of sexual sadism applied in prison settings. *Sexual Abuse: Journal of Research and Treatment, 14*, 301–11.

Marshall, W. L., Kennedy, P., Yates, P. & Serran, G. (2002). Diagnosing sexual sadism in sexual offenders: reliability across diagnosticians. *International Journal of Offender Therapy and Comparative Criminology, 46*, 668–677.

Marshall, W. L. & Laws, D. R. (2003). A brief history of behavioural and cognitive behavioural approaches to sexual offenders: Part 2. The modern era. *Sexual Abuse: Journal of Research and Treatment, 15*, 93–120.

Marshall, W. L. & Serran, G. A. (2000). Improving the effectiveness of sexual offender treatment. *Trauma, Violence, and Abuse, 1*, 203–22.

Marshall, W. L. & Yates, P. (2004). Diagnostic issues in sexual sadism among sexual offenders. *Journal of Sexual Aggression, 10*, 21–7.

Marziano, V. (2002). Child molesters ITs. Unpublished doctoral thesis. University of Melbourne.

McCann, J. T. (1992). Criminal personality profiling in the investigation of violent crime: recent advances and future directions. *Behavioral Sciences and the Law, 10*, 475–81.

McGrath, M. G. (2000). Criminal profiling: is there a role for the forensic psychiatrist? *Journal of the American Academy of Psychiatry and the Law, 28*, 315–24.

McKenzie, C. (1995). A study of serial murder. *International Journal of Offender Therapy and Comparative Criminology, 39*, 3–10.

Megargee, E. I. (1970). Undercontrolled and overcontrolled personality types in extreme antisocial aggression. In E. Megargee & J. Hokanson (Eds), *The Dynamics of Aggression* (pp. 108–20). New York: Harper and Row.

Meloy, J. R. (2000). The nature and dynamics of sexual homicide. *Aggression and Violent Behavior, 5*, 1–22.

Meloy, J. R., Gacono, C. B. & Kenney, L. (1994). A Rorschach investigation of sexual homicide. *Journal of Personality Assessment, 62*, 58–67.

Miethe, T. D. & McCorkle, R. (1998). *Crime Profiles: The Anatomy of Dangerous Persons, Places, and Situation.* Los Angeles: Roxbury.

Millon, T. (1983). *Millon Clinical Multiaxial Inventory Manual.* Minneapolis, MN: Interpretive Scoring Systems.

Millon, T. (1994). *Millon Clinical Multiaxial Inventory–III Manual.* Minneapolis, MN: National Computer Systems.

Millon, T. & Davis, R. D. (1996). *Disorders of Personality: DSM-IV and Beyond.* New York: John Wiley & Sons, Inc.

Milsom, J., Beech, A. R. & Webster, S. D. (2003). Emotional loneliness in sexual murderers: a qualitative analysis. *Sexual Abuse: Journal of Research and Treatment, 15*, 285–96.

Milsom, J., Webster, S. & Beech, A. (2001). *Childhood, adolescent and adult emotional loneliness in sexual murderers.* 20th Annual Meeting of the Association for the Treatment of Sexual Abusers, San Antonio, Texas.

Money, J. (1990). Forensic sexology: paraphilic serial rape (biastophilia) and lust murder (erotophonophilia). *American Journal of Psychotherapy, 44*, 26–36.

Mosher, D. L. (1988). Aggressive sexual behavior inventory. In C. M. Davis, W. L. Yarber & S. L. Davis (Eds), *Sexuality Related Measures: A Compendium* (pp. 9–10). Lake Mills, IA: Graphic.

Mosher, D. L. & Anderson, R. D. (1986). Macho personality, sexual aggression, and reactions to guided imagery of realistic rape. *Journal of Research in Personality, 20*, 77–94.

Myers, W. C. (2002). Overview of sexual homicide. In W. C. Myers (Ed.), *Juvenile Sexual Homicide* (pp. 15–48). San Diego, CA: Academic Press.

Myers, W. C. & Blashfield, R. (1997). Psychopathology and personality in juvenile sexual homicide offenders. *Bulletin of the American Academy of Psychiatry and the Law, 25*, 497–508.

Myers, W. C., Burgess, A. W., Burgess, A. G. & Douglas, J. E. (1999). Serial murder and sexual homicide. In V. Van Hasselt & M. Hersen (Eds), *Handbook of Psychological Approaches with Violent Offenders: Contemporary Strategies and Issues* (pp. 153–72). New York: Kluwer Academic/Plenum.

Myers, W. C., Burgess, A. W. & Nelson, J. A. (1998). Criminal and behavioral aspects of juvenile sexual homicide. *Journal of Forensic Sciences, 43*, 340–7.

Myers, W. C. & Monaco, L. (2000). Anger experience, styles of anger expression, sadistic personality disorder and psychopathy in juvenile sexual homicide offenders. *Journal of Forensic Sciences, 45*, 698–701.

Myers, W. C., Reccoppa, L., Burton, K. & McElroy, R. (1993). Malignant sex and aggression: an overview of serial sexual homicide. *Bulletin of American Academy of Psychiatry and Law, 21*, 435–51.

Nichols, H. R. & Molinder, I. (1984). *Manual for the Multiphasic Sex Inventory.* Tacoma, WA: Crime and Victim Psychology Specialists.

Nicole, A. (2002). *Du viol au meurtre sexuel: appréhension du développement personnel et de la trajectoire criminelle.* Practical Training Report, Université de Montréal.

Novick, J. & Novick, K. K. (1994). Externalization as a pathological form of relating: the dynamic underpinning of abuse. In A. Sugarman (Ed.), *Victim of Abuse: The*

Impact of Child as Adult Trauma (pp. 343–81). New York: International Universities Press.

Novick, J. & Novick, K. K. (1996). A developmental perspective of omnipotence. *Journal of Clinical Psychoanalysis, 5,* 129–73.

Novick, J. & Novick, K. K. (2000). Love in the therapeutic alliance. *Journal of Psychoanalytic Association, 48,* 189–218.

O'Donohue,W., Letourneau, E. J. & Dowling, H. (1997). Development and preliminary validation of a paraphilic sexual fantasy questionnaire. *Sexual Abuse: Journal of Research and Treatment, 9,* 167–78.

Ouimet, M. (1998). L'agression sexuelle, la violence et les infractions aux lois sur les drogues: un portrait statistique. In G. Lemire, S. Brochu, P. Noreau, J. Proulx & G. Rondeau (Eds), *Le Recours au Droit Pénal et au Système Pénal pour Régler les Problèmes Sociaux.* Montréal: CICC, Université de Montréal.

Ouimet, M., Guay, J.-P. & Proulx, J. (2000). Analyse de la gravité des agressions sexuelles de femmes adultes et de ses déterminants. *Revue Internationale de Criminologie et de Police Technique et Scientifique, 53,* 157–72.

Perris, C., Jacobsson, L., Lindström, H., Von Knorring, L. & Perris, H. (1980). Development of a new inventory for assessing memories of parental rearing behaviour. *Acta Psychiatrica Scandinavica, 61,* 265–74.

Petee, T. A. & Jarvis, J. (2000). Analyzing violent serial offending. *Homicide Studies, 4,* 211–18.

Pinizzotto, A. J. (1984). Forensic psychology: criminal personality profiling. *Journal of Police Science and Administration, 12,* 32–40.

Pinizzotto, A. J. & Finkel, N. J. (1990). Criminal personality profiling: an outcome and process study. *Law and Human Behavior, 14,* 215–33.

Pithers, W. D. & Cumming, G. F. (1996). Relapse prevention: a method for enhancing behavioral self-management and external supervision of the sexual aggressor. In B. K. Schwartz & H. R. Cellini (Eds), *The Sex Offender: Corrections, Treatment and Legal Practice* (pp. 1–32). Civic Research Institute.

Pithers, W. D., Beal, L. S., Armstrong, J. & Petty, J. (1989). Identification of risk factors through clinical interviews and analysis of records. In R. Laws (Ed.), *Relapse Prevention with Sex Offenders* (pp. 77–87). New York: Guilford Press.

Pithers, W. D., Kashima, K. M., Cumming, G. F., Beal, L. S. & Buell, M. M. (1988). Relapse prevention of sexual aggression. In R. Prentky & V. Quinsey (Eds), *Human Sexual Aggression: Current Perspectives* (pp. 244–60). New York: New York Academy of Sciences.

Pithers, W. D., Marques, J. K., Gibat, C. C. & Marlatt, G. A. (1983). Relapse prevention with sexual aggressives: a self-control model of treatment and maintenance change. In J. G. Greer & I. R. Stuarts (Eds), *The Sexual Aggressor: Current Perspective on Treatment* (pp. 214–39). New York: Van Norstrand Reinhold.

Polaschek, D. L. L. & Ward, T. (2002). The implicit theories of potential rapists. What our questionnaires tell us. *Aggression and Violent Behavior, 7,* 385–406.

Porter, S. & Woodworth, M. (2001). *In cold blood: Motivation and sexual dynamics of Canadian homicides as function of psychopathy.* 26th Annual Meeting of the International Academy of Law and Mental Health, Montreal, Canada.

Prentky, R. A. & Burgess, A. W. (2000). *Forensic Management of Sexual Offenders.* New York: Kluwer Academic/Plenum.

Prentky, R. A., Burgess, A. W., Rokous, F., Lee, A., Hartman, C., Ressler, R. & Douglas, J. (1989). The presumptive role of fantasy in serial sexual homicide. *American Journal of Psychiatry, 146,* 887–91.

Prentky, R. A., Knight, R. A., Sims-Knight, J. E., Strauss, H., Rokous, F. & Cerce, D. (1989). Developmental antecedents of sexual aggression. *Development and Psychopathy, 1,* 153–69.

Proulx, J. (2001). *Sexual preferences and personality disorders of MTC-R3 rapists subtypes.* 20th Annual Conference, Association for the Treatment of Sexual Abusers (ATSA), San Antonio, Texas.

Proulx, J., Aubut, J., McKibben, A. & Côté, M. (1994). Penile responses of rapists and non-rapists to rape stimuli involving physical violence or humiliation. *Archives of Sexual Behavior, 23,* 295–310.

Proulx, J., Beauregard, E. & Nicole, A. (2002). *Developmental, personality and situational factors in rapists and sexual murderers of women.* Paper presented at the 21st Annual Conference of the Association for the Behavioral Treatment of Sexual Abusers, Montreal, Canada.

Proulx, J., McKibben, A. & Lusignan, R. (1996). Relationship between affective components and sexual behaviors in sexual aggressors. *Sexual Abuse: Journal of Research and Treatment, 8,* 279–89.

Proulx, J., Ouimet, M., Lussier, P. & Boutin, S. (2003). *Criminal career parameters in four types of sexual aggressors.* 22nd Annual Conference of the Association for the Treatment of Sexual Abusers (ATSA), St Louis, Missouri.

Proulx, J., Pellerin, B., McKibben, A., Paradis, Y., Aubut, J., & Ouimet, M. (1997). Static and dynamic predictors of recidivism in sexual aggressors. *Sexual Abuse: A Journal of Research and Treatment, 9,* 7–27.

Proulx, J., Perreault, C. & Ouimet, M. (1999). Pathways in the offending process of extrafamilial sexual child molesters. *Sexual Abuse: Journal of Research and Treatment, 11,* 117–29.

Proulx, J., St-Yves, M., Guay, J.-P. & Ouimet, M. (1999). Les agresseurs sexuels de femmes: scénarios délictuels et troubles de la personnalité. In J. Proulx, M. Cusson & M. Ouimet (Eds), *Les Violences Criminelles* (pp. 157–85). Saint-Nicolas, Québec: Presses de l'Université Laval.

Quinsey, V. L. & Chaplin, V. L. (1982). Penile responses to nonsexual violence among rapists. *Criminal Justice and Behavior, 9,* 372–81.

Quinsey, V. L., Rice, M. E. & Harris, G. T. (1995). Actuarial prediction of sexual recidivism. *Journal of Interpersonal Violence, 10,* 85–105.

Rada, R. T. (1978). *Clinical Aspects of the Rapist.* New York: Grune & Stratton.

Ressler, R. K. (1993). *Chasseur de Tueurs.* Paris: Presses de la Cité.

Ressler, R. K., Burgess, A. W., & Douglas, J. E. (1988). *Sexual Homicide: Patterns and Motives.* New York: Lexington.

Ressler, R. K., Burgess, A. W., Douglas, J. E., Hartman, C. R. & D'Agostino, R. B. (1986). Sexual killers and their victims: identifying patterns through crime scene analysis. *Journal of Interpersonal Violence, 1,* 288–308.

Ressler, R. K., Burgess, A. W., Hartman, C. R., Douglas, J. E. & McCormack, A. (1986). Murderers who rape and mutilate. *Journal of Interpersonal Violence, 1,* 273–87.

Revitch, E. (1965). Sex murder and the potential sex murderer. *Diseases of the Nervous System, 26,* 640–8.

Revitch, E. (1980). Gynocide and unprovoked attacks of women. *Corrective and Social Psychiatry, 26,* 6–11.

Revitch, E. & Schlesinger, L. (1981). *The Psychopathology of Homicide.* Springfield, IL: Charles C. Thomas.

Revitch, E. & Schlesinger, L. (1989). *Sex Murder and Sex Aggression: Phenomenology, Psychopathology, Psychodynamics and Prognosis.* Springfield, IL: Charles C. Thomas.

Roberts, J. V. & Grossman, M. G. (1993). Sexual homicide in Canada: a descriptive analysis. *Annals of Sex Research, 6,* 5–25.

Rossmo, D. K. (1993a). *Multivariate spatial profiles as a tool in crime investigation.* Paper presented at the Workshop on Crime Analysis Through Computer Mapping, Chicago, IL.

Rossmo, D. K. (1993b). Target patterns of serial murderers: a methodological model. *American Journal of Criminal Justice*, *17*, 1–21.

Rossmo, D. K. (1994). A primer on criminal geographic targeting. *IALEIA Journal*, *9*, 1–12.

Rossmo, D. K. (1995a). Strategic crime patterning: problem-oriented policing and displacement. In C. R. Block, M. Dabdoub & S. Fregly (Eds). *Crime Analysis Through Computer Mapping* (pp. 1–14). Washington, DC: Police Executive Research Forum.

Rossmo, D. K. (1995b). *Geographic profiling: target patterns of serial murderers*. Unpublished doctoral thesis, Simon Fraser University, BC, Canada.

Rossmo, D. K. (1996). Targeting victims: serial killers and the urban environment. In T. O'Reilly-Fleming (Ed.), *Serial and Mass Murder: Theory, Research and Policy* (pp. 133–53). Toronto: Canadian Scholars' Press.

Rossmo, D. K. (1997). Geographic profiling. In J. L. Jackson & D. A. Bekerian (Eds), *Offender Profiling: Theory, Research and Practice* (pp. 159–75). Chichester: John Wiley & Sons, Ltd.

Rossmo, D. K. (1998). Target patterns of serial murderers: a methodological model. In R. M. Holmes & S. T. Holmes (Eds), *Contemporary Perspectives on Serial Murder* (pp. 199–217). Thousand Oaks, CA: Sage.

Rossmo, D. K. (2000). *Geographic Profiling*. Boca Raton, FL: CRC Press.

Rossmo, D. K. (2001). *Evaluation of geographic profiling search strategies*. Paper presented at the meeting of the American Society of Criminology, Atlanta, GA.

Roussillon, R. (2002). Décomposition 'clinique' du sadisme. *Revue Française de Psychanalyse*, *66*, 1166–80.

Safarik, M. E., Jarvis, J. P. & Nussbaum, K. E. (2002). Sexual homicide of elderly females: linking offender characteristics to victim and crime scene attributes. *Journal of Interpersonal Violence*, *17*, 500–25.

Salfati, G. (2000a). *Homicide and sexual homicide: an investigation of crime scene behaviours and offender characteristics*. 52nd Annual Meeting of the American Society of Criminology, San Francisco.

Salfati, G. (2000b). The nature of expressiveness and instrumentability in homicide: implications for offender profiling. *Homicide Studies*, *4*, 265–93.

Salfati, G. & Canter, D. V. (1999). Differentiating stranger murders: profiling offender characteristics from behavioral styles. *Behavioral Sciences and the Law*, *17*, 391–406.

Schlesinger, L. B. (2000). Serial homicide: sadism, fantasy and a compulsion to kill. In L. B. Schlesinger (Ed.), *Serial Offender: Current Thought, Recent Findings* (pp. 3–22). Boca Raton, FL: CRC Press.

Schlesinger, L. B. & Revitch, E. (1997). *Sexual Dynamics of Anti-Social Behavior*. Springfield, IL: Charles C. Thomas.

Scully, D. (1990). *Understanding Sexual Violence: A Study of Convicted Rapists*. New York: Routledge.

Seto, M. C. & Kuban, M. (1996). Criterion-related validity of a phallometric test for rape and sadism. *Behaviour Research and Therapy*, *34*, 175–83.

Shaw, S. (1998). *Applying environmental psychology and criminology: the relationship between crime site locations within offences of murder*. Unpublished undergraduate thesis, University of Plymouth, England.

Shipley, W. C. (1940). A self-administering scale for measuring intellectual impairment and deterioration. *Journal of Psychology*, *9*, 371–7.

Simon, L. M. J. (2002). An examination of the assumptions of specialization, mental disorder and dangerousness in sex offenders. *Behavioral Sciences and the Law*, *18*, 275–308.

Siomopoulos, V. & Goldsmith, J. (1976). Sadism revisited. *American Journal of Psychotherapy*, *30*, 631–40.

Smith, S. & Braun, C. (1977). Necrophilia and lust murder: report of a rare occurrence. *Bulletin of the American Academy of Psychiatry and the Law*, 6, 259–68.

Soothill, K., Francis, B., Sanderson, B. & Ackerley, E. (2000). Sex offenders: specialists, generalists – or both? A 32-year criminological study. *British Journal of Criminology*, 40, 56–67.

Spitzer, R. L., Feister, S., Gay, M. & Pfohl, B. (1991). Results of a survey of forensic psychiatrists on the validity of the sadistic personality disorder diagnosis. *American Journal of Psychiatry*, 148, 875–9.

Stoller, R. J. (1978). *La Perversion, forme érotique de la haine*. Paris: Payot.

Stone, M. H. (1994). Early traumatic factors in the lives of serial murderers. *American Journal of Forensic Psychiatry*, 15, 5–26.

St-Yves, M. (2002). Interrogatoire de police et crime sexuel: profil du suspect collaborateur. *Revue Internationale de Criminologie et de Police Technique*, 1, 81–96.

St-Yves, M., Granger, L. & Brien, T. (1998). *Scénario délictuel et lien avec la victime chez les agresseurs sexuels de femmes adultes*. Unpublished document.

St-Yves, M., Proulx, J. & McKibben, A. (1994). *QIDS: Questionnaire informatisé sur la délinquance sexuelle*. Unpublished document.

Swigert, V. L., Farnell, R. A. & Yoels, W. C. (1976). Sexual homicide: social, psychological, and legal aspects. *Archives of Sexual Behavior*, 5, 391–401.

Tamura, M. & Suzuki, M. (1997). Criminal profiling research on serial arson: examination of circle hypothesis estimating offender's residential area. Reports of the National Research Institute of Police Science. *Research on Prevention of Crime and Delinquency*, 38, 1.

Tedeschi, J.T. & Felson, R. (1994). *Violence, Aggression, and Coercive Actions*. Washington, DC: American Psychological Association.

Tedeschi, J. T. & Norman, N. (1985). Social mechanisms of displaced aggression. In E. J. Lawler (Ed.), *Advances in Group Processes: Theory and Research* (pp. 29–56). Greenwich, CT: JAI Press.

Thornton, D., Mann, R., Webster, S., Blud, L., Travers, R., Friendship, C. & Erikson, M. (2003). Distinguishing and combining risks for sexual and violent recidivism. In R. Prentky, E. Janus, M. Seto & A. W. Burgess (Eds), *Understanding and Managing Sexually Coercive Behavior* (pp. 225–35). New York: Annals of the New York Academy of Sciences.

Thornton, D. & Shingler, J. (2001). *Impact of schema level work on sexual offenders' cognitive distortions*. Paper presented at the 20th Annual Conference, Association for the Treatment of Sexual Abusers, San Antonio, Texas.

Turvey, B. E. (1998). Deductive criminal profiling: comparing applied methodologies between inductive and deductive profiling techniques. *Criminal Profiling Research Site*: http://www.criminalprofiling.ch/article2.html.

Turvey, B. E. (2001). *Criminal Profiling: An Introduction to Behavioral Evidence Analysis* (Second edition). San Diego, CA: Academic Press.

Verma, A. (2001). Construction of offender profiles using fuzzy logic. In G. M. Godwin (Ed.), *Criminal Psychology and Forensic Technology: A Collaborative Approach to Effective Profiling* (pp. 49–59). Boca Raton, FL: CRC Press.

Vetter, H. (1990). Dissociation, psychopathy and the serial murderer. In S. A. Egger (Ed.), *Serial Murder: An Elusive Phenomenon* (pp. 73–92). New York: Praeger.

Ward, T. (2000). Sexual offenders' cognitive distortions as implicit theories. *Aggression and Violent Behavior*, 5, 491–507.

Ward, T., Hudson, S. M., Johnston, L. & Marshall, W. L. (1997). Cognitive distortions in sex offenders: an integrative review. *Clinical Psychology Review*, 17, 479–507.

Ward, T. & Keenan, T. (1999). Child molesters' implicit theories. *Journal of Interpersonal Violence*, 14, 821–38.

Ward, T., Louden, K., Hudson, S. M. & Marshall, W. L. (1995). A descriptive model of the offense chain for child molesters. *Journal of Interpersonal Violence*, 10, 452–72.

Warren, J., Hazelwood, R. & Dietz, P. (1996). The sexually sadistic serial killer. *Journal of Forensic Sciences*, 41, 970–4.

Warren, J., Reboussin, R., Hazelwood, R. R., Cummings, A., Gibbs, N. & Trumbetta, S. (1998). Crime scene and distance correlates of serial rape. *Journal of Quantitative Criminology*, 14, 35–59.

Warren, J., Reboussin, R., Hazelwood, R. R., Gibbs, N. A., Trumbetta, S. L. & Cummings, A. (1999). Crime scene analysis and the escalation of violence in serial rape. *Forensic Science International*, 100, 37–56.

Watkins, J. G. (1984). The Bianchi (LA hillside strangler) case: sociopath or multiple personality? *International Journal of Clinical and Experimental Hypnosis*, 32, 67–101.

Wechsler, D. (1981). *Wechsler Adult Intelligence Scale – Revised*. New York: Psychological Corporation, Harcourt Brace Jovanovich.

Weiss, J. (1993). *How Psychotherapy Works: Process and Technique*. New York: Guilford Press.

Weiss, J. (1998). Bondage fantasies and beating fantasies. *Psychoanalytic Quarterly*, 67, 626–44.

West, D. J. (1983). Sex offenses and offending. In N. Morris & M. Tonry (Eds), *Crime and Justice. A Review of Research* (Vol. 5, pp. 183–233). Chicago: University of Chicago Press.

Widiger, T. A. & Trull, T. J. (1994). Personality disorders and violence. In J. Monahan & H. J. Steadman (Eds), *Violence and Mental Disorder* (pp. 203–26). Chicago, IL: University of Chicago Press.

Wilson, P., Lincoln, R. & Kocsis, R. (1997). Validity, utility and ethics of profiling for serial violent and sexual offenders. *Psychiatry, Psychology and Law*, 4, 1–12.

Wilson, P. & Soothill, K. (1996). Psychological profiling: red, green or amber. *Police Journal, January*, 12–20.

Winnicott, D.W. (1958). *Through Pediatrics to Psychoanalysis*. New York: Brunner Routledge.

Winnicott, D. W. (1971). *Playing and Reality*. New York: Brunner Routledge.

Winnicott, D. W. (1986). *Home is Where We Start From: Essays by a Psychoanalyst*. New York: Norton.

Wolfgang, M., Figlio, R., Tracy, P. & Singer, I. (1985). *The National Survey of Crime Severity*. Washington, DC: US Department of Justice, Bureau of Justice Statistics.

World Health Organization (1992). *The ICD-10 Classification of Mental and Behavioural Disorders: Clinical Descriptions and Diagnostic Guidelines*. Geneva: World Health Organization.

Yarvis, R. M. (1990). Axis I and Axis II diagnostic parameters of homicide. *Bulletin of the American Academy of Psychiatry and Law*, 18, 249–69.

Yarvis, R. M. (1995). Diagnostic patterns among three violent offender types. *Bulletin of the American Academy of Psychiatry and Law*, 23, 411–19.

Yates, E., Barbaree, H. E. & Marshall, W. L. (1984). Anger and deviant sexual arousal. *Behavior Therapy*, 15, 287–94.

Zagury, D. (2002). Les serial killers sont-ils des tueurs sadiques? *Revue Française de Psychanalyse*, 66, 1195–213.

Zipf, G. (1950). *The Principle of Least Effort*. Reading, MA: Addison Wesley.

Zadeh, L. A. (1965). Fuzzy sets. *Information Control*, 8, 338–53.

INDEX

age, victim 10, 170, 171
aggressive dyscontrol murderer 125
aggressive fantasies 16
Aggressive Sexual Behaviour Inventory 217
aggressivity 15
alcohol 4, 24, 31, 35, 41, 73, 86, 92, 96, 135–6
anal sex 108, 112
anger 4, 24, 73, 74, 177
    pre-crime/crime-phase 86, 94–5, 96
anger-excitation rape/murder 126, 178
anger-retaliatory rape/murder 125, 178
angry murderers
    case study 139–40, 226–7
    characteristics 125, 128, 131–3
    crime phase 133–4
    post-crime attitudes 137–8
    pre-crime phase 134–7
animals, cruelty towards 21, 109
antisocial personality disorder 17, 21, 54–6, 64
Antisocial Personality Questionnaire (APQ) 165, 172
attachment, inadequate 30–1
atypical sexual behaviours during childhood 36–7, 42–3
autoerotic activities 31
avoidant personality disorders 111, 135

Bayesian Belief Network 199–200, 201
behavioural try-outs 138
Berkowitz, David ('Son of Sam') 196
biological theories 12–13, 21
bipolar disorder 13
Boolean logic 200
borderline personality disorder 17, 53, 56–8, 64, 135, 137
Boston Strangler 195
brain damage 21, 108
Bundy, Ted 9, 26

case studies
    angry murderers 139–40, 226–7
    marginality 151–3
    overcontrol 153–4
    personality disorders 66–8
    sadistic murderer 138–40, 225
    sexual aggressor 46–7, 82–3, 150–1
    sexual murderers 47–50
    sexual offender treatment programme 225–8
    violent polymorphism 149–50
catathymic murderer 14, 125
CATCHEM database 199
Chikatilo, Andrei 207
child physical abuse 30
child sexual abuse 13, 30
childhood 167–8
chronically overcontrolled personalities 154

Clarke Sex History scales 112
classical (respondent) conditioning 13
classification of sexual murders 176–80
    clinical description 178–9
    pragmatic 176–7
    statistical description 179–80
    theory-led 177–8
cluster analysis 198
Coercive Sexual Fantasies Questionnaire
    217
cognitive behavioural theory (CBT) 189
cognitive distortion 73, 214
commuter hypothesis 206
compulsive sexual murders 14, 100, 125
Computerized Sex Offenders Questionnaire
    (CSOQ) 27, 129
conduct disorder, childhood 161–2
confinement, unlawful 108
conflict resolution 221–2
coping strategies 15, 31
crime pattern theory 203
crime scenario, analysis 10, 217–20
crime-scene profiling 196–7
criminal acts, definition 72
criminal career 32, 38, 43–4
Criminal Code of Canada 9–10
Criminal Geographic Targeting (CGT)
    algorithm 207
criminal profiling 193–211
    crime-scene profiling 196–7
    evaluative studies 201–2
    evolution 195–201
    geocriminology and geographical profiling
        of sexual murders 202–10
    inductive vs. deductive 194–5
    psychological profiling 195–6
    statistical profiling 197–201

daydreaming 35, 41
deductive profiling 194–5
definition of sexual murder 9–10
Derogatis Sexual Functioning Inventory
    112
developmental characteristics 20, 21
developmental factors 29–32, 33–7, 45
    sexual aggressors 29–30
    sexual murderers 30–2
developmental profiles 37–8, 43
developmental variables 68
deviant sexual fantasies 13, 14, 15–17, 24,
    25, 37, 43, 74, 86, 92, 93, 96, 136–7
disorganized murderer 125, 134, 136,
    176–7, 196

dissociative syndrome 13, 17, 53, 57, 63
distance-decay function 203–4
drug abuse 24, 35, 41, 73, 86, 136
DSM-III 52, 55, 64
DSM-III-R 110, 113
DSM-IV 52, 54, 55, 59, 64, 107
    axis I mental disorders 60
    axis II mental disorders 60, 61
dual-path prediction model of sexual
    coercion of women 30
Duffy, John ('Railway Rapist') 198
duration of crime 86
dysfunctional family relationships 13

education 36, 42
EMBU 163–4
emotional isolation 30
empathy deficits 68, 214
empirical model 44–5
endocrinological factors 12, 13
entitlement, feelings of 15
environmental criminology 202–10
epidemiology 11–12
epilepsy 12, 13
erectile difficulties 109
erotophonophilia 12
escalation models 75–8
ethnicity 161
exhibitionism 17, 31, 33, 109
Exner system 55
exposure to inadequate models 33–4,
    38–9
expressive murder 198

Facet Theory 198
familial violence 41
fetishism 17, 25, 109
firearms 24
forensic history 166–7
functional MRI 232
fury murderer 1275
fuzzy logic 200–1

genetic factors 12, 13
geocriminology (environmental criminology)
    202–10
geographical mobility 204–5
geographical profiling of sexual murders
    202–11
    application to police investigations
        205–7
    program 207–8
    value of 208–10

grievance murderer 125
guilt 68, 137, 221–2

hostile masculinity 30
humiliation rape 110
humiliation victimization 86, 108, 120

implicit theories (IT) 179–80
    categorization of sexual murderers
        by 186–8
    dangerous world 181–2
    entitlement 183–4
    uncontrollable male sex drive 182–3
    women are unknowable/women are
        dangerous 185
    women as sex objects 184–5
inappropriate behaviours, childhood 30, 33,
    35–6, 41–2, 96
incest 40
incidence
    of serial killers 3, 101, 160
    of sexual offenders (England and Wales)
        159
inductive profiling 194–5
instrumental murder 198
integrative models 94
intentional factors in sexual assault
    73–4, 85–6
intervention goals 222–5
intrafamilial assaults 74
IQ 21, 25, 165

Jack the Ripper 195

Kelly, Mary 195
kidnapping 108
Kolmogorov-Smirnov test 207

least effort, principle of 203
limbic system, trauma to 12
logistic regression analysis 76–8, 199, 201
loneliness 16
lust murder see sadistic murder
lying, habitual 31, 35, 94

Mad Bomber 195
marauder hypothesis 205–6
mass murder 10
mass murderer, definition 100
masturbatory activities 15, 17, 36
matricentric rage 14–15
matricide, symbolic 14
matrix of repetition 218

McVeigh, Timothy 100
mental map 203, 208
Millon Clinical Multiaxial Inventory (MCMI)
    52, 56, 59–60, 61–2, 64–9, 116, 135, 230
MCMI-I 115
MCMI-III 164–5, 168, 172
Minnesota Multiphasic Personality Inventory
    (MMPI) 21, 52, 55, 113
mixed murderer 126, 177
Montreal Study of sexual murders 26–8
    methods 26–8
    objectives 26
    procedures 27–8
    subjects 26–7
mood disorders 63
motivational model (FBI) 15–17, 30, 32, 45, 88,
    94–5
motivations 126, 175–90
MTC-R-3 110, 114, 197
Multidimensional Assessment of Sex and
    Aggression (MASA) 164, 166, 167, 217,
    230
multidimensional scaling 198
Multiphasic Sex Inventory (MSI) 164, 230
multivariate statistical analysis 76–8
mutilation
    postmortem 108
    sexual 108, 188

narcissistic personality disorders 54–6, 64, 137
Nazism 109
negative reciprocity 71–2
negativity, prevalence of 218
neurological factors 12, 13
neuropsychological dysfunction murderer
    126
nonserial sexual murderers
    life histories in Quebec vs. USA 101–3
    sexual aggressors of women and 19–24
    serial sexual murderers and 24–5
nonsexual assault 2

obscene phone calls 109
obsessive-compulsive disorder 17, 53, 57–8,
    63
offence characteristics 170–1
omnipotent illusion 222
operant conditioning 13–14
organized murderer 125, 133, 134, 136,
    176–7, 196

paedophiles 32
paranoid ideation 53

paraphilias 17, 21, 24, 25, 31, 95
parental violence 30
personality assessment 168–70
personality disorders 17, 54–7, 57–9, 64–6, 111
   case studies 66–
personality profile 96
phallometry 232
phobias 35, 41
phone-sex services 36
pornography 4, 31, 36, 109, 120
power-assertive rape/murderer 126, 177
power-reassurance rape/murderer 126, 177–8
pre-crime characteristics 23
pre-crime/crime-phase anger 86, 94–5, 96
pre-crime/crime-phase sexual arousal 86
PRESS system 199
process of fascination 218–19
property, crime against 2, 93, 96
psychiatric history 168
psychodynamic approaches 14–15
psychological characteristics 22
psychological profiling 195–6
psychological theories 13–17
psychopathy 17, 51, 54–6, 58
Psychopathy Checklist – Revised (PCL-R) 162
psychopathy scale (PCL-R) 55, 56
psychosis 52–3
psychotic disorders 62–3

rage 4, 14
   matricentric 14–15
   see also anger
rape murderer 126
rational choice theory 23, 72
rebelliousness 15
relapse prevention 214
relational problems and guilt, early 221–2
relationship to victim 161, 165–6
remorse 68, 137
resistance 97
respondent conditioning 13
Rigel 207–8
Rorschach tests 56
routine activities theory 203
Ryan, Michael 100

Sade, Marquis de 1, 107
sadism 1, 2, 4–5, 21
   aetiological and developmental factors
     108–9
   definition 107, 215–16
sadistic impulses 177
sadistic murderers 10, 177

case studies 138–40, 225
characteristics 125, 127, 131–3
crime phase 133–4
elimination of a witness 146
link between criminal career and 147–54
neutralization of victim resistance 146
post-crime attitudes 137–8
pre-crime phase 134–7
rage and vengeance 145–6
role of sadism in sexual murder 146
sadistic sexual behaviours, emergence of 31
sadistic sexual offenders 107–22
   adult daily life 109–10
   phallometric profile 110
   pre-crime and crime phases 112
   psychopathological profiles 110–12
   vs. nonsadistic sexual offenders 112–14,
     115–19, 120–2
sadomasochism, child 221
SALVAC 209
Schedule for Nonadaptive and Adaptive
   Personality (SNAP) 57, 65
schema-focused treatment 189
schizoid personality disorder 17, 57, 58, 111,
   135
schizophrenia 17
schizotypal personality disorders 57
self-esteem 16, 35, 94, 121, 172
self-regulation 221–2
serial killers 1–2, 3, 99–105
   definition 100
   deviant sexual fantasies in 103–4
   incidence 3, 101, 160
   life histories in Quebec vs. USA 101–3
   relationship to victim and premeditation
     104–5
serial murder 10
serial sexual murderer, definition 100
Sex Fantasy Questionnaire (SFQ) 217
sex of victims 10
sex offender treatment programmes 159–60
sexual abuse, childhood 40
sexual aggressors 3–4, 148–9
Sexual Arousability Inventory 217
sexual assault 5, 92
sexual-assault decision trees 78, 85
   attack outcome 78–80, 84
   attack severity 80–2
sexual gratification 14
sexual history 167
sexual murder 10, 14
   definition 100, 215–16
sexual nuisance offences 109

sexual offender treatment programmes
    213–28
  analysis of crime scenario 217–20
  analysis of victim function 219–20
  case studies 225–8
  clinical issues 220–5
  early relational problems and
    guilt 221–2
  effectiveness 213–15
  initial evaluation 216–17
  intervention goals 222–5
  therapeutic framework 216–17
sexual promiscuity 30
sexual sadism 17, 53–4, 63
  definition 107–8
sexual tension 14
sexually motivated murderer 178, 189
sexually-triggered/aggressive control
    murderer 126, 178–9, 189
sexually triggered/aggressive dyscontrol
    sexual murderer 179, 189
sexually triggered-neuropsychological
    dysfunction 179
Shipley Institute of Living Scale 163, 165
situational factors in sexual assault 68, 73–5,
    86, 92
Smallest Sample Analysis (SSA) 198
Smallest Space Analysis 198
social conflict 19
social isolation 15, 16, 21, 31, 35, 41, 94,
    95, 161
social skills deficits 73, 214
sociodemographic characteristics 20
socio-historical theory of serial sexual murder
    18
sociological theories 18–19

Special Hospitals Assessment of Personality
    and Socialisation (SHAPS) 165
Speck, Richard 100
spree murderers, definition 100
statistical profiling 197–201
strangulation 24, 186
Sutcliffe, Peter William (Yorkshire Ripper)
    205

temper tantrums, adolescent 21, 120
testimony 10, 11
testosterone deficits 12, 21
torture 108
transvestism 21, 25
trauma-control model 31, 88, 95

vengeance, desire for 15, 74, 86
VICAP 209
victim behaviour 71–2
victim characteristics 68, 170–1
victim humiliation 86, 108, 120
victim, relationship to 86, 161, 165–6
victim resistance 73–4, 84, 85, 86, 92, 93
victimization 33, 34–5, 39–40, 96
  childhood 167
voyeurism 17, 21, 25, 33, 109

weapons, use of 74, 86, 92, 97, 108
Wechsler Adult Intelligence Scale – Revised
    163
witchcraft 109
witness elimination murderer 125, 126
Wolfgang severity score (NSCS) 38

Yorkshire Ripper (Sutcliffe, Peter William)
    205